Cultures and Crimes

So that however it may be mistaken, the end of law is not to abolish or restrain, but to preserve and enlarge freedom; for liberty is to be free from the restraint and violence of others, which cannot be where there is no law; and not, as we are told, *a liberty for every man to do as he lists*. But a liberty to dispose and order freely as he lists his person, actions, possessions and whole property within the allowance of those laws under which he is, and therein not to be subject to the arbitrary will of another, but freely follow his own.

John Locke, *An Essay Concerning the True Original Extent and End of Civil Government* (1690)

Cultures and Crimes
Policing in Four Nations

Norman Dennis
George Erdos

Civitas: Institute for the Study of Civil Society
London
Registered Charity No. 1085494

First published January 2005

© The Institute for the Study of Civil Society 2005
77 Great Peter Street
London SW1P 2EZ
Civitas is a registered charity (no. 1085494)
and a company limited by guarantee, registered in
England and Wales (no. 04023541)

email: books@civitas.org.uk

ISBN 1-903 386-38-1

Typeset by Civitas
in Palatino

Printed in Great Britain by
The Cromwell Press
Trowbridge, Wiltshire

Dedicated to

Audrey Dennis
Julia Jane Hodkinson and Robert and Sarah
John David Dennis and Max

Children and grandchildren to be proud of
A wife beyond compare

Contents

Authors

Norman Dennis was born in 1929. He spent his childhood in various working-class neighbourhoods during the depression years in Sunderland, at that time a town famous for its ships, marine engines, glass works and colliery. A crucial and benign year was spent at the beginning of the 1939-45 war as an evacuee with one of his three brothers in a coal-miner's family in the small pit village of Leasingthorne, County Durham. Admitted from Bede Grammar School, Sunderland, to Corpus Christi College, Oxford, he preferred to study at the London School of Economics of Tawney, Popper, Ginsberg and Laski. He has been a Ford Fellow, Rockefeller Fellow, Leverhulme Fellow, and Fellow of the Center for Advance Study in Behavioral Sciences at Palo Alto, California. At the Universities of Leeds, Bristol, Birmingham, Durham and Newcastle upon Tyne, since the nineteen-fifties he has carried out participant-observation and survey research into the changes taking place in working-class communities against the background of wider cultural changes, paying special attention to the four countries England, France, Germany and the United States. He is currently a colleague of George Erdos in the School of Biology (Psychology) at the University of Newcastle upon Tyne. He has been a member of the Labour party since the mid-nineteen-forties, when he joined the Sunderland Labour League of Youth.

George Erdos is senior lecturer in the School of Biology (Psychology) at the University of Newcastle upon Tyne. He is a chartered occupational psychologist. He is currently studying the cultural and community relationships that have been relatively successful, comparing one society with another, in producing personal freedom, mutual trust, willing co-operation and an adequate and secure standard of living for all participants—the central concerns of English ethical socialism as articulated by R. H. Tawney. Dr Erdos is intimately acquainted with the repressive systems of both national-socialist Germany and communist Hungary. With Norman Dennis, he argues in this book that England is a nation that, compared with most others in the past and today, has enjoyed in its various communities and associations a culture and practice of relatively high levels of freedom of expression and low levels of coercion. The greatest internal threats to personal liberty originate with law-breakers in the state and violators of rules of good conduct in neighbourhoods and organisations.

Foreword

A few years ago Norman Dennis wrote that crime had been growing unchecked in this country since 1955. The reason he put forward for the rise was the collapse of a multi-faceted culture of civic harmony, not least the dismantlement of life-long monogamy as the basis of child rearing and the core of adult duties. He followed Burke in arguing that, if a society is to continue in existence, a controlling power upon the will and appetite must be placed somewhere, and the less there is within, instilled by a society's culture, the more there must be from without, enforced by a society's police. From the mid-1950s to the early 1990s both the 'power within' and the 'power without' were diminishing. While cultural constraints were being discarded, in relation to the number of crimes they had to attend to, police numbers were not keeping pace and police powers were declining.

Dennis attacked the widely propagated view that to the extent that material standards rose and equality of material outcomes was established, neither the inculcation of a culture of law-abidingness nor the presence of a preventive police force would be necessary. But it was not until July 2004 that Prime Minister Blair publicly recognised that the problem of law and order was cultural as well as controlling and material. In introducing the Labour government's policies to recreate 'confident communities in a secure Britain' he said that the five-year plan marked 'the end of the liberal, social consensus on law and order'. He said that the post-1960s society of different lifestyles had 'spawned a group of young people who were brought up without parental discipline, without proper role models and without any sense of responsibility to or for others'. 'Here, now, today', he said, 'people have had enough of this part of the 1960s' consensus'. People did not want a return to old prejudices and ugly discrimination. But they did want 'rules, order and proper behaviour'. They wanted a community where 'the decent law-abiding majority' was in charge.[1]

In the 132 pages of the government's five-year plan to 2008, *Confident Communities in a Secure Britain*, the conception of 'culture' is thin in the extreme. All research shows that the key element in keeping children and young people from crime and disorder has been, and is, their being born into and brought up by a family of their own biological parents, who before the conception of their child were in a self-chosen and socially approved and sanctioned relationship of life-long monogamy. *Confident Communities* itself points out that, as contrasted with two per cent of the general population, 25 per cent of all prisoners were in local authority care as children,[2] their parents having failed to provide, or never having created, a marital family home.

But the word 'family' appears in *Confident Communities* only where 'family' can only mean any household arrangement of a single adult or partners in any relationship, together with children of whatever provenance—in such clichéd phrases as 'families and communities', 'the well-being of individuals and families', 'support for families' etc. *Confident Communities* says that children are protected from the temptations of crime if they enjoy the benefits of a 'secure and stable environment with role models and constructive activities'.[3] But a secure and safe environment is a very general set of circumstances. The Home Office concedes no preference to the safe and secure environments created by the family of marriage operating as *a privileged cultural institution*. Children's Centres, not the family home, are mentioned as giving the child 'the best start in life'.[4] 'Marriage' is mentioned only once—in a negative reference to it. 'More checks will be made on suspicious marriages' to ensure that rules of entry are not abused.[5] The words 'parent' and 'parenting' appear only in connection with failed parents—'mentoring schemes', the expansion of 'parenting support', 'parenting programmes', 'Acceptable Behaviour Contracts' between young people, their parents and local agencies, 'parenting orders for those who cannot or will not face up to their responsibility', 'family group conferencing' and so forth.[6] Many youngsters who get into trouble with crime had 'the bad example of a parent who had offended'.[7]

'Civil society', 'active citizenship', 'proactively strengthening communities', 'community cohesion' are all terms that in the context in which they appear in *Confident Communities* give no hint that spousehood and parenthood were and are still the social roles central to any neighbourhood that actually functions as a community, and to the fulfilment of practical civic responsibilities. Traditionally, *Confident Communities*, says, the Home Office refrained from 'proactively trying to strengthen the communities in which problems of crime appeared'. Since 1997, however, the Home Office says that it has seen 'active citizenship and more cohesive communities as essential parts' of its 'core business'.[8]

While one explicit objective of the five-year law-and-order plan is 'creating stronger families',[9] and 'families' are placed by the Home Office 'at the heart of' the partnership effort to reduce crime,[10] Home Office action conspicuously excludes promoting marriage, as does the 'family-supporting' actions of other government departments.[11] The

Government had earlier considered emphasising the importance of the family based on marriage, but the champions of that view were defeated by those who argued that the Government should not 'interfere with lifestyle choices', as if taking no responsibility for your own children were on a par with opting for a holiday in Spain over one in the Lake District.

The reason put forward by Norman Dennis to explain the separate problem of why the rise in crime proceeded unchecked from the mid-1950s to the early 1990s was that it was almost universally dismissed by England's public intellectuals as a fable created by ill-informed people in the throes of moral panic. The problems of the growth of crime had not been faced, he wrote, 'because it has been systematically and successfully denied that there were such problems'. But he saw many signs in 1993 that the 'pernicious consensus' of denial was beginning to crumble under the sheer weight of inescapable brute facts. If his book played any part in hastening its collapse, he wrote, it would have served its purpose.[12]

Whether or not *Rising Crime and the Dismembered Family* itself had any influence, the fact is that the 'moral panic' consensus no longer exists among public intellectuals, though its pallid sibling 'the exaggerated fear of crime' still stalks the corridors of the Home Office and an occasional column of the quality press, or sits sipping coffee in university common rooms with forlorn veterans of the student movements of the 1960s.

In place of moral panic we have something almost as bad, a wholesale, ramifying and perhaps in part fabricated confusion in and about the crime statistics. This fact on the one hand makes it possible for almost anyone to secure a respectful media hearing for almost any case he or she, in good faith or bad faith, chooses to put. On the other hand it feeds a generalised apathy about the search for better data and the rejection of worse data on crime, and tempts the layman to choose the safe simplicity of indiscriminate cynicism about all statistically-based arguments.

There are two sets of crime figures, those of 'police recorded crime' and those of the British Crime Survey. The figures of police recorded crime have been published annually since 1857. The annual volumes note in detail the effects on the figures of changes in the description of incidents that are recorded as a crime. There is now no way of discovering what differences existed over time in the recording practices in one police force compared with another. It is inherently unlikely, however—in practical terms, impossible—that a trend of generally rising crime could have been either concealed or exaggerated over all police forces in any particular year, or over a series of years. It is virtually certain, therefore, that whatever the defects of figures as a measure of the absolute volume of crime, they fairly represent the growth or diminution of crime over the years. There was a slight break in the police-recorded crime series in 1997/98, when the first of two new sets of counting rules were introduced. The difference was that they were 4,598,327 crimes on the old system, and 4,481,817 on the new system. The figure 4,598,327 is part of the series running back, with some interim adjustments of the same kind, to 1857. The second of the new sets of counting rules, introduced in April 2002, but begun to be implemented in some forces before that date and not fully implemented in some forces after that date, made a larger difference. Using this second new recording system, the National Crime Recording Standard (NCRS), the number of police-recorded crimes in 2003/04 was 5,934,580, instead of the 5,341,122 that the first new set of counting rules would have shown. The figure of 5,341,122 is part of a consistent series running back to 1997/98.[13] Because the figures are defective as a measure of the absolute volume of crime in any given year, that does not mean that they are defective for all purposes. And although there have been breaks in the series, the figures retain their value as measures of the trend of increases and reductions in crimes over the years.

In this volume Norman Dennis and George Erdos look at these police-recorded trends in the crime rate. Supporting the Prime Minister's remarks about the importance of culture in controlling or engendering crime is the fact that, in the England and Wales of 1955, poor, unequal and uneducated by present-day standards, fewer than 500,000 crimes were recorded by the police. By the end of the 1960s there were over 1.5 million. By the end of the 1970s there were 2.7 million.[14] The steeply rising trend in crime predated the Thatcherite 1980s by 25 years, and proceeded in its upward course as relentlessly through times of low unemployment as through times of high unemployment. Throughout the period, of course, the standard of living was steadily improving, and educational opportunities were expanding rapidly.

The police-recorded crime figures peaked at 5,591,717 in 1992. The falling trend preceded the election of a Labour government by five years. But in 2003/04 there were still well in excess of five million crimes on the low count, and just under 6 million on the high count.

The British Crime Survey (BCS) has produced crime figures based on a sample survey of between 11,000 and 38,000 adults living in private households, who have reported to investigators on the incidents of crime of which they personally or their homes have been victims in the previous year. The series has been annual only in this century. The BCS does not take account of crimes committed against under-16s, sexual offences, fraud or so-called 'victimless' offences such as drug dealing.[15] On the basis of the samples, the estimate was that 11,041,000 BCS crimes were committed in 1981. In 2003/04 the estimate was that 11,716,000 were committed. BCS crime, like police recorded crime, had peaked in the mid-1990s (19,353,000 in 1995).[16]

While all these figures are perfectly useful, in the most important context for public discussion today, the brief radio or television interview, the scope is considerable for being confused, or inadvertently or deliberately sowing confusion, or both. A random example suffices. The following is the verbatim account of the discussion on the BBC's Today programme of the newly published crime figures for the year 2003/04.

The discussion centred on the rise of 12 per cent in the year in all violent crime, according to police records, from 991,603 cases to 1,109,017 cases. It did happen to be the fact that almost all of it was a paper and not a real rise, explicable by the change in what incidents had to be recorded as violent crimes. To pursue the 12 per cent rise in the year specifically in violent crime, as distinct from categories of crime that had risen in frequency, was therefore to pursue a pure red herring. And to restrict the discussion to changes since 1997 was to adopt an entirely misleading perspective. The falls in the high volume crimes, and thereby the fall in the overall crime figure, owed little to the police, even less to local authorities, and hardly anything at all to an improvement in morals, the main causes of the fall in crime in the nineteenth century. They were the result mainly of increasing the prison population from 1993 onwards (a Conservative policy not reversed by the Labour Government after 1997), a less trusting attitude towards property and personal safety, and improved security devices installed by householders in their homes and by manufacturers in their cars. Those parts of the discussion that did not deal with the crime figures have been deleted.

John Humphrys Crime has fallen. We've had the biggest sustained fall in the number of crimes committed since the seventee ... er, the nineteenth century, down nearly 40 per cent (*sic*) over the past nine years ... That's one way of reading one set of figures being published today. But other figures tell a different story and violent crime—and that's what worries some people the most—has risen. It's up by 12 per cent—and that's because of drink.

Stephen Green, Chief Constable of Nottinghamshire Well, the general consensus is that the *figures* say that violent crime is falling. In our view go to any town or city centre and the problem is there, visible before your eyes. Town and city centres are being denied to most members of communities because they are now the domain of young people who are under the influence of drink and are misbehaving ...

Humphrys ... What do you make of these figures, Mr. Davis?

David Davis, Shadow Home Secretary Well, they are as confusing as we're used to getting from the Home Office. But the raw truth is, as you've already said, violent crime has gone up by 12 per cent—up above a million now. The British Crime Survey, which the Home Office prefers to use, doesn't include murder; doesn't include crimes against under-16s—some of the fastest-growing crimes, mobile [phone] muggings; doesn't include drug abuse, up 16 per cent; doesn't include rape, up seven per cent; doesn't include shoplifting, double. So, it's a silly survey to use. The real figures are the recorded figures. And these show, as you said, a very large increase in violent crime.

Humphrys But most of it is accounted for by kids pushing and shoving each another when they're drunk on Friday and a Saturday night, if we are to believe the figures ...

Davis Well, no. That doesn't add up either. I mean, serious wounding is up by eight per cent. That's not pushing and shoving. Racially-aggravated wounding up 11 per cent. Sex offences up eight per cent. Rape up seven. These are not minor issues. They're very important. And people listening to your programme will just simply not recognise this picture the Home Office is trying to put out of violent crime going down.

Humphrys It's not what the Home Office is trying to put out. It's the British Crime Survey—which in the past, incidentally, has often shown quite the opposite. They have shown more crimes than the official figures have shown.

Davis Well, the reason the British Crime Survey was set up was in order to try to indicate whether there has been under-reporting, and often you find that with minor crimes. And, I think, you know, there may be an argument for that with something like harassment, for example. But the primary, major crimes and violent crime, where people are *not* not going to report them, the recorded crime is the most important. ...

Hazel Blears, Home Office Minister ... But let's get the story straight here today. We've got a five per cent fall in crime, 30 per cent fall since 1997. You know, this is pretty good work by the police, the people out there on the front line. And if you look at the British Crime Survey, which David says is a silly survey, it's actually the way we have counted crime for decades in this country. If you look at that and the recorded crime figures in terms of burglary, vehicle crime, robbery—all of them down. There's actually half a million fewer people getting burgled than there was a few years ago. So credit where it's due, you know. These are pretty good figures ... Stephen Green is right ... The figures today are extremely good —crime down five per cent last year and down by a third in the last few years.

Humphrys But you know—you quote Stephen Green a lot and he said, ha, he said that people are not going to recognise the picture from these figures. If you can't go into your town centre on a Friday or Saturday night because of drunken yobs making life absolutely impossible for you, what kind of society are we living in?

Blears Well, exactly. And I think this is the responsibility of all of us. It's not simply a matter for government. It's about our own attitudes. ... But the story today—let's just not get away from this—is actually very good crime figures. Crime down five per cent. Burglary down 42 per cent over the last few years. Vehicle crime down as well. And domestic violence down 12 per cent again. So this is good news. And I just want to give a bit of credit to the police out there and people in local authorities working really hard to try to make communities safer. There's more to do ... But let's give them a pat on the back and say, 'Well done!'[17]

There is no way to clear up this confusion in a few phrases or to place our problems of crime and disorder in a proper perspective with a sound bite. But here, in *Crimes and Cultures*, Norman Dennis and George Erdos try to keep complication and contention over the figures to a minimum by concentrating on one category of crime, robbery. Their historical accounts of crime and policing widen the time perspective. Their studies of crime and policing in the United States, Germany and France widen the perspective geographically. Their studies of culture take us beyond the usual discussion of crime and poverty. And they compare the information provided by crime and police statistics with the reports of social observers and with what can be inferred from contemporaneous novels, poems and other sources of information on how people conducted themselves at the time and in the place.

The book is a gauntlet thrown down to the received ahistorical, provincial and materialistic wisdom and fashionable scepticism of the criminological establishment, especially in government.

David G. Green

Preface

One of the first and firmest things taught to students of criminology is that the official figures of police-recorded crime are misleading. Definitions of what does or does not constitute a crime or misdemeanour have changed from time to time. New crimes have been made possible by technical progress—there was no car crime in the middle of the nineteenth century. The proportion of unreported crimes, the 'dark figure', is high for some offences, such as shoplifting, lower for others. The proportion of all crimes committed that are reported to the police has changed over time. In the case of particular offences, the proportion of victims reporting them to the police have gone up considerably. There have been changes in the formal rules that lay down what crimes reported by the public should be recorded by the police, as well as changes in the informal practices of particular police forces and particular police officers.

All these are empirical matters. Some of them can be taken into account easily, some with difficulty, some not at all. But the impression that we have gained from our everyday discussions with colleagues, and others, is that the necessary statistical scepticism of experts has consolidated itself further afield into something of a social axiom or general state of mind: that the official figures of police-recorded crime are totally defective.

This axiom, as such, absolves those who accept it from getting to know what the record actually shows; it can be taken as a dispensation from making any effort to find out what effect particular changes or practices have actually had on the police-recorded figures of overall crime, or on the figures for particular offences. In some cases the axiom leads straight to the blatant and lazy *non sequitur*, that because the raw recorded figures cannot impeccably prove there has been a steep increase in actual crime in the past half-century, this impeccably proves that there has *not* been a steep increase in actual crime in the past half-century.

In spite of the widespread disposition to dismiss the police-recorded figures as for all purposes fatally flawed, we shall nevertheless start by using them. Examining the credence that they can be properly accorded will be a large part of the work of this book.

The figures of crimes recorded by police forces in England and Wales show a remarkable break from about 1955 in the country's history of law and order and policing.

CULTURES AND CRIMES

From 1857 until after the Great War it was rare for recorded crimes in England and Wales to breach the barrier of 100,000 a year. The trend line of Figure 1—the broken line—shows great stability around the figure of 90,000 a year. The population of the country was rising. This represented, therefore, a substantial fall in the crime rates per 100,000 population—or as in those days they used to calculate it, per million population.

Figure 1
Crime figures lie between 80,000 and 105,000 for 65 years
All crimes recorded by the police, 1857 to 1921

Thousands

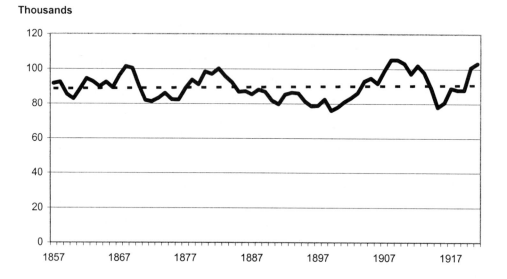

Source: Judicial Statistics England and Wales; Criminal Statistics England and Wales

Figure 2 is on the scale of millions, not the thousands of Figure 1. It relegates figures as small as 100,000 to the depths of the graph. The scale of millions used in Figure 2 means that variations of a few tens of thousands from one year to another are not registered, only the general upward movement of the line. But at the time, the responsible authorities in all areas of national life were deeply worried by what was to them, on the official figures, a perturbing increase.

Figure 2
**Between the wars crime rises from its stable level
of about 100,000 to 300,000
All crimes recorded by the police, 1919 to 1939**

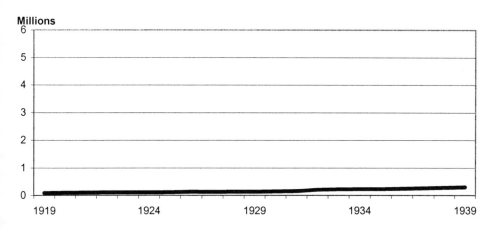

Source: Criminal Statistics England and Wales

After the Second World War, however, it looked as if the widespread expectation would be fulfilled, that the country would return to its century-long normality of civil peace and (in the belief that the figures broadly represented reality) low crime rates. In the early years of Keynesian full employment, renewed programmes of slum clearance and council house construction, social security benefits and a National Health Service, the annual figures of recorded crime stabilised, and indeed tended to fall. (Figure 3.)

Figure 3
In the late 1940s and the 1950s there were about 500,000 crimes a year
All crimes recorded by the police, 1948 to 1957

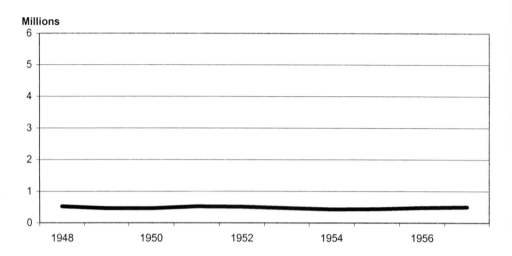

Source: Criminal Statistics England and Wales

But then, alarming at the time, the figures doubled in a decade. (Figure 4.)

Figure 4
In the 1960s crime more than doubles
All crimes recorded by the police, 1960 to 1970

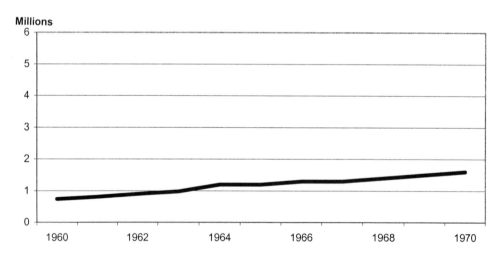

Source: Criminal Statistics England and Wales

In the next 20 years the numbers of recorded crimes mounted year by year. (Figure 5.)

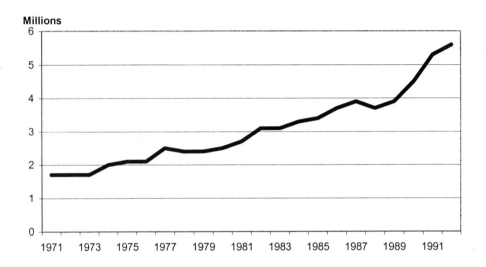

Figure 5
In the 1970s and the 1980s crime continues to rise
All crimes recorded by the police, 1971 to 1992

Source: Criminal Statistics England and Wales

In the early 1990s the crime figures fell. Figure 6 shows the figures up to the year ending March 2003. It shows a break in the line. The subsequent jump in the figures is the result of incidents being recorded as crimes under the new counting rules that would not have been classified as crimes under the previous recording rules. On both the old rules and the new rules, the figures remained at an historically very high level.

Figure 6
From about 1993 at about 5,000,000 a year
All crimes recorded by the police 2000/01

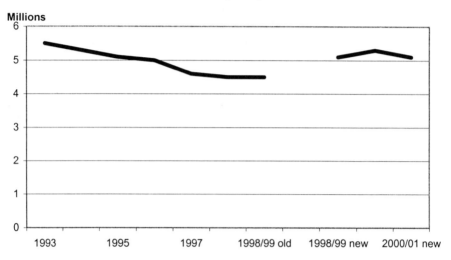

Source: *Criminal Statistics England and Wales*

While the annual totals of all recorded crime were pulled back from
the very high levels reached by the 1990s, robbery continued to
increase into the early twenty-first century. (Figure 7.)

Figure 7
Robberies: Police recorded robberies, 1857 to 2002/03

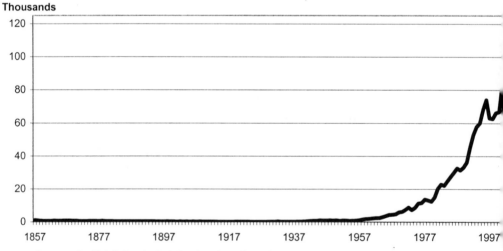

Source: *Judicial Statistics England and Wales; Criminal Statistics England and
Wales; and Crime in England and Wales*

The following statistics are striking. In 1893 the annual number of recorded robberies in England and Wales fell below 400. There were then never as many as 400 recorded robberies a year in the whole of England and Wales until 1941. In stark contrast, from February to December 2001 there were never as few as 400 recorded robberies a month in the London Borough of Lambeth alone. (Figures 8 and 9.)

Figure 8
From 1893 to 1940 there were never as many as 400 robberies a year

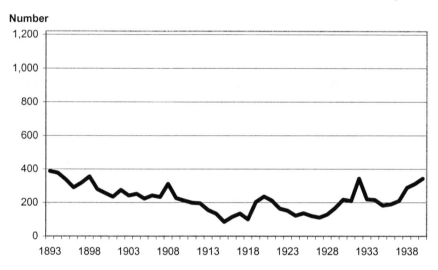

Source: Judicial Statistics England and Wales; Criminal Statistics England and Wales

Figure 9
From February 2001 to December 2001 there were never fewer than 400 robberies a month in Lambeth alone

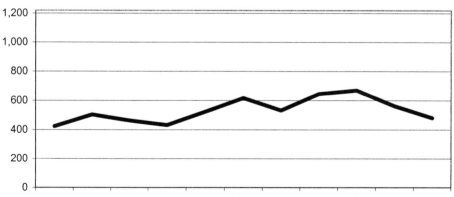

Source: http://www.met.police.uk/crimestatistics/index.htm

Yet during this period of rising crime—again, with the caveat, if the figures do mean anything, a caveat we shall spend some time exploring—there was hardly any response in terms of matching police numbers to the numbers of criminals.

Figure 10 shows the fall in police numbers and the rise in robberies at the end of the 1990s and the beginning of the 2000s.

Figure 10
Police numbers fall. Robberies rise
Falls in police numbers, 1998 to 2000. Rises in Robberies, 2000 to 2002

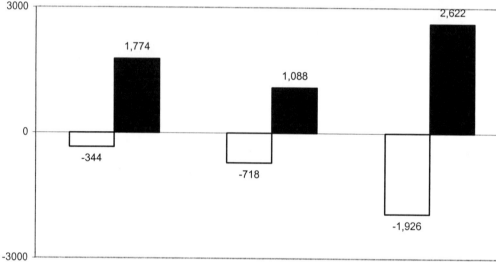

Note: Police scale: one unit equals one police officer.
Robbery scale: one unit equals ten robberies.

Figure 11 shows the number of police officers and the number of crimes in 1960 and 1977.

Figure 11
Before the 1960s' cultural revolution and after
Police strength and crime, England and Wales, 1960 and 1977

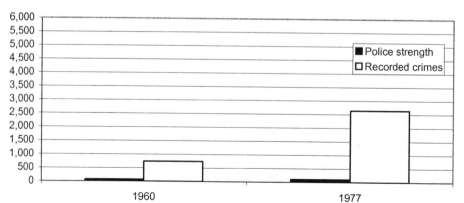

Source: Criminal Statistics; Annual Abstract of Statistics

Figure 12 continues the story to 1986.

Figure 12
Philips to PACE
Police strength and crime, England and Wales from 1977 to 1986

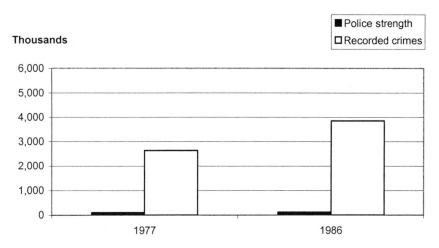

Source: *Criminal Statistics; Annual Abstract of Statistics*

The overall picture of police-officer numbers and crimes in the past century and a half are shown in Figure 13.

Figure 13
Crimes and police numbers, England and Wales, 1868 to 2003

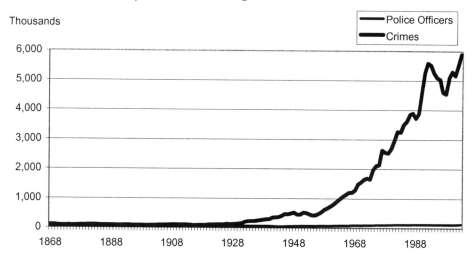

Source: *Judicial Statistics England and Wales; Criminal Statistics England and Wales; Annual Abstract of Statistics* and Home Office papers 17/98 and 10/02

Magnifying the bottom right-hand corner of Figure 13, Figure 14 shows an actual fall in police numbers in the 1990s, before the numbers were increased at the beginning of the 2000s.

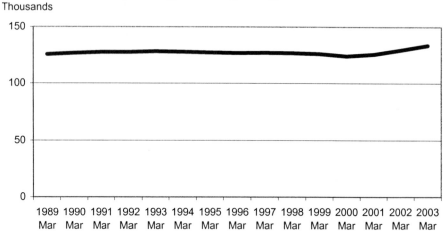

Figure 14
Police numbers 1989 to 2003
Total police officer strength, England and Wales

Source: *Annual Abstract of Statistics*; Home Office papers 17/98 and 10/02

Similar developments in disorder and crime seem to have occurred in other countries. There, too, in the first half of the 1950s it looked as though the theory that crime had been caused by harsh working conditions, unemployment, war, poor housing, social insecurity and so on was being validated by events. With peace, prosperity, better schools and housing, improved educational opportunities, full employment and social security, crime rates stabilised. In the false dawn of the early 1950s they actually fell.

In Berlin, there were seven times more robberies in 1946 than there had been before the war. Money had lost its value, respect for property was shattered and people felt it was useless to go to the police at all. Trains and lorries were cleared of their loads in transit. Farmhouses and fields were looted by raiding parties. Yet from 1947, as economic and political conditions improved, crime rates declined.[1]

In the United States the sociologist Daniel Bell welcomed the same trend of declining crimes rates as a permanent characteristic of a post-war prosperous democracy. Murder rates in the 1950s were half those of the 1930s, and the crime of kidnapping had practically disappeared.[2] But in the late 1950s and 1960s, with incomes still rising, a narrowing of the gap between the rich and the poor, an unbroken succession of years of extremely low unemployment and the provisions of the welfare state, the crime rate surged upwards.

In France, the decade from 1955 to 1964 saw an increase in the crime rate of 70 per cent. In the Netherlands the increase was 54 per cent. In Sweden, the social-democratic model of steady economic prosperity, enlightened laws and penal innovation, the increase was 44 per cent. In Italy it was 40 per cent. The 'earnest and disciplined Germans', along with the Austrians, also experienced a sharp rise in the crime rate, of 26 per cent in the Federal Republic and 25 per cent in Austria.[3]

Writing at that time, Sir Leon Radzinowicz, Wolfson Professor of Criminology at the University of Cambridge, concluded that the hard facts of the 1960s and 1970s had put it beyond dispute that a 'relentless upsurge in crime' was now being caused, not by economic deprivation, but by economic affluence.[4] A rapid increase in crime, out of all proportion to anything that had been seen in Britain, certainly since mid-Victorian times, was coincident with personal liberation, material well-being and the extension of state as provider of at least a subsistence income, of council housing and new towns, of health services and education free at the point of delivery, and other economic and town planning services and controls.

While these improvements were under way, various other aspects of civic society were also undergoing rapid change. The state, in the pursuit of worthy political causes, or in the remedying of obvious evils, intentionally or inadvertently damaged or destroyed moral and institutional capital that it could not restore when the costs appeared alongside the gains. The most obvious example was the dismemberment of the family in the West as an institution based on life-long monogamy for the procreation and raising of children. The male was now brought up largely freed from the expectation that his main adult concern would be maintaining a home for a lifetime with the mother of their children.

But according to hegemonic opinion this could have had no effect on the frequency with which young men expressed their freedom from such adult burdens in irresponsible violence and crime, because violence and crime, it was claimed, were not occurring any more frequently. The almost unchallenged view of the influential intelligentsia in the universities, and the broadsheet and public-service media of communication, was that crime had not increased from the late 1950s to the mid-1990s. According to the social-affairs consensus, the high and increasing figures did not reflect any real increase: they were an artefact of the moral panic of the unenlightened public fanned by the gutter press; they were due to more reporting of the same amount of crime; they were due to the interest of the police in exaggerating the crime figures so that their own numbers would be expanded; they were due to more incidents being reclassified as crimes, and so forth. The contributions that all or any of these factors might have made to the increase in the figures were treated without further examination as if they explained the whole of the increase in the figures.

The conventional wisdom of the social-affairs intelligentsia in the second half of the twentieth century was: there had been no significant increase in crime, so there was no need to seek any causes of an increase in crime, least of all to seek causes that put in question the benefits of lone-parenthood, freely chosen pre- and extra-marital sexual activity, abortion, divorce on demand and so forth.

We were led by the consideration of these crime figures and these social changes to examine in greater detail the experience of the English people during the period covered by these statistics, and to compare the experience of England with that of the United States, Germany and France. In particular, we wanted to explore what had happened over time in these four countries within the triad of (i) the 'internalisation' of values (a process that, when successful, renders control unnecessary, the individual being guided by his 'conscience'), (ii) informal community controls to the extent that internalisation fails and (iii) police control to the extent that there is a failure of both self-control and community control.

Culture, Law and Order and the Police

To be members of the same society means, by definition, to share a certain sameness of views about what is true about human nature; about social organisation; about the history of the society; and about the relationship between life in this world and (if it is believed there is one) an existence after death.

To be members of the same society also means a certain sameness in beliefs about what should be done about the perceived real world. Some things are perceived as being beneficial, to be preserved or improved upon. Others are perceived as harmful, to be combated or eliminated. These cultural judgements, made upon cultural perceptions of reality, constitute, roughly speaking, the shared morality of the members of the same society.

By definition, being 'a member of the same society', whether on the large-scale of the nation or the small-scale of family, school or local community, means that there is a certain sameness in self-image. 'Our lot don't do that sort of thing.' 'That's what we do.'

Some of 'our lot' do what they ought not to do, or don't do what they ought to do. But the self-image, and the controls that other members of the society exercise on all other members to live up to the image, affect everyone's conduct, even where it only takes the form of the group's special form of hypocrisy or bravado.

A 'certain' sameness is necessarily a vague phrase. All societies are internally differentiated. The sameness of belief always consists, therefore, in a degree of consensus that differences exist for sound empirical and moral reasons: the varieties of human nature being —believed to be—what they are; what we now call the laws of physics being what they are; the possible forms of efficient social organisation being what they are; the nature and the stated will of the deity or deities being what they are.

The life span of some societies is months or years. Of others it is a generation or two. Of others it is centuries or millennia. The continued existence of a large-scale society depends upon there being a sufficient degree of agreement between both the rich and the poor that the rich as a body, though not all of them as individuals, are rightly rich: the rich and the poor agree that the poor are unavoidably poor, even if they are poorer than they should be, and it is fruitless to try to change things very much. There is sufficient agreement on what part trying to get rich should play in a person's life, and on the circumstances within which poverty is a virtuous state. The powerful and the powerless agree that the powerful are deservedly powerful, and agree on what conditions must exist, or what procedures must be followed, to secure a valid entitlement to power. There is sufficient agreement on what procedures are empirically and morally available if conflicts are to be effectually contained, conducted and composed. As an aspect of this, there is sufficient agreement on who can legitimately use how much force for what purposes in what circumstances.

A 'certain' sameness is a vague phrase also because the 'sameness' in some societies consists in agreeing that there should be wide scope for individuality and for freedom from public scrutiny of one's beliefs and conduct. It is necessarily a vague phrase because societies change over time. In the course of a thousand years the content of a nation's culture or, say, a church's culture alters, sometimes at a slow, some- times at a fast pace. The distribution of income and power changes. The old bases of consent change. But the sameness results from the fact that remnants of the old ways are preserved for a shorter or longer period in the process of change, leaving the stamp of the old society on the new.

A 'certain' sameness is necessarily vague, again, because of the fact that, although over a long enough period any large-scale society can lose its own characteristics and take on those of another (and superficial changes of dress and industrial technique can be introduced by a conqueror or dictator overnight), societies cannot develop from year to year, or decade to decade, in any direction they or their leaders choose. They can develop only along the lines that the existing attitudes and skills of their members and the structure of their institutions make possible. That, at any rate, has been the case up to now with regard to the major cultures of the world. No doubt with contemporary means of communication, and given the economic power and military might of the United States, all the processes that foster a culture of strict rules in the world of work, and unrestrained self-indulgent choice outside it, will be greatly speeded up.

The phrase 'sufficient agreement' is also necessarily vague. What was 'sufficient' is known only after the event. But in general it remains true that a society on a large scale or a small scale ceases to exist when its members lose the capacity to agree on what facts are true and what conduct is good.

One possibility is that the society does literally cease to exist for all practical purposes. On a small scale, the society of husband and wife ceases to exist when they can no longer contain their disagreements. The structure of uncles, aunts, cousins created for their children by their marriage is enfeebled. On a larger scale, within a religious denomination, say, or a political party, the beliefs that once held the church or the party together can fade. Offices are filled by mediocrities or no one at all can be persuaded to take office. Members leave. New members are not attracted. The organisation disappears when the death of the last few loyal members obliterates it even as the subject of bitter or wistful reminiscence.

Societies can cease to exist altogether on the scale of a national state. The state of Prussia once covered a land area larger than modern Germany. There is no longer a Prussia even as a place on a map. It lingers passively in the Prussian archive of the state library of Berlin and, partly a revival of Prussian culture, in the statue of Frederick the Great restored to its place Unter den Linden. It lingers actively in a shop in Potsdam main station displaying Prussian memorabilia, run by a voluntary association of Prussian patriots. The East German Communists put great efforts into rewriting history and destroying buildings and monuments in order to replace even the memories of old beliefs and morals. But the job can be, and is, done as well without falsification by embracing an ignorance of history to oneself, and inducing historical amnesia in others.

Schisms are a second possibility. There are two or more parties or sects where there was one before.

A third possibility is the gradual or swift replacement of one set of beliefs about what is factually true and morally laudable—one culture—by a different set of beliefs—by a different culture, without a change in name. 'Marriage', for example, has retained its name, but it is no longer heterosexual monogamy with the focus on the procreation and rearing of the children of the life-long marriage. It has moved steadily towards being a civic or religious certification of any 'stable relationship' for any period of time between any two people who seek the certification.

A religious body might continue for a time with a set of doctrines that would not have been recognised even as Christian in the religious body with the same name 40 years before. The assumptions of fact and value that sufficiently united members of a political party in the 1930s might be present in a highly transmogrified form in a new party that nevertheless retains the party's title in the 2000s.

Any national culture at any particular point of its development has its characteristic perceptions of the facts of human nature and its own theories about what forms of social organisation work well or poorly as these bear upon the effectual and morally justifiable use of force. Whatever else a 'state' is, it is a potential user of violence. Its peculiar nature as an association is that, first, there is attached to its lawfully established proceedings the ultimate sanction of unconditional compulsion. Secondly, this unconditional compulsion applies to everyone within its geographical area.[5] As Weber said, the state cannot be defined in terms of its ends. There is scarcely a task that one state or another has not taken in hand. The state can be defined only in terms of the specific means available to it, namely its monopoly of the legitimate use of violence within a given territory.[6]

It is never, therefore, a matter of an organisation either being a state or not being a state. It is a matter of its place on a continuum. A state exists to the extent that a set of people are accorded the right by the population to use publicly approved and publicly regulated force against all other users of force. At one extreme there is widespread and deep support for the way in which the state uses its coercive power—the state enjoys a high degree of legitimacy. At the other extreme there is a grudging acceptance of the state and all its abuses because of the belief that a free-for-all for criminal gangs and war-lords would be still worse. When it loses all legitimacy of its monopoly of the use of violence then sociologically speaking it ceases to exist as a state, whatever label it continues to be given.

The state might approve the use of some degree and type of physical violence by some private individuals in some circumstances. Teachers might be permitted by the state to detain pupils, and use a minimum of physical restraint when they attempt to evade detention, where the intention is to maintain the good order of the class or school. Parents might be permitted by the state to smack their children on certain parts of their bodies where the intention is to make their children behave 'properly'.

But the state can withdraw such delegated powers—perhaps or probably under the influence of the belief about human nature and social organisation that such physical restraint or chastisement is ineffectual, or counterproductive, or always abused. The state again becomes the sole arbiter of the detail of when, what and how much restraint and physical force will be used to keep or—if the cultural definition of the facts of human nature and social organisation that led to the abolition of the delegated powers was erroneous in actual fact—restore order among the children once kept in order by teachers and parents.

The state might condone and overlook, where it does not actually approve, a fight without weapons or boots at a football match or in the back street behind a pub, where one man is fighting one other man under the gaze of spectators ready to intervene in the interests of the community's conception of 'fairness'. One of the men has, say, sworn in the presence of a woman or a child. The state might regard this as a legitimate part of the rough and ready machinery of local social control.

But here, too, the state can withdraw its implicit delegation, perhaps because cultural changes on various grounds of perceived fact and value have led to an obliteration of the distinction between private force used to uphold community standards, and private force used for selfish and anti-social purposes. But when these informal controls are banned, the risks attendant upon attempts even to admonish what a person regards as the bad behaviour of others in public—swearing, littering, spitting, insulting, speeding, making a row—become excessive. He or she is too likely to secure no support from anyone else, and perhaps get a knife in the neck or a kick in the head as the reward for possessing a sense of civic responsibility.

The British state used violence for external purposes far less in the second half of the twentieth century than it had in previous centuries. During the century of internal civil peace from the mid-nineteenth to the mid-twentieth century, to give a few examples, the British state was busy quelling the Indian Mutiny 1857–59, or fighting the Second

Afghan War 1878–80, or attempting to subdue the Boers, or shelling the German lines on the Somme in 1916, or firing on the crowd at Amritsar in 1919, or sinking the Bismarck or bombing Hamburg or Dresden during the Second World War, or fighting against Irish nationalists. Courts martial and Royal Commissions document some of the abuses and excesses in the use of violence at the disposal of the British state.

Internally, British people were also using state-tolerated private violence to uphold community values far less in the year 2004 than they were during the century of civil peace from the mid-nineteenth century to the 1960s. Committees of inquiry and the records of the criminal courts document some of the abuses of this state-tolerated private violence.

The certain sameness in perceptions, morality and self-image expresses itself, then, in average differences in actual conduct between members of one society and another—one football team or another, one army or another, people from one country or another—given the same objective circumstances. The emphasis is on the word average. Around the average there is variety in the reactions of human beings that make up any society, and a more or less large overlap between what is found in one society compared with another.

All Americans have a wide range of beliefs, morals and modes of reacting in given situations that they share with everybody else in the world. Large numbers of human beings are nevertheless distinctly American in their beliefs and modes of conduct. All Texans have a wide range of beliefs, morals and modes of conduct that they share with everybody else in America. Large numbers of Americans are nevertheless distinctly Texan.

It is curious but not unusual to find people who insist that differences of culture are socially insignificant, and that it is morally obnoxious to suggest that they are, and then in the next breath are violently anti-American, and vehemently object to a president of the USA because he is Texan. They object to the way that the—in some discernible sense—typical Texan and—in some discernable sense—typical American thinks about things and does things.

At the level of a society that is a national state or an anthropologically distinct society, perceptions of reality and judgements of morality have to do with religion; with the production and distribution of food, dwellings, clothing, medicines; with sex and procreation; with defence against outside aggressors; with the control of breakers of its own laws; with the acquisition of technical skills; with education into how to behave in ways considered necessary for the efficient functioning of

xxxiv   CULTURES AND CRIMES

the society; with the amenities of social intercourse; with how differences empirically can and morally must be handled, and so forth.

So far this is purely a matter of definition of what 'a society' is. Like any other definition of a social phenomenon, it concerns a continuum. At one extreme there is the pure case of a set of people who are completely at one with one another. At the other extreme, the complete absence of society, there is a set of individuals who bear no resemblance to one another and who agree on nothing. In real life, any particular society lies somewhere along this continuum from unbroken solidarity to complete fragmentation, the point where the set of people cease to form a society to the slightest degree. People form a society, just as any society is also a state, to the extent that their perceptions of reality, their morality and their actual conduct meet the criteria of the definition.

Social anthropologists have made it their special business to study examples of populations that have developed with widely different ways of coping with the various problems of human survival. Ruth Benedict contrasted the chronic blame culture of the Dobu of eastern New Guinea, the chronic one-up-manship and individualism of the Kwakiutl of the south-west coast of Canada, and the extreme peacability, conformism and communality of the Zuni of New Mexico. She was careful to emphasise that even in the most conformist society, the Zuni (one of the most conformist societies of which we have knowledge), there remained a great deal of difference in the way different individuals responded to given situations.[7]

In some cases, anthropologists have concentrated on populations with identical genetic distributions. Perhaps the most famous example is that of three small New Guinea tribes living within a few miles of each other. They were similar in that they were all hunter-gatherers. But in some respects they were vastly different. The Mundugumor were selfish, violent and unsociable. Arapesh life was amiable, peaceable and co-operative. Among the Tchambuli the women were competitive and aggressive go-getters, while the men were more or less useless ornaments, gossiping and being nice to one another, and beautifying themselves at home. The feminine character was created by culture, not by biology.[8] Mead's studies of adolescence purported to show that it was possible for a culture to cope without great difficulty with the transition from childhood to adulthood, because Samoan culture accomplished this.[9]

Ruth Benedict's, *The Chrysanthemum and the Sword* is a study of Japan at the end of the 1939–45 war. Her argument was that, with its overall and internally various distributions of genetic traits, Japan could organise itself in ways that any other large society had organised itself, and achieve what any other society had achieved. In Ruth Benedict's view, this applied not only to Japan, but also to any other open society with a large population, and to any open and large group within each open and large society. Life began on earth by seeking sustenance from the environment by reflex actions built into the genetic make-up. It developed by finding ways of building-on the genetic capacity to respond to experience by using the more flexible mechanisms of culture.[10]

Every culture, like every human being, has its praiseworthy qualities. Every culture, like every human being, brings suffering to its members through its own defects, or makes others suffer from them. It may be that in some ultimate sense all cultures are equally blameworthy and equally meritorious—that *overall* there is nothing to choose between any culture that exists or has ever existed. But different populations have varied, and do vary enormously in what they have ever attempted, and in what they ever have achieved or ever can achieve, given the world-view, the morality, the knowledge and the skills characteristic of its members—that is to say, given their cultural heritage.

Clearly in modern times there were certain things that Europeans wanted to do, were able to do and succeeded in doing. There were other societies with their own world-views, morals, knowledge and skills—their different cultures—who did not want to do these things. Or, if they dreamt of doing them, their cultures did not create in sufficient numbers the people with the motivational, moral and technical capacities to make the dream come true. Whether or not they were right in retaining their culture in the face of European hegemony, or perishing along with their culture, is an entirely separate matter.

The dominance of Western European cultures since the end of the fifteenth century is clearly seen in the conquest by Europeans first of the high seas and then of much of the land area of the globe. 'Dominance' is used here, of course, in the objective sense and not the moral sense of superior. European cultures were dominant in that they attained the objectives of Europeans, however morally repugnant or sublime their objectives and methods were compared with those of opponents who were operating with the world-view, morality, skills and knowledge provided by their own cultures.

Europeans all but eliminated the Siberians and the Amerindians and seized their lands. Europeans conquered India and Indonesia. By the end of the nineteenth century most of Africa was incorporated into the British, French, Portuguese and Belgian empires, and China had been made to submit to various humiliating demands of different European powers.

At the beginning of the period of European world hegemony, agriculture was still the major source of wealth. European culture had made Europeans richer than their contemporaries. The heavy plough had been gradually developed during the late Roman and early medieval period until it was capable of efficiently turning and draining the soils of the high rainfall zone of northern Europe. A series of small improvements in detail and in ancillary equipment, together with an increasing use of other machines, particularly water- and windmills, kept productivity rising.

Technical efficiency correlates with knowledge, and knowledge correlates with literacy. By the early fifteenth century Europeans were certainly as literate as anyone else, if not more literate, but from the mid-fifteenth century Gutenberg's method of printing by the use of movable type put European literacy far ahead of that of other cultures. From the publication of Gutenberg's Mazarin Bible in 1456 until the twentieth century the gap in technical knowledge between the West and the rest of the world grew at an ever-increasing rate.

But economic growth depends also on the existence of attitudes that drive people to engage in certain types of activity. Weber's thesis is well known. According to Weber, Calvinism was a crucial variant within European culture in the early stages of the development of its potent cultural element—industrial capitalism. Calvinism demanded that pious men and women should work actively in the world and not languish in a monastery. All men and women should work for the glory of God and not for their own physical gratification. (Weber called the combination of these two features of Calvinism 'this-worldly asceticism'.) Calvinists believed, furthermore, that only a chosen few would enjoy everlasting life in Heaven. Most would suffer everlasting torment in Hell. But, crucially for the motivations that Calvinism produced, the choice of Heaven or Hell did not lie with the individual. Everyone had been already predestined by God for either Heaven or Hell. Good behaviour did not improve one's chances of entering Heaven. But it was at least certain—almost certain—that evil-doers would not be found among the elect of God. Calvinists could never therefore at any time allow themselves the moral luxury of misbehaviour, for that was the one proof that they could not be among those predestined for eternal felicity.

These elements in Calvinism as a culture were therefore extremely well-suited for the production of both conscientious and frugal working men and women, and trustworthy and innovative entrepreneurs who would invest their profits in further growth and not waste them in social display and personal indulgence.

By the time Weber produced his thesis in 1904, of course, Calvinism had long lost its former pre-eminence as the motivator of either capitalists or workmen. Weber was interested in the traces of the influence of Calvinism that remained in the United States in the early years of the twentieth century. But Weber argued that capitalism no longer needed Calvinism. Capitalism was quite capable of producing for itself, he said, the increasingly non-religious, and even anti-religious motivations, morals and skills—the distinctive culture —required for its own continued success.[11]

Europe carried all before it from the end of the fifteenth to the end of the nineteenth century because of its cultural attitudes. The first of these attitudes was that in trying to achieve any particular purpose, a variety of different ways existed. The second was that to achieve any particular purpose some ways were better and some were worse than others. The third was that still better ways remained to be discovered. At the opposite extreme to this European attitude, that better ways ought to be imitated or invented, is the attitude that current practices are a gift from the gods from the beginning of time, and change is sacrilegious.

'Better ways' are not only a matter of the technical improvement in the use of material resources. They are also a matter of the way in which material resources are deployed.

Cortes and Pizarro conquered empires with a handful of men. Each had only a dozen harquebusiers that had to be reloaded after each shot. This weapon could not have been decisive in battles involving thousands of men. Their possession of horses was a factor in their conquests. Swords of Spanish steel were much more deadly than the stone maces and wooden clubs of the Aztecs and Incas.

But the decisive difference lay in cultural factors. The Aztecs fought to get captives for sacrifice. For them, a battle was a matter of dashing up to the enemy's lines and pulling out a prisoner. The Spaniards fought to destroy the opposing army as a cohesive force. Whatever the moral virtues of one cultural concept or another, for winning battles the European concept was clearly superior.

The importance of a superior culture of management as well as superior technical skills comes out just as clearly in the British conquest of India. At the battle of Plassey in 1757, 800 British soldiers and 2,200 Indian auxiliaries defeated a Bengal army of 50,000 men. As far as fire power was concerned, the advantage lay with the Bengalis. They had 53 field-pieces against the British 12, and they had enough French advisers to get reasonable if not perfect use out of their guns. Clive won the battle of Plassey through the skilful use of extremely meagre resources. European dominance at Plassey, as elsewhere, was based on the possession of a particular culture of decision-making.

In an eloquent comment on the Emperor Decius's appointment of Valerian as censor, Gibbon points to the futility of attempts by any state at any time to control conduct without sufficient willing support from its subjects or citizens. The state can make a benign contribution only when most individuals most of the time accept the state's specific controls, and condemn others when they violate them. It is impossible, Gibbon says, for the state to exercise its authority with benefit or even with effect if virtuous citizens become rare, and if unforced public opinion ceases out of cowardice or folly to condemn vice.

In the absence of a sufficiently strong sense of honour and virtue in the minds of the people; where there is not sufficient reverence for public opinion; and without a host of 'decent prejudices' about what is good and what bad conduct, the state's structures of control sink into 'empty pageantry' or become officious excuses for merely 'vexatious oppression'.[12]

Benign societies, as distinct from dominant societies, are exceptional, and their creation is a slower and more uncertain process than their destruction. Whether he or she is born into a relatively benign society or not is, from the point of view of the given individual, a matter of the purest chance. On the first page of *The Decline and Fall of the Roman Empire* Gibbon formally acknowledges that fact, by giving thanks that he had the good fortune of living in a culture of science and philosophy and, in what was rarer still, 'in a free and civilized country'.[13]

Adam Smith shared Gibbon's view that a state's ability to support benign, and suppress malign conduct depends heavily upon the prior existence of a population that holds the same conceptions of what is good and evil, and accepts the desirability of the particular rules that the state enforces. For Smith, a society is precisely a set of people who willingly abide by the same rules, including the rules that define the private sphere—the rules of personal liberty—and how the people who break the rules or invade the private sphere should be punished. A largely unconscious familiarity with and acceptance of its rules of justice are as necessary to the functioning of a society as are the rules of grammar to the mutual comprehensibility of the society's language, 'precise, accurate and indispensable'.[14]

But a benign society also requires the widespread practice of other virtues. The rules of justice benignly prohibit us from hurting our neighbour. But what Saint-Just later called 'the cold rule of justice',[15] though crucial, is a very limited element in a benign society. The rules of justice, Smith wrote, might sometimes be fulfilled by simply 'sitting still and doing nothing'. At the most, the bare rules of justice require no more than 'the exchange of good offices according to an agreed evaluation'. The virtues that go beyond justice present us with ideas of the perfection we ought to aim at in our social conduct. If justice is the grammar of morality, benevolence is comparable to the loose and vague rules of language that are laid down for the attainment of what is 'sublime and elegant' in composition. When benevolence is widespread, social life is not just fair, it is happy; society does not just survive, it flourishes.

In Smith's view, however, benevolence is a component of human nature. Providence has imposed upon human kind a 'piece of deceptive folly', he says, that drives them through their benevolent conduct to seek the approbation of other people:

> It is well that nature imposes upon us in this manner. It is this deception that rouses and keeps in motion the industry of mankind. It is this which first prompted them to cultivate the ground, to build houses, to found cities and commonwealths, and to invent and improve all the sciences and arts which enable and embellish human life, which have entirely changed the whole face of the globe, have turned the rude forests of nature into agreeable and fertile plains, and made the trackless and barren ocean a new fund of subsistence and the great highroad of communications to the different nations of the world.

Adam Smith insisted that the success of 'free markets' themselves, no less than the efficacy of states, depends upon our acting, not simply selfishly, and not even simply with a rigid sense of justice, but 'according to the dictates of our moral faculties'. To the extent that we follow this natural inclination, we pursue the most effectual means of promoting the happiness of mankind, 'and may therefore be said in some sense to co-operate with the Deity and to advance, as far as is in our power, the Plan of Providence'.[16]

Smith's view of human nature was thus far less pessimistic than was Gibbon's, and his view of economic progress was as optimistic as Marx's.[17] His optimism seems to be based on the sense he shared with Gibbon, that he was already living in a morally benign and economically successful community. His society required relatively little internal use of the coercive action of the state; and small applications of the state's coercive power, when exercised, were effective.

Beneficence, for Smith, then, is just as important, if not more important, than the mechanism of markets free from force and fraud in leading people 'as if by an Invisible Hand' to promote the welfare of others as well as their own well-being. Without such pre-existing beneficence, the state can do little to combat resulting evils, much less create a moral society.

A person's attachment to his social group depends upon his feeling that, without his having to do anything himself, the particular orders he is asked to comply with, the specific rules under which the orders are given, by whom, in which circumstances, and the processes under which the rules have been made, will be beneficial to him, if only in general or in the long run, or indirectly as they do or will benefit others he cares about. This is as true of a member of a voluntary group, no matter how petty, as it is of a citizen of a country. In a parliamentary democracy, the order might be that he stop his car. The rule might be that the police may or must stop a car exceeding a certain speed limit on a certain stretch of road. The method of making such a rule is by a regulation introduced by a particular government. The regulation derives its authority from the Act of Parliament under which it is made. The government derives its authority from the fact that compliance with electoral laws has resulted in a majority of MPs being of the government's party. The Act of Parliament derives its authority from its passage having been in compliance with the word and the spirit of the rules of debate and all other aspects of constitutional procedure.

These considerations can be thought of as five circles of acceptance of, support for, trust in, or attachment or loyalty to the association of which he is either voluntarily, or without any choice in the matter, a member. The most important such association—not a voluntary association—is the state of the country of which he is a resident or citizen.

The first circle would represent his trust in the people whose immediate orders, or other actions, on behalf of the group, actually impinge directly upon him in the here and now. A particular police officer stops and searches a particular young man on a particular pretext. The police officer might behave politely or impolitely; he might be acting within the rules or in breach of the rules. If the young man comes from a community that does not trust the police, he will object to even a polite and legal stop-and-search.

The second circle represents his trust in the current incumbents of those positions in the association, the occupancy of which carries with it the authority, if proper procedures are followed, to make the rules that permit or require that particular orders be issued or other actions taken in the circumstances specified by the rules.

The third circle represents his trust, not in persons, but in the group's impersonal systems and procedures. These include the system of the offices that incumbents occupy, the procedures of election or appointment that must be followed to have the offices duly filled, and the 'operating rules', as Easton calls them, that constitute in writing or by tradition the ways in which members of the group are expected to behave as officers or in the rank-and-file.[18] It is possible, indeed quite normal, to be dissatisfied with the way one has been treated by a particular official on a particular occasion or many officials on many occasions; to think that this or that particular rule is redundant or ridiculous; to abhor and despise the current holders of political and administrative office, expecting nothing but harm to result from their use of power and yet have full confidence and undiminished trust that the system is the one that, on the whole, does produce the best results. When faith in the institutions is lost, this is much more serious than loss of faith in the people who have made the current rules, and the people who are enforcing them.

The fourth circle represents adherence to the group's culture, the ideas about, and the moral judgements on, human nature and history that sustain its set of social arrangements. Members of one group, for example, believe as a matter of fact, and approve as a matter of value, that people develop their innate capacities, and do most good for others, only if they are compelled to exert themselves. Members of another group, by contrast, believe that people develop best, and contribute most to society, when they are left to make their own choices—the 'natural identity of interests' postulated in one form or another in world-views otherwise as various as those of Locke's liberalism, Godwin's anarchism and Marx's communism. Members of one group believe that the exercise of power is ennobling. Members of another believe that power corrupts. In one culture the belief reigns that human nature is the same the world over; in another, that human nature is infinitely various the world over; in yet another that national or other group differences are deep and ineradicable, men and women, working-class and bourgeois, English and French. Members of one group believe that people are fundamentally equal in their abilities, and inequalities of achievement are entirely and solely the creation of circumstances that speaking empirically can, and speaking morally must, be altered. Progress is inevitable and a blessing; progress is a chimera and its pursuit is a curse. Instructions necessary for a good life are contained in this or that sacred text; no existing or conceivable lifestyle choice is superior to any other conceivable lifestyle choice. One culture inculcates the virtues of thrift and self-control, another the virtues of extravagance and self-indulgence. One encourages the notion that personal hardships are the fault of assignable perpetrators who must be blamed and made to pay; others encourage the notion that the same hardships are one's own fault or the result of unassignable accident, and must be endured.

Fifthly and finally, there is the circle of attachment, trust and loyalty that encloses actions, orders, decisions, rules, incumbents, constitutions and culture, namely, trust in and attachment to the group, whether the group is a country or a community or association within it. On the level of the country, a citizen or resident of a country might feel that he has been badly treated by a particular person or persons on one or many occasions. He might believe that the current laws are damaging to his interests. He might feel that the present office-holders will always issue orders and make rules that are damaging to his interests. He might feel that the country's current culture, or melange of cultures, will continue to throw up such actions, decisions, rulers and institutional arrangements. He can yet feel that, because of the possibilities lying within it cultural heritage and the basic potentialities of the community's population, the community of which he is a member will eventually produce the culture, institutions and personnel who will act as the agents of his and the general welfare, or at least the welfare of future generations.

As Walter Bagehot said in discussing the dignified and efficient parts of the English constitution in the nineteenth century, 'every institution must first win the loyalty and confidence of mankind and then employ that homage in the work of government'. Trust, the willingness of the rank-and-file to let the authorities get on with the business of producing and implementing decisions, can be envisaged as a stock that accumulates or diminishes in response to a citizen's experiences of actions, commands, decisions and rules. The sociologist Talcott Parsons dealt with this point in a similar way. One of the most important 'returns' on the prudent 'expenditure' of power, he argued, is trust. Trust directly affects a leadership's capacity to rule without the extra efforts involved in mobilising prior approval or in controlling disorder.[19] The less cultural cohesion there is in within a society, the more expensive it is to govern, and the less scope there is for the lax systems of individual rights and liberal freedoms that are possible in consensual societies, where trust replaces control.[20]

At one notional extreme on the continuum of trust in the government of a society (never reached in real life) there is no need for coercive control at all, as in the imagined 'higher state of communist society'. Behaviour is no longer confined within 'the limits of what is permitted by the police'.[21] No police are needed, the state 'withers away' and the 'administration of things replaces the government of men'.

At the other notional extreme, also never reached, only control can make the society function at all, because trust is completely absent, and alienation has replaced it. Alienation from the incumbents of office means that they are believed to be all out for themselves. Alienation from the operating rules means that they are believed to be rigged. Throwing the rascals out only means making room for another set of rascals. 'The conductor changes, the music remains the same.' Alienation from the group's culture means that its noblest aspirations are dismissed as the piety of buffoons and the lies of frauds. With such alienation from the group's actions, decisions, incumbents, institutions and philosophy of life, there are no barriers on the passive side to apathetic withdrawal, apostasy, desertion, voluntary exile or secession, and on the active side no barriers but brute power to sabotage and nihilistic or collective terror.

With these very general remarks on the meaning of culture in mind, attention can now be turned to the cultures of England, the United States, Germany and France, as these have tended to produce or suppress crime and dissent.

Part I

England

1

Political Disorder in England
before the Nineteen-Sixties

The territory of present-day England was definitely united as early as the reign of Edgar (958–975). 'Never had England seemed so strong or so peaceful' as under Edgar and his 'Primate minister', Dunstan. The same culture was propagated by Oswald from the See of York in the north of England as by Ethelwold from the See of Winchester in the south. 'After-times looked back fondly to "Edgar's Law", as they called it', in other words to aspects of England's past and future political culture as they shaped themselves in the hands of Edgar's ministers.[1] The people of the whole of England had developed by the tenth century a national consciousness of being members of a single society. The present border between England and Scotland was finally fixed as far back as the reign of Henry III, when by the Treaty of York (1237) Alexander II renounced Scotland's claims to Northumberland, Cumberland and Westmoreland.

In the middle of the nineteenth century, when Germans were struggling to achieve national unity of lands stretching far over present-day Poland into Lithuania, 'from the Meuse to the Memel, from the Etsch to the Belt', English poets took national solidarity for granted in their incantation of place names familiar to all English people, as part of their own country from time immemorial:

Night sunk upon the dusky beach, and on the purple sea;
Such night in England ne'er had been nor ne'er again shall be,
From Eddystone to Berwick bounds, from Lynn to Milford bay,
That time of slumber was as bright, as busy as the day;
For swift to east, and swift to west, the warning radiance spread—
High on St. Michael's Mount it shone—it shone on Beachy Head:
Far o'er the deep the Spaniard saw, along each southern shire,
Cape beyond cape, in endless range, those twinkling points of fire.
The fisher left his skiff to rock on Tamar's glittering waves,
The rugged miners poured to war, from Mendip's sunless caves,
O'er Longleat's towers, o'er Cranbourne's oaks, the fiery herald flew,
And roused the shepherds of Stonehenge—the rangers of Beaulieu,
Right sharp and quick the bells rang out all night from Bristol town;
And, ere the day, three hundred horse had met on Clifton Down.[2]

As a remedy for the injustice and disorder that had grown under Edgar's predecessor Edmund, Edgar elaborated a system of primitive police for the 'hundreds' of families headed by a freeman in a village or group of villages. The hue and cry was to be raised after a thief—probably a horse or cattle thief—by order to the senior 'hundred man'. The hundred man passed the order for hue and cry to each senior 'tithing man', the head of each group of ten freemen in the hundred. All the freemen in the hundred were thus mobilised to ride out after the thief, under pain of fines or, in the last resort, outlawry. If the thief escaped into another hundred, the hundred man there was informed, and responsibility for hue and cry was passed to him, and so to the next hundred.[3]

Edgar's measure built on the cultural notion of those early times that policing is a matter for the ordinary people of the small community taking responsibility for the system of just and fair laws.

Policing can be oppressive control imposed by an alien body of men, in the interests of a predatory minority, but it need not be. Edgar's cultural conception and his institutional form of policing has reappeared with the authority of the state in, for example, the lawfully constituted posse of the Wild West. It has appeared in many times and places, without the authority of the state, where legal controls over criminals have not been established or have become corrupt or feeble. Unauthorised vigilante groups of otherwise law-abiding citizens in those circumstances have organised themselves to enforce on violators the laws that conduce to the perceived common good. Usually they have disbanded when the state has established or re-established its ability to control crime. In notorious cases, however, the vigilante group has fallen under the control of criminals and become itself a significant problem for the equitable enforcement of law and order.

Two centuries of largely foreign rule soon followed Edgar's reign. But the centralising government first of the Danes, especially under Canute, then of the Normans, especially under William I, and then of the Angevins, especially under Henry II (their reigns preceded or followed by those of assorted tyrannous or manipulated incompetents) had the effect of strengthening both the consciousness of and loyalty to a national culture and its political, religious and social institutions. The meaning of loyalty to the national 'social order', to the point of giving one's life for it, was pungently expressed by the Earl of Surrey when the social order of England was in dire contention, during the Wars of the Roses. When he was asked why he had fought for Richard III at the battle of Bosworth Field (1485), the Earl of Surrey answered, 'He was crowned my king, and if the Parliamentary authority of England set the crown upon a stock, I would fight for the stock. And as I fought for him then, I will fight for you when you are established by the same authority'.

By the middle of the thirteenth century the most distinctive and pervasive feature of English culture had firmly established itself, the English Common Law.[4] The Common Law, 'not made, but begotten out of immemorial custom', was the law of the land. Until the late twentieth century, when the law of the European Union overrode any English law, there was no question of Roman law becoming dominant in English courts.

The great distinguishing feature of the Common Law was that law was conceived of as an independent entity, to which the monarchy itself was subject.[5] Roman law justified much more easily than the Common Law government by an enlightened and benign monarch or élite dealing with an ignorant and wayward mass. The Common Law, by contrast, embodied the notion that the sovereign governs by laws established by negotiated charters, or in accordance with nation-wide arrangements that have proven their worth in their actual results over the course of time.[6]

Roman law was more sympathetic to rational uniformities and to what Jakob Burkhardt calls the 'terrible simplifications' of bureaucrats. The Common Law was more sympathetic to equitable practical outcomes and the dictates (if not always the forms) of common sense.[7]

Max Weber regarded the distinction between an oversimplified politics and a politics that paid adequate attention to the actual richness of any situation in the real world, as being of far more importance than any distinction between 'left-wing' and 'right-wing' politics. Some politicians and political theorists stick to a principle or to a few principles. It does not matter if the consequences are disastrous for other people. They have stuck to their principles, and that is enough for them. *Fiat justicia, ruat cælum.* Let justice be done, though the skies fall—on everybody.

There are other politicians, however, who bring to bear on the empirical problems with which they have to contend an adequate number of relevant principles. Crucially, they measure their success, not by the conformity of their results to the principles that animated their original policies, but on the principles that justify or condemn the actual results of their policies. Weber called these responsible politicians. In the middle of the Great War he courageously went on public record to tell the German public that Britain's successes for centuries had their basis in the politics of responsibility, and Germany was failing because of the preponderance of conviction politicians.[8] In 1918, when the war was lost, he warned that the principled politics of both the German left and the German right, the politics of the naïve literati as he called it, would lead within ten years to 'a polar night of icy darkness and hardness, no matter which group triumphs now'. He was out by five years.[9]

Roman law is not necessarily less sympathetic to the abstract idea of democracy than the Common Law. In his *Democracy in America* Tocqueville made an early attempt to solve the puzzle of why the pure democracy of the Jacobins had ended in Napoleonic authoritarianism, while the United States and the muddled unwritten constitution of England had produced both consent and liberty.[10] The democracy that Roman law traditions favour is the simple 'yes' and 'no' of the mass electorate—the democracy of the plebiscite—the form that Weber labels, indeed, 'cæsarian' democracy. The plebiscite, Weber writes, is 'the specifically cæsarian technique of control', and the apathy of the electorate and the activism of the leadership mean that all forms of democracy, unchecked, drift in that direction.[11]

At best, if the electorate proves so ill-informed as to return the wrong result on any occasion, then there will be new inputs of persuasion from the 'enlightened' leadership and new plebiscites until the 'right and rational' result is obtained. At worst, and in modern times not infrequently, 'democracy' simply as one person one vote has deteriorated into 'totalitarian democracy'.[12] Hannah Arendt saw the emergence of a mass of people 'free of all principles and so large numerically that they surpassed the ability of the state and society to care for them' as the raw material with which, under a régime simply of one person one vote and none of the other elements of democratic consent and liberty, became available to be manipulated by self-righteous bureaucrats or by corrupt demagogues no less than by honest governments.[13]

These assertions about the antiquity of an English national consensus, about the content and influence of cultural perceptions of reality, and cultural evaluations of what is perceived as reality, are all references to matters of fact. Whether those perceptions of fact and morality were themselves right or what the facts of national solidarity or the content of the culture at a given time were is one question. It is an entirely different question whether then or now, in themselves or in their consequences, it was a good thing or a bad thing that these were indeed the facts. And facts can only be established or demolished *ad rem*, by the facts, never *ad hominem*, by showing some characteristics of those who have asserted them. Whether particular statements can be attributed to 'Whig historians', or 'Communist ideologues', or 'feminists', or white or black men or women, or old or young people, in itself confirms or refutes nothing.

This is not a brief history of England. The sole intention is to establish first, that people who have lived in the territory, neither more nor less, now called England, have been subjected as a single political unit to experiences common to successive generations for a thousand years. Secondly, it is to establish that, by whatever processes, these experiences resulted in a society that has had its baronial wars, religious wars and class conflicts, but that, compared with the internal conflicts of other societies, was exceptionally consensual—whether or not the reason was, as Arendt suggests, that English statesmen had the 'good sense' to draw a sharp line between colonial methods and normal domestic policies, unlike France and Germany, where an attempt was made to 'imperialise the whole nation'.[14]

The worst and most famous massacre to occur in England in modern times followed a peaceful and well-organised demonstration held on St Peter's Fields, Manchester, in August 1819. Eleven people were killed and hundreds injured by the swords of the mounted volunteers of the Manchester Yeomanry. This massacre, the Battle of Peterloo, provoked an immediate revulsion of feeling throughout England. There were numerous meetings in many parts of the country, strongly supported not only by the working-class, but by middle-class and aristocratic protesters.[15] One of the aristocratic protesters was Lord Fitzwilliam, who organised a demonstration against the massacre at the cost of his lord-lieutenancy of Yorkshire.[16] On the continent, the Holy Alliance of Prussia, Austria and Russia was pursuing—and was to pursue until 1848—unremitting policies of censorship, espionage and the military subjugation of revolutionary movements. In England, Peterloo had the effect of making the rising generation permanently disgusted with violence as a means of controlling domestic dissent.[17]

In May 1833, shortly after the foundation of the Metropolitan Police in its modern form, the National Union of the Working Classes held an open meeting off Calthorpe Street, by the Gray's Inn Road. The meeting does not seem to have been turbulent, but the new 'Peelers' under Inspector Thomas closed off the area and set about the demonstrators with staves. A constable named Cully died from a knife wound in his back. The attacker was acquitted. The coroner's jury returned a verdict of justifiable homicide.[18] The Metropolitan Police learned early that physical violence was available to it for the control of crowds only on occasions of patently dangerous unrest.

In 1848 and 1849 revolutions and their suppression in all the major countries of western Europe except England resulted not in 11 deaths, as in Manchester in 1819, but in hundreds of deaths In 'the year of revolutions', England experienced no revolutionary deaths at all. The most serious disturbances were in Bradford. On 29 May 1848 the Mayor had to issue a proclamation and to order the employment of dragoons as well as the policemen and special constables. Many people were injured, but no one was killed in the clashes.[19]

The first half of the nineteenth century was much freer from repressive violence than the continent. After 1848 it became freer still. That civil peace characterised English life as early as mid-1844 is confirmed by Engels's own 'evidence' that England was not just on the brink of civil war, but already engaged in one. For any reasonable reading of his own evidence proves just the opposite. Engels's evidence that 'in this country, social war is under full headway' was—the 'shocking' crime rates that he deduced from his reading of three editions of the *Manchester Guardian*, and one day's edition of *The Times*. By present-day standards they amount to a tiny number of trivial incidents. What he reports as evidence that there was a crime problem verging on civil war in 1844 is clearly beyond the wildest dreams of civil peace for any English town in 2004.[20]

In 1855 the railings of Hyde Park were torn down in the course of a demonstration protesting at Parliament's proposal to impose Sunday closing on shops—a measure the working people objected to. Being at work all the week, including a full day's work on Saturdays, Sunday shopping was convenient for them. Marx wrote of the event that there was no doubt that 'the English revolution began yesterday in Hyde Park'. But reading his own account, the striking impression it has on a modern reader is the extreme peaceabililty of the enormous crowd. Marx describes how Inspector Banks and 40 constables made their way through the crowd to the speakers' platform and told them to desist, and the crowd to disperse—which they did.[21]

Reviewing its history from 1868 to 1968, the British Trade Union Congress (TUC) included among its first illustrations a drawing by the nineteenth-century cartoonist George Cruikshank, whose work appeared in such critical journals as the *Scourge* and the *Satirist*. Cruikshank's 'British Beehive', dated 1867, was the symbol of the *Beehive*, a labour journal.

It showed the 'British Beehive' with the army, the navy and volunteers at its base, supporting the rest of society, not at the apex dominating it. The mercantile marine is at the second level. The next level shows cabmen, ostlers, pavoirs, boatmen, coal heavers, coster mongers and so forth. Above them are depicted tailors, boot makers, weavers, carpenters, smiths, masons, bricklayers and engineers. Above them are the retailers of meat, bread, vegetables, cheese, jewellery, clothes and books. At the next level are inventors of work for men and boys, mechanics, workers in agriculture, and girls and women at work. Above them come medical science, schools, literature, art, colleges and chemistry. Above them Cruikshank places religious denominations and the courts of criminal law and equity, then the Lords and Commons. At the top level is the 'royal family by lineal descent'. The drawing is embellished with labels that add the information that the Queen, the Lords and the Commons are 'the pillars of the state', that the 'British Beehive' has a 'free press, honest and independent', and that there is 'freedom to all religious denominations'.

The comment made by the TUC in 1968 on Cruikshank's 'British Beehive' was that it shows 'the gulfs between the governors and governed in 1867'. It certainly shows that there was a stratified society in 1867. But it does not suggest that there were society-rending disagreements either over the fact of stratification, or over who occupied the lower and higher positions, or over the suitability of their qualifications for occupying them. The text of the TUC's centenary volume also shows clearly that its taken-for-granted cultural view in 1968 was that in the century since 1868 the only sharp disagreement had been over how good a deal the workers in the lower echelons were getting. The TUC's story, told by itself—presenting, that is, its own perception of reality—was that Britain's politicians, clergymen, academics, inventors, journalists and trade unionists working with one another (or against one another as the case may have been), within the context of British 'ways of doing things', i.e. British culture, had succeeded in vastly improving the political and material conditions of all the working class and some of the middle class.

Some disagreements in the century 1868 to 1968 had ended in violence. On the side of the workers, there were a handful of cases of what would now be called terrorism. The TUC's centenary volume discussed only one example. During a strike in 1866 a tin of gunpowder was used to blow up the house of a non-unionist. The perpetrators received little or no support from the labour movement of the time. The Association of Organised Trades in Sheffield and the London Trades Councils applied to the Home Secretary, and a special Commission was set up at their request to clear trade unionism of any association with the 'Sheffield Outrages' as they were called then and have been ever since.[22]

Charles Dickens's *Hard Times* is based on his experience of a strike in Preston in 1854 that he covered as a reporter for *Household Words*. The novel is a merciless exposition of the inhumanities fostered and sanctioned by the utilitarian view of the world and its moral evaluation of its perceived world. But a subplot is the struggle between the corrupt union official Slackbridge and the upright and doomed Stephen Blackpool. Slackbridge tries to discredit Blackpool at a union meeting. 'There were general groans and hisses, but the general sense of honour was much too strong for the condemnation of a man unheard. "Be sure you're right, Slackbridge!" "Put him up!" "Let's hear him!" Such things were said on many sides. Finally, one strong voice called out, "Is the man heer? Is the man heer, Slackbridge, let's hear the man himseln, 'stead o' yo". Which was received with a round of applause.'[23]

Lasalle, the father of German socialism, taught that to treat an opponent fairly was the first duty of man. Whether that made him a good or bad leader of the German workers is not relevant here. The German workers, he said, should look to England to see the ideal put into practice. In England, he wrote, 'opposing forces fight like gentlemen'. Sombart, in quoting Lasalle, remarks that England was the home of a working class that before 1850 had been disorderly, but was now persistent, businesslike, calm and above all self-confident.[24]

When unskilled labour roused itself in the late 1880s it proceeded along the same path. *The Times* reported that in the London dock strike of 1889 for the 'dockers' tanner' there was no reference to revolution 'except in the peaceful spirit of Thomas More'.

> *John Burns*: Now, lads, are you going to be as patient as you have been?
> *The crowd*: Yes!
> *Burns*: As orderly as you have been?
> *The crowd*: Yes!
> *Burns*: Then march off five deep past the dock companies' offices and keep to the left hand of the street.[25]

Charles Booth believed that by the 1890s the material for civil disorder was found only in the 1.25 per cent of the population of the East End, and a lower percentage elsewhere.[26] Keir Hardie's vision was to 'waken in the worker a consciousness of his manhood, not of his class'.[27] Looking back from the mid-1960s to later Victorian times, Asa Briggs wrote that English trade unionists had been engaged in the task of 'building with care and vision a co-operative commonwealth'.[28]

We often hear Robert Roberts's account of the slums of Salford in the first quarter of the twentieth century cited as evidence that what may have been true of the skilled working class was not true of the unskilled, and that the slum working class at least was held down by force. When Roberts simply says that the policeman was viewed with 'fear and dislike' it is in the context of denying that he was seen as a 'social worker', or as a 'counsellor or friend' of the slum dweller, not to allege that the police force was an active instrument of state coercion. Roberts said that the unskilled worker did not need to be coerced. He was 'conformist' in his respect for the criminal law and 'chauvinistic' with regard to the English constitution, (i.e., he was not merely a patriot, but a rabid patriot). He went on 'accepting his lot unchanged'.[29]

Roberts gives an account of a visit to Salford of Tom Mann during the notorious times of suffragette, Irish Unionist and working-class unrest before the Great War. Since the days of the dock strike of 1889 Tom Mann had come to adopt the position of the syndicalists, who followed the doctrines of Sorel, as presented in his *Reflections on Violence*.[30] Mann led the dockers' strike of 1911, which brought gunboats to the Mersey and cavalry to Liverpool. He was active in the Cambrian Combine strike in South Wales in the same year, and his 'Don't Shoot!' leaflet led to his arrest for incitement to mutiny.[31] As a result of his Salford speech, Mann was arrested and sentenced to six months in prison. 'In fact, he only served six weeks', Roberts writes, 'and told the press on his release that he had been "treated well".' 'Authority saw little menace in syndicalism.' Roberts adds a further opinion that coincides with that of Arendt: the English authorities, he says, were 'wily enough not to make martyrs'.[32] One thousand disaffected people from Manchester and Salford might cheer the syndicalist. 'But city and borough together held close on a million people, for the most part solid in their allegiance to society as it was ...'

Roberts might be right or wrong in the account he gives. The English might or might not have been dismally misguided in not following the French example of the Commune of 1871 with its bloody aftermath of thousands of dead workers; or that of the Bolsheviks in 1917; or the revolutionaries of the *Spartkusbund* in Germany in 1918, whose best-known leader, Rosa Luxemburg, was executed 'in accordance with martial law' and thrown into a Berlin canal as the first step in the death dance of inter-war Germany.[33] But his account confirms the view that the culture of the working class was not one of opposition, least of all violent opposition, to the authorities; nor of the authorities to the working class.

The fundamental importance attributed to volunteers and the mercantile marine in Cruikshank's 1867 cartoon may have been connected to the emergence at that time of many organisations like the Volunteer Life Brigade (VLB). A culture is characterised by the extent to which it elevates certain social types; and if it does seek to elevate them, what social types it does seek and succeed in representing as heroes and heroines. The success of the VLBs was itself connected with the importance in Victorian culture of Grace Darling. At great risk to their own lives, in an open rowing boat in a violent storm, she and her father rescued five passengers from the *Forfarshire*, wrecked off Bamburgh in 1838. The first Volunteer Life Brigade was established in Tynemouth in 1864. A group of men at South Shields—typically at the Mechanics Institute—decided to follow suit. When volunteers were called for, 140 men enrolled. There were eventually 500 Volunteer Life Brigades around the coast of Britain, dependent from first to last only on voluntary labour and on voluntary financial contributions.[34]

The continuity of culture in spite of all political or philosophical attempts to diminish its importance or obliterate its memory is well illustrated by this story. When the *Tenterten* of Sunderland was wrecked on the south pier of the Tyne in 1866 those rescued included a small girl. The rescue was the subject of Watson's painting 'Saved'. In 1946 a woman in her eighties standing in front of the picture in the South Shields Watch House was heard to say simply: 'I was that child'.[35]

There was thus in Cruikshanks's time a close familiarity with the difference between voluntarily risking one's own life for the sake of strangers in the mines, at sea or on the coast, and a secret attack on fellow-workers—not to speak of the contrast with robbers, burglars and other (to them) clearly anti-social elements. This is what made, and to some extent what still makes, the cultural atmosphere in working-class areas so inhospitable to the post-modernist doctrine of sheltered academics and journalists, that it is difficult to make distinctions of a moral kind between different cultures, cultural elements or lifestyle choices.

On the side of the violence of the state against the workers, Alfred Linnel, 'the first English socialist martyr', died of injuries sustained when he was part of a crowd of demonstrators trying to force its way past the police cordon into Trafalgar Square in November 1887. Two miners were shot dead in a riot in West Yorkshire in 1893. Two bystanders were shot dead in a riot by striking railwaymen in Monmouthshire in 1911 by troops correctly following the procedures of the Riot Act. The culture of victimisation was so weak in the Labour movement that the Miners' Federation of Great Britain immediately condemned the rioters in West Yorkshire as 'the worst enemies of the miners' cause'.[36] The two deaths in 1893 and the two in 1911 are not even mentioned in the TUC's centenary volume.

William Morris wrote of the Trafalgar Square death of Alfred Linnel:

They will not learn: they have no ears to hearken.
They turn their faces from the eyes of fate,
Their gay-lit halls shut out the skies that darken,

But lo! this dead man knocking at the gate.
Not one, not one, nor thousands must they slay,
But one and all, if they would dusk the day.

As G.D.H. Cole, the Labour historian and activist, rather dryly remarked 62 years later, 'his warning was without basis: the revolution was not at hand'.[37]

In 1921 and 1922 demonstrations of the unemployed were often dispersed by the police. Mounted police batoned the crowd severely in Sunderland on 21 September 1921. The Recorder of Liverpool, from his place on the bench, publicly rebuked his local police for their violence. Cole called these actions of the police 'uncharacteristic extravagances'. Cole adds that these uncharacteristic extravagances were 'soon brought to an end'.

The unemployed who took part in the Hunger Marches of the 1920s and 1930s, Cole writes, were 'never violent':

> They paraded in military formation, it is true, and in considerable numbers, but they wrecked no buildings and they seized no food; their banners were as often Union Jacks as Red Flags; as a marching song they preferred, for both sentiments and tune, 'Colonel Bogey' to the 'International'. ... The conservative capitalist and the conservative Labour leader were both, consciously or unconsciously, beginning to look back to a period of peace before the war, of two party government, prosperity and calm progress. Circumstances enabled them to take some steps towards their ideal.[38]

In 1944 George Orwell wrote approvingly of the 'gentle-mannered, undemonstrative, law-abiding English':

> An imaginary foreign observer would certainly be struck by our gentleness; by the orderly behaviour of English crowds, the lack of pushing and quarrelling... And except for certain well-defined areas in half-a-dozen big towns, there is very little crime or violence.[39]

The alarming if slow realisation by those who disparage English culture that Orwell had favourable things to say about it has led them to reappraise his reputation as one of the most honest and accurate observers of twentieth-century life.[40]

K.B. Smellie, a professor at the London School of Economics respected by and popular with the students of the late 1940s and early 1950s, wrote of the English that the life of the town has given them:

> a discipline, which is unsurpassed because for the most part self-imposed and which has made them amenable and loyal to sensible leadership in new conditions or in any emergency. The pattern of life in a wartime air raid shelter was as orderly as that of the group of pilgrims in Chaucer's *Canterbury Tales*.

Professor Smellie continues:

> there can be little doubt that the life of towns has steadily improved. ... Drunkenness has fallen steadily. So too has public violence. ... From the Yahoo habits of

eighteenth-century London we have passed into an almost Houyhnhnm rationality of orderly processions and patient queues. And, almost certainly with the passing of violence, drunkenness and squalor, has gone much cruelty as well. Personal relations are more gentle and, as one observer has said, 'the contemporary English would appear to have as unaggressive a public life as any recorded people'.[41]

If we consider civil unrest outside of the boundaries of England, 38 MacDonalds were murdered by Campbells loyal to King William in the Glencoe massacre of 1692. Lord Macaulay convinced the nineteenth-century English that it was one of the great crimes of history. On the orders of their general, the Duke of Cumberland, the English and Scots regiments loyal to Kind George cut the throats of their rebel Stuart prisoners at the battle of Culloden in 1746. Hundreds were killed. But there was little public approval for Cumberland's ferocity. News of Culloden was received in England with shame, and Cumberland was reviled as 'Butcher' and 'Nolkejumskoi'.[42] In the Punjab in 1919 the Amritsar Massacre cost the lives of nearly 400 Indians, when British troops fired on a crowd that was protesting against the extension of emergency powers to control subversion. In England it remained a *cause célèbre* for the left as an outstanding example of bloody repression up to the 1960s and beyond. General O'Dwyer was nevertheless condemned by the British Government for the part he played in suppressing the demonstration; and when Mr Justice McCardie expressed the view in the case of *O'Dwyer v Nair* that General O'Dwyer had been unjustly condemned by the government, his remarks led to vehement protests in the House of Commons, and a motion was tabled for his removal from the bench.[43]

The grievances of the Irish against the English are manifold. On Cromwell's orders, English and Irish royalists stormed the city after the garrison refused to surrender, and killed 2,500 of the defenders of Drogheda in 1649. In hindsight, the potato famine of the 1840s in its causes and consequences should have been handled quite differently. But few allege that the failure of the English to deter the Irish from their choice of depending upon the monoculture of the potato, and the failure of the English to supply life-giving aid when the potato crops were blighted, were strands in any policy of hostility to, much less the genocide of, the Irish by the English.

But since Drogheda there has been nothing remotely comparable in extent with the Armenian massacres, 'the saddest of all the countless horrors associated with the great war of 1914'. The sum total of persons massacred by the Turks in Armenia in 1917 will never be known, but Grant and Temperley write in their standard history of Europe 1789 to 1939 that 'it can hardly be wrong to reckon that something like 600,000 persons perished... '.[44] Millions of fellow-citizens were slaughtered on the orders of Nazis and Bolsheviks, by people who either shared the Nazis' or Bolsheviks' cultural conceptions of truth and virtue, or who were working within a culture that had not created institutions that kept Nazi and Bolshevik culture at bay.

At the beginning of the twentieth-first century, failures to develop a culture of internal stability have manifested themselves in the slaughter of thousands of fellow-citizens in the Balkans, and hundreds of thousands of fellow-citizens in many countries of sub-Saharan Africa and elsewhere. In other places the death toll is less dramatic, but relentless. According to Le Monde, between 100,000 and 150,000 were killed in Algeria between 1992 and 2003, most of them civilians, as the price of a 'merciless war' waged between the state and Islamists.[45] According to western diplomatic sources, also reported in Le Monde, in mid-2003 an average of 30 people a week were being assassinated in the course of the armed struggle between the Algerian state and the Islamic Salvation Front (FIS).[46]

Contrasting one atrocity with larger atrocities does not detract from its intrinsic seriousness. But given the unending daily toll of atrocities in some societies, the notion that 'all cultures are equally good and equally bad' must depend very largely upon a misreading of the historical and contemporary records of the world-views and achievements of one culture compared with those of others.

In the early 1950s the noted anthropologist Geoffrey Gorer set out the problem he had to solve if he were to give an adequate account of the English national character. In public life today, he wrote,

> the English are certainly among the most peaceful, gentle, courteous and orderly populations that the civilized world has ever seen... the control of aggression has gone to such remarkable lengths that you hardly ever see a fight in a bar (a not uncommon spectacle in most of the rest of Europe or the USA), [and] football crowds are as orderly as church meetings.

Still in 1955, it was this, to use Gorer's words, 'orderliness, gentleness, and absence of overt aggression' that puzzled the anthropologist. His explanation was that the English had modelled themselves generally on the character of the Peelite police officers they personally knew. 'I wish to advance the hypothesis', Gorer wrote,

> that one of the techniques by which the national character of a society may be modified or transformed over a given period is through the selection of personnel, for institutions which are in constant contact with the mass of the population in a somewhat superordinate position. If the personnel of the institution are chosen chiefly for their approximation to a certain type of character, rather than for specific intellectual or physical skills, if persons of this type of character have not hitherto been consistently given positions of authority; and if the authority of the institution is generally felt to be benevolent, protective or succouring, then the character exemplified by the members of this institution will to a certain degree become part

of the ego ideal of the mass of the population, who will tend to mould their own behaviour in conformity with this ideal, and will reward or punish their children in the light of this pattern which they have adopted.

As generations pass, the attempt to approximate to this ideal will become less and less conscious, and increasingly part of the unconscious mechanisms that will determine the content of the super ego or ego ideal; with the consequence that a type of character that might have been... very uncommon in the society when the institution was first manned will subsequently become... common in, and even typical of, the society, or of those portions of it with which the members of the institution are in most continuous contact or from which its personnel are drawn.

The institution which I propose to examine in detail is the English police ... I should like to suggest that, increasingly during the past century, the policeman has been for his peers not only an object of respect, but also a model of the ideal male character, self-controlled, possessing more strength than he ever has to call into use except in the gravest emergency, fair and impartial, serving the abstractions of Peace and Justice rather than any personal allegiance or sectional advantage.

This model, distributed throughout the population has, I suggest, had an appreciable influence on the character of the population during recent decades, so that the bulk of the population has, so to speak, incorporated the policeman or woman as an ideal, and become progressively more self-policing... If this hypothesis is true, then what started out as an expedient to control great criminality and violence of large sections of the English urban population has resulted in a profound modification of the character of this population. ...

There is not yet comparable evidence to show whether the communist party member in the USSR or China is producing analogous results. The communist party members are publicly connected with the whole apparatus of state power... and this... may interfere with the processes of identification by the powerless; for, it would seem, it is by means of the more-or-less complete and more-or-less unconscious identification with the members of the admired and succouring institution that the characters of the mass of the population are gradually modified and transformed.[47]

Were not a word of that true, the fact that it was written by an eminent academic, and not attacked by his peers at the time, would still constitute it as evidence of the leap made into a different culture a few years later.

2

Crime in England before the Nineteen-Sixties

To leap centuries freely, therefore, and pass to more recent times: in the second half of the nineteenth and the first half of the twentieth century England remained, internally, a society that compared with its peers had few problems of social order, and compared with the past half century suffered few problems of crime.

Crime in the middle of the nineteenth century

Engels

'With the extension of the proletariat', Engels wrote of the state of affairs in 1844, 'crime has increased in England, and the British nation has become the most criminal in the world.' The conclusion that any reader today will draw from the evidence Engels adduces to support that statement, however, is that the crime rate in 1844 must have still been very low by present-day standards. 'I look at a random heap of English journals lying before me', Engels writes. 'There is the *Manchester Guardian* for October 30, 1844, which reports for three days that in Salford a couple of boys had been caught stealing, and a bankrupt tradesman tried to cheat his creditors.' Reports are 'more detailed' for the neighbouring towns. In Ashton in the course of three days there were two thefts, one burglary and one suicide. In Bury there was one theft. In Bolton there were two thefts and one revenue fraud. In Leigh in the course of three days there was one theft. In Oldham there was one theft, one fight between Irish women, one non-union hatter assaulted by union men, one mother beaten by her son, one attack upon the police and one robbery from a church. In Stockport there was discontent of working men with wages, one theft, one fraud, one fight and one wife beaten by her husband. In Warrington there was one theft and one fight. In Wigan there was one fight, and one robbery from a church.

In London, he writes, the position is much worse so far as crime is concerned. In a *single day*, according to reports Engels gleaned from *The Times*, there was in the whole of London no fewer than one theft, one attack upon the police, a sentence upon a father requiring him to support his illegitimate son, the abandonment of a child by his parents and the poisoning of a man by his wife. 'Similar reports', he says, 'are to be found in all the English papers.'

If England, on that evidence, was the most criminal country in the world, the rest of the world must have been remarkably free from crime.[1]

However well or poorly these reports reflected the real crime rates in 1844, Engels's assumption from his own experience of English life was they did reflect the real crime rates. He was not the most incompetent of observers of social life. People in the twenty-first century who insist that crime rates in the middle of the nineteenth century were really about as high or higher than current crime rates have to explain why they know better than the reported figures what the figures really were, and why their claim to know what the truth was about mid-nineteenth-century crime is superior to that of Engels's.

The 'moral panic' argument of the last part of the twentieth century, that crime was not growing, and that it was a feature of all societies to become increasingly distressed in each generation in the face of an unchanging level of crime, is comprehensively contradicted by writers in the second half of the nineteenth century. Already in 1848 John Stuart Mill had addressed the question of the probable future of the working class. The future of liberal democracy depended upon the degree to which working people could be made into rational beings. Contrasting the experience of England with that of the authoritarian powers of Europe in the course of the 'year of revolutions' 1848, his conclusions were that past trends were favourable and promised further improvement.[2]

Mayhew

The principal descriptive source of crime in London in the middle of the nineteenth century is Henry Mayhew's eyewitness accounts, given in the four volumes of his *London Labour and the London Poor*.[3]

In 1850 London was in a state of rapid population growth. Universal educational provision lay 20 years ahead, and universal, compulsory and free education lay 40 years ahead. Town planning, council housing, social security and the welfare state all lay in the remote future. Public health legislation was in its infancy, and modern-style policing had been in existence for about 20 years. According to the common criminological theory that crime is caused by social, political and economic deprivation, these high levels of deprivation must have been associated with very high crime rates.

Yet what do Mayhew's direct observations reveal about crime in Victorian London? He does not deal with the respectable working class. His observations are restricted to those elements of the mid-nineteenth-century working class that were freest of the pressures and controls of respectable society—the street people of the metropolis. In contrast to the early twenty-first century, when all personal property must be carefully supervised at all times, Mayhew tells us that during the day the goods on costermongers' stalls and barrows were left 'almost entirely unwatched, the policeman and the market-keeper only passing at intervals'. After business was finished, the goods would be left exposed all night, 'with nobody to see to them'. Yet, according to Mayhew, thefts were 'rarely heard of'. The costermongers' stables were sometimes used to store goods that the donkeys would not spoil. The stables seldom had even a latch, much less a lock. But the goods were (Mayhew uses the strong word) never stolen.[4]

Judicial Statistics provided estimates made by the police of the 'number in the criminal classes' in their areas at about the time Mayhew was carrying out his investigations. All the police forces in the country reported a grand total in the criminal classes of 135,766. Included in the criminal classes were all the known prostitutes (2,037 under the age of 16, and 28,743 aged 16 and older), all known vagrants and tramps (23,353), and all suspected persons (37,688) The number of 'thieves and depredators' in England and Wales in 1859 was put at 39,538.[5]

In the accounts he gives of the costermongers' 'low and disorderly' pastimes of drinking, gambling and boxing, Mayhew shows that there was a high degree of self-regulation, requiring adherence to rules of decency, honour and fair play when dealing with other people. Boxing 'rarely' led to quarrelling.[6] At playing cards for money, 'we play fair among ourselves—aye, fairer than the aristocrats'.[7] In playing 'three up' (betting on how three ha'pennies will fall) a ruined player was made a gift by the others of 2*d* for every shilling lost.[8]

Mayhew's account of the costermongers' gambling presents not only a picture of self-regulated fair play, but an implicit acceptance of the authority and power of the police or indeed any respectable passer-by to stop them gambling in public.

'It would be difficult to find in the whole of this numerous class a youngster who is ... not a desperate gambler. ... Every attempt by the police to check this ruinous system has been unavailing. ... Many a lad has gone down to the gambling ground with a good warm coat on his back and his pocket filled from Saturday night's market, will leave it at evening penniless and coatless.'[9] 'The spots generally chosen for the

Sunday's sport are in secret places ... where a scout can give quick notice of the police. ... Between Lambeth and Chelsea, the shingle on the left side of the Thames is spotted with small rings of lads, hidden behind the barges. One boy ... is always on the look-out, and even if a stranger should advance, the cry is given ... Instantly the money is whipped-up and pocketed. ... If during the game a cry of "Police!" should be given ... instantly a rush at the money is made by any one in the group, the costers preferring a stranger should have it rather than the policeman.'[10]

At the costermongers' dances, Mayhew reports, it was 'not often' that there was any violation of 'decorum'. '"The women", I was told by one man, "doesn't show their necks as I've seen ladies do in them there pictures of high life in the shop winders."'[11] Only a minority of costermongers' families were created by formal marriage but, according to Mayhew, the woman in each family, however formed, was 'rigidly faithful' to the man. 'Chance' children, children unrecognised by any father, were 'rare'.[12]

The work ethic was strong. It was a marvel to many of this class, Mayhew writes, that there actually were some people who did live without working.'[13] The costermongers' attitude to hardship was stoical. 'To flinch from expected suffering', Mayhew says, 'is scorned.'[14]

Figure 2.1
Population rises from 18 million to 38 million
England and Wales, 1851 to 1921

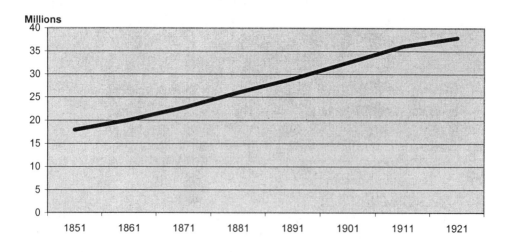

Source: Decennial Censuses

Crime in the second half of the nineteenth century

Statistics of crimes recorded by the police

From 1857 we have the annual figures of indictable crimes recorded by the police, that is to say the more serious crimes. There are strong deficiencies in the figures as a measure of the absolute amount of crime. But the deficiencies are much reduced when the figures are used to show the *trend* of the volume of crime.

As contrasted with 5.9 million crimes in England and Wales in a population of 52 million in 2002/2003, there were 88,000 crimes in a population of 20 million in 1861. From 1857 until after the First World War, by which time the population of England and Wales had more than doubled to 44 million, the total number of crimes never rose above 106,000, and in 1899 had fallen to as low as 76,000. The trend line 1857 to 1921 has a barely discernable upward slope.

Social commentators

Popular and serious Victorian novelists frequently refer to improvements in working-class social behaviour. Near the start of her novel *Felix Holt the Radical*, published in 1866, George Eliot observes that the 'brawny pauperism' of the 1830s was one of England's 'departed evils'.[15] One of the great novels of working-class life is Charles Kingsley's *Alton Locke*. In it Kingsley attributes to the Chartists the 'rapid improvement' in the morals of English workers. The Chartists, he said, were the 'great preachers and practisers of temperance, thrift, chastity, self-respect and education'.[16]

A perennially popular novel like *Treasure Island*, published in 1883, must appeal to the cultural preferences of its readers. There is an account near the beginning of the book of the confrontation between the pirate Billy Bones and the magistrate Dr Livesey. Bones is staying at the 'Admiral Benbow', no longer paying his bill for his bed, board or rum. He terrorises all the customers into silence when he speaks. Jim Hawkins, the publican's son, believes that the worry and fear of having this unpleasant guest hastened the death of his father. One day the doctor pays a visit. Bones does not know Livesey at all.

> The captain at last clapped his hand upon the table before him in a way we all knew to mean—silence. The voices stopped at once, all but Dr Livesey's; he went on as before, speaking clear and kind ... The captain glared at him for a while, flapped his hand again, glared still harder, and at last broke out with a villainous low oath: 'Silence, there, between decks!'

> 'Were you addressing me, sir?' says the doctor; and when the ruffian had told him, with another oath, that this was so, 'I have only this to say to you, sir,' replies the doctor, 'that if you keep on drinking rum, the world will soon be quit of a very dirty scoundrel!'

The old fellow's fury was awful. He sprang to his feet, drew and opened a sailor's clasp knife, and ... threatened to pin the doctor to the wall.

The doctor never so much as moved. He spoke to him, as before, over his shoulder, and in the same tone of voice, rather high, so that all the room might hear, but perfectly calm and steady:

'If you do not put that knife this instant in your pocket, I promise, upon my honour, that you will hang at the next assizes.'

Then followed a battle of looks between them; but the captain soon knuckled under, put up his weapon, and resumed his seat, grumbling like a beaten dog.

'And now, sir,' continued the doctor, 'since I now know there is such a fellow in my district, you may count I'll have my eye upon you day and night. I'm not a doctor only, I'm a magistrate; and if I catch a breath of complaint against you, if it's only a piece of incivility like tonight's, I'll take effectual means to have you hunted down and routed out of this. Let that suffice.'

Soon after, Dr Livesey's horse came to the door, and he rode away; but the captain held his peace that evening, and for many evenings to come.[17]

In this tale of what English people in 1883 thought should happen, and could plausibly have happened a century earlier, lawful violence was effective as a threat, because it was regarded by everyone as a real and justifiable one, and the forces of law and order were able to prevail to such an extent that a knife drawn on a magistrate could be dismissed by him merely as 'a piece of incivility'. It is difficult to think of an account even being offered today, though fictional, of a civilian facing down a violent drunkard in a public house in that way.

In the same year that *Treasure Island* was published, Robert Giffen delivered his Presidential Address to the Statistical Society. He showed that there had been a fall from 24,000 people committed for trial in 1839 to 15,000 in 1883, even though the population of the country had doubled.[18]

Alfred Marshall considered the question in the 1880s that Mill had considered at the end of the 1840s—whether the conduct of the working class indicated that there would be more problems of social order in the future or fewer. His findings were that the skilled working men were becoming more courteous, gentle, thoughtful and able. They were embracing their private and accepting new public duties. They were, he wrote, 'steadily becoming gentlemen'.[19] Arnold Toynbee spoke of the very great 'moral advances', as he called them, in England's industrial towns in 'temperance, in orderly behaviour, in personal appearance'. The English working class was entering the 'citizen' stage.[20]

Beatrice Potter—later Beatrice Webb—frequently visited her working-class relatives in the cotton town of Bacup, Lancashire, in the 1880s. She recorded in her diary, from her day-to-day impression as first hand, that the working-class families of Bacup were 'more refined in their motives than the majority of the money-getting and money-inheriting class'. She speaks of 'the ordinary Bacup workman, with his fair mindedness, and the kindliness of his view of men and things'.[21]

J.A. Hobson, a socialist economist prominent in his day, whose book on imperialism was acknowledged by Lenin as being the basis of his own works on that subject, took a view of the exceptional conduct of members of the tiny underclass that was also robustly judgemental. So far as circumstances permitted, he said, they imitated the habits of the upper leisure class, 'the same unaffected contempt for the worker ... the same sex license'. Their criminal parasitism on the rest of society and their destructive treatment of other people and property counted in the aggregate of social waste out of all proportion to their small numbers.[22]

Engels's remarks on England in 1892 are as suggestive as evidence of how low English crime rates as were his original remarks on the 'high' rates in 1844. In his preface to the 1892 reissue of *The Condition of the Working Class* Engels says that improvements since 1844 meant that the shocking state of things described in that book 'belongs today, in many respects, to the past, as far as England is concerned'.

He had to explain the good conduct of the English as he observed it at the end of the nineteenth century in Marxist terms. 'The law of modern political economy' he adduced was that 'the larger the scale on which capitalist production is carried on, the less it can support the petty devices of swindling and pilfering that characterise its earlier stages'. The low and falling crime rate was a necessary feature of capitalism. It required an honest and law-abiding working class, and it therefore created it.[23]

In his introduction to *Socialism: utopian and scientific*, Engels explains how this Marxian law of modern political economy had operated in such a way as to produce the respectable, relatively crime-free, English working class. 'The first and foremost of all moral means of action upon the masses', he wrote, 'is and remains—religion.' 'Regardless of the sneers of his Continental compeers', the English capitalist had successfully used religion to bring about the 'signal triumph of respectability'. The Englishman was the 'model workman' for capitalist success, modest in claiming rights for himself, and solicitous of the interests of his employer.[24]

Booth's Life and Labour of the People in London

In the course of his study of life in the East End of London at the end of the nineteenth century, Charles Booth lived there incognito as a boarder on three occasions. 'I can only speak as I have found: wholesome, pleasant family life, very simple food, very regular habits, healthy bodies and healthy minds—affectionate relationships of husbands and wives, mothers and sons, elders and children, of friend with friend.' On the basis of the 13 volumes of statistics and other first-hand reports of the full study, this 'very agreeable picture', as he called it, reflected the state of affairs in the nine-tenths of the population of the East End that were not middle class.[25]

In the East End, Booth reported, 91 per cent of the population was composed of the working class, plus the unemployed or the unemploy-able. The higher grade of labourer and artisan made up 13.5 per cent of the population. By far the largest class were those labourers who had 'a regular income and a good deal of property'. They made up 42 per cent of the population of the East End. The standard of living of these two sections of the working class was fairly secure. If their opportunities were improved by even a small extent, Booth said, succeeding generations—and even his own generation—would see 'a glorious structure arise, to be a stronghold of social progress'. Below these classes were the 22 per cent of the population who were 'the poor', as he defined the category. But by choosing that term, Booth said, he did not mean to imply that the people his researchers placed in that category were 'in want'. They were not rich, and life was an unending struggle. But they were 'neither ill-nourished not ill-clad, according to any standard that can be reasonably used'. Their income, though barely so, was sufficient for an independent life, and a decent life. Below them the 'very poor' made up the remaining 13 per cent of the population of the East End. Only some of these 'and I think not a very large percentage' would be described by anyone, 'including themselves' as being in distress. But they were the part of the popula-tion that was in want. Some suffered from physical or mental handi-caps. Others suffered because they lacked 'prudence or sobriety'.[26]

Booth said he had chosen the East End of London in order to confront England's most serious domestic social problems. The East End of London was acknowledged by all to contain 'the most destitute population in England'. He found to his satisfaction that the 'danger-ous classes' amounted to 1.25 per cent of the population of the East End. These were the few people, he said, who provided the bullies, the loafers and criminals for the urban scene. They fouled the reputation of the poor, the unemployed and handicapped and the whole working class.[27]

It has not been generally thought in the social sciences for many years that this is what Booth said he found (and perhaps a majority of social scientists think and teach that he said something very like the opposite). Fortunately it is easy to consult his volumes to confirm that these were indeed his conclusions: what is written remains.

Figure 2.2
Criminal underclass, East End of London, 1892

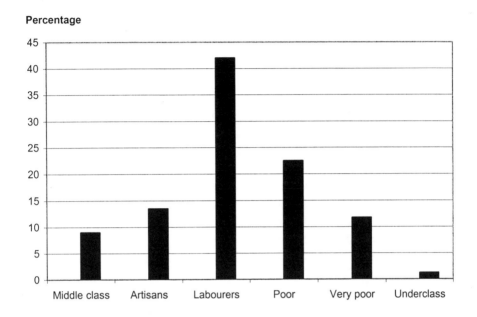

Percentage

Source: Booth's *Life and Labour*

Edwardian times

The statistical summary 1857 to 1907

In the half century that followed the publication of the first crime figures in 1857, the population of England and Wales nearly doubled from 19 million to 34 million, but the number of crimes remained almost the same—not just the crime rate per 100,000 of the population. *Criminal Statistics 1908* reviewed the course of crime over this period, with this conclusion:

> Crime has increased very little in the past half century, and taking into account the greater opportunities open nowadays to an individual of criminal tendencies through the greater profusion of wealth and personal possessions on the one hand, and on the other hand the reduction (by the decrease in the average length of sentences) in the periods for which he is forcibly restrained from crime, it may reasonably be inferred that the members of the predatory classes are appreciably fewer than in 1857 in spite of the fact that in the interim population has almost doubled.

The police in England and Wales estimated that on the first Tuesday in April 1908 there were 4,255 habitual criminals at large in England

and Wales—0.0125 per cent of the population. *Criminal Statistics* stated that the offences committed by habitual criminals varied little in number from year to year. There were reasons to believe, the report said, that they were tending to decrease. Nor was there any good reason to suppose, the report said, that the standard of honesty among respectable people was being lowered. The pervasive tone is a settled confidence that England was indeed becoming steadily a still more safe and civilised society.[28]

In 1906 the 15 million more people than in 1857 annually committed only 228 more offences of violence against the person than in 1857—and in 1906 the total number of offences of violence against the person was, by present-day standards, the incredibly low figure of 2,546. By contrast, the number of offences of violence against the person was 256,000 in 1997-98—the year before new counting rules inflated the figures in subsequent years and enabled the government to say that increases did not reflect a real rise, that they were an artifact of these statistical changes.[29]

Some commentators dismiss these figures as an illusion. According to them, cultural changes affecting the English have led them to become more sensitive to violence against the person. There is not more violence, only more reporting of criminal violence (especially rape), and more violence being treated as being criminal (especially domestic violence). The rising crime figures are therefore proof, according to them, that English society has become more sensitive to and less tolerant of violence, not more violent.

But these figures under the heading 'offences of violence against the person' do not include sexual offences. They are counted in a different category. The fact that rape and other sexual assaults are now more likely to be reported to the police, therefore, is not relevant here.

Domestic incidents of violence against the person ought to have been included in the violence figures. In addition to the 2,500 cases of violence against the person recorded by the police in 1906 there certainly would have been a large number of assaults by men on women in the home that were not recorded.

It is theoretically possible that in addition to the exposed number of cases of violence in 1906, 2,500, there were 253,500 cases of domestic violence that were regarded as normal and non-criminal then, but that we now regard as violence against the person, making the actual figure 256,000 in 1906, the same as the figure on violence against the person in the late 1990s. It is theoretically possible that there were 2,535,000, or 25,350,000 cases of domestic violence annually, or any figure far above that, with every husband beating his wife several time every day with the famous stick no thicker than a man's thumb. No statistics exist that can ever now tell us.

Very few people who were husbands and wives in 1906 were still alive in the 1970s, when claims began to multiply that domestic violence was the norm in Victorian and Edwardian England. All we have to depend on are some indecisive indications from reports of social observers at the time and reminiscences in writing that generalise about working-class life at the turn of last century.

It is clearly not true that the law in principle ignored domestic violence. Nor is it true that wives had no means of escape from a violent marriage. Since 1895 a wife could obtain a separation order on the grounds of her husband's persistent cruelty. The wife was given an incentive by the law to report her violent husband to the police by the granting of a separation if he was convicted of assault on her. In 1902 the husband's habitual drunkenness was added to the grounds for legal separation. During the years 1895-99 there was an annual average of 600 applications for these matrimonial orders. The annual averages for 1900-04, 1905-09 and 1910-14 were 1,400, 2,200 and 2,200 respectively. In the interwar period the annual averages remained stable at about 2,800 a year.[30]

Robert Roberts's The Classic Slum

Allegations of widespread and socially approved wife-beating are almost exclusively the product of publications dating from the late 1960s that are hostile, from one viewpoint or another, to the institution of the life-long monogamous family with children. Contemporary accounts that make such allegations are almost impossible to find. Where sources are quoted in post-1960s accounts, they invariably turn out to be very defective as evidence, and sometimes do not support the case for wife-beating as a normal occurrence at all. As crucial first-hand evidence in this field, a view has been attributed to Roberts, since the first appearance in 1971 of his book on the Salford slums between 1900 and 1925, that in the privacy of their slum homes men were brutal to their wives by community consent, and parents to their children. If not there, then where? The Cambridge sociologist Peter Marris, for example, claimed that Roberts showed that men in the home were 'petty tyrants, remote and harsh'.[31]

Roberts's actual comments on the issue are as follows: 'Despite poverty and appalling circumstances parents brought up their children to be decent, kindly and honourable ... It is such people and their children who deny indignantly (and I believe rightly) that the slum life of the industrial North in this century, for all its horrors, was ever so mindless and uncouth as superficial play or novel would have later generations believe.' There were of course, Roberts says, 'low characters'. But they formed a small minority, and played no part in setting the standards of the neighbourhood.[32]

That passage taken by itself is not strong evidence that men did *not* beat their wives. It could be evidence that Roberts was simply blind as a male of his generation to the phenomenon that is now condemned as domestic violence. But it certainly cannot be said to be evidence provided by Roberts that domestic violence was rife or even common.

'Home', Roberts adds, 'however poor, was the focus of all the child's love and interests ... songs about its beauties were ever on people's lips. ... Few walls in lower-working-class homes lacked 'mottoes attesting to domestic joys: "East, West, home's best"'.[33] That does not sound like a place where fathers were routinely assaulting mothers. The reality may have been different, but if it was different, it was not the reality that *Roberts* was reporting.

Let us accept any figure, no matter how large, put forward by those who claim that violence against the person is really no higher now than a century ago because domestic violence went unreported then. Let us concede every inch of ground in this whole controversial area of non-existent statistics, where all we have are reports of contemporary observers then (many of them men, white and middle class) and the assertions of partisans now.

The proponents of 'greater sensitivity' would still have to show that the scale of recent rises in the short period from one year to the next is owing to greater sensitivity from one year to the next, and not to real rises in the rate of violent crime. There were 24,000 cases of serious violence against the person in 1997-98, and it took only one year to raise the number by a further 3,000 to 27,000 in 1998-99. By contrast the total number of all cases in 1906, serious and not so serious, was only 2,500, and it had taken 50 years to raise the figure by 228.

The proponents of the 'greater sensitivity' view would have to show, too, how greater sensitivity explains the rise since 1906 in the recorded figures of *non-domestic* violence. Domestic violence is now among the most strongly condemned of all crimes. In the Metropolitan Police statistics it was one of only three classes of crime that in 1999-2000 were specially monitored. There were 44,000 domestic incidents of violence against the person. The figure of cases of non-domestic violence against the person in London alone in 1999-2000 was 112,600.[34] The figure of all cases of violence against the person in the whole of the country in 1906 was 2,500.

On violence in public, what the crime figures showed, commentators confirmed. Engels said of crime in England in 1844 that most offences were not of violence, but against property, 'as in all civilized countries'.[35] The fact that he makes this point about 'all civilised countries' only in passing makes it all the more telling. A passing remark by Lenin is also of great interest for the same reason. It shows that he took for granted, and that his readers took for granted, that criminal violence outside the home at least, was at a low level in the cities of Western Europe before the Great War. 'We are not utopians', he writes in *The State and Revolution*, 'and we do not in the least deny the possibility of excesses on the part of individual persons, or the need to suppress such excesses. But ... no special machine, no special apparatus of repression is needed for this; this will be done by the armed people itself, *as simply and readily as any crowd of civilised people, even in modern society, parts two people who are fighting, or interferes to prevent a woman being assaulted.*'[36] Lenin's comments are in accordance with the statistics. They cannot be taken to suggest that the people he was describing as a contemporary observer were more tolerant of violence against the person than we are. It seems strange that nearly a century later some commentators have the confidence to feel that they can not only dismiss the figures, but that they know better what was going on in the great cities of Europe in 1917 than someone whose whole career was spent in criticising what could be criticised about them.

Dean Inge, famed in his time as an unsentimental social critic, wrote in 1917 that the Great War had awoken a sense of fear for the integrity of the home and the safety of women and children. This was a feeling, he wrote, 'to which modern civilised man had long been a stranger'.[37] The same view is intimated in the *obiter dicta* of writers of fiction. In the first of the modern spy thrillers, *The Riddle of the Sands* published in 1903, Erskine Childers remarks in passing that all thoughtful observers of the time knew that the most striking feature of modern democracy was the improvement in the common sense conduct of the general population. Conspicuous proofs of this abounded in history, he wrote.[38]

During the first 20 years of the twentieth century the total number of indictable offences recorded by the police in England and Wales fluctuated, but rarely rose above 100,000. The population of England and Wales rose from 33 million in 1901 to 38 million in 1921. The number of crimes rose from 90,000 in 1901 to 103,000 in 1921. In a 20-year period of fluctuating crime figures, that is, five million more people ended by contributing 13,000 more crimes a year to the criminal statistics. Compared with just over 100,000 crimes in the whole country in 1921, in the year 2000-2001 there were just under one million crimes in London alone.[39]

Between the two world wars

One difficulty faced by those who deny that England was a society that enjoyed a very low crime rate in the second half of the nineteenth century and the first half of the twentieth is the fact that statistics uniformly contradict them. But statistics can always be shown to be in some way defective, or can be complicated beyond comprehension by those in control of their production or presentation. There is another difficulty that such people face, however, perhaps more formidable than the statistics. It is the fact that it is difficult for them to find support for their case in the materials of contemporary observers.

Harry Daley's This Small Cloud

Eye-witnesses of the interwar period give accounts that cannot be reconciled with those of the 'moral panic' school. In reading the memoirs of Harry Daley, for instance, it is difficult to see how they could be the product of anything but a low-crime London. If they are all pointless invention, it is difficult to see what motivated Daley to write them, for his politics (or at least the politics of his eminent friends) and personal situation would themselves have led him to emphasise the extent of crime and political unrest.

Daley's father, who had been brought up in the Poplar orphanage, had risen to be skipper of a fishing smack at Lowestoft. Like the sons of other fishermen, during the summer holidays Harry went with his father from the age of seven on working trips to the Dogger Bank, in the middle of the North Sea. Harry says that, for him and the other boys, each year it was 'holiday paradise'.

Harry went on to join the Metropolitan Police. He was homosexual. In his early days as a young constable at Hammersmith he became very friendly with A.J. Ackerley, who became a talks producer at the BBC, and through him with a group of friends who were 'very much to the left'.[40] Through Ackerley, Daley became acquainted with members of London's literary and artistic élite, among them Raymond Mortimer, Duncan Grant, and E.M. Forster. There is a portrait of Daley in his constable's uniform by Duncan Grant. E.M. Forster developed an affair with Daley, and sometimes accompanied him on his night patrol of Hammersmith's streets, which were deserted except for a few costermongers' barrows 'and a friendly police *protecting* the public'.[41] If anything happened, even at the dead of night, the slightest disturbance brought people streaming out of their houses, with the policeman at the centre of everything.

This is rather a different picture from that which is used to explain the low figures of recorded crime in those days and to explain away the high recorded crime figures today—that of a population then too hardened by the constant occurrence of crimes to bother to report them to the police, as contrasted with our modern sensitivity to offences that registers every triviality with the authorities.[42]

Daley went to Peel House to start his police training in March 1925, and 'from the first day enjoyed being a policeman'.[43] 'Viewed from the outside', he wrote as an old man, 'policemen now seem very unpopular.' He said that he had never seriously sensed this in his 25 years of service from 1925 to 1950. 'How many times have I seen a crowd, staring in attitudes of anxiety ... look up with relief at my approach? Hundreds of times. ... In the poorer districts of London, people in trouble run to the police station continually, as people ran to the vicarage in Victorian villages. At Wandsworth police station, where I finished my service, a truthful sign could have been displayed over the door, as over the portal of a fairy-tale castle—No person came here for help and went away uncomforted.' In his very early days, he says, minor bribery was a commonplace, 'if bribery can ever be classed as minor', and at that time, in the late 1920s, he occasionally saw prisoners struck by police officers.

> But in my third or fourth year of service general bribery in the uniform branch was ruthlessly stamped out. At about the same time violence died a natural death as the standard of recruits improved and better types were promoted. After having a rough time in the street, some policemen naturally were often inclined to have a poke back. But it had to be quick, for soon the impartial station officer and gaoler would be present and beating up would not be tolerated. ... Many people imagine they have seen violent treatment of prisoners in the street. ... Order your grandmother to bed as an experiment; if she refuses to go, try to make her against her will. You will be surprised at the violent appearance of the scene, especially if granny is artful enough to trip you up at the top of the stairs. ... Violent policemen were a minority, even among the old-timers ... Collectively we could often intimidate the remaining bullies [among his police colleagues] to curb their natural aggression.[44]

Of his first posting, to Chiswick, Daley says that he 'got no cases, and felt that he never would'—though there was plenty of non-criminal business in the localities to keep him busy.[45] Later he was posted to Hammersmith, and again his mild worry was that he could not get a criminal case. 'We were all expected to work, and indeed I was anxious to gain police court experience. It was very difficult. Drivers without lights would cry, "How kind of you—thank you so much" ... Drunks were never so drunk but they could mumble, "I only live round the corner, mate", and even ask for a helping hand home ... The public often intimidated young coppers into interfering against their better judgement. For instance, it takes courage to walk past a gang of happy, noisy youths, when the whole street waits and watches to see what you are going to do.' There were one or two unpleasant characters at each police station who did register cases. The description that Daley gives of how they did so, however, confirms the picture of a low-crime London. The Metropolitan Police Act entitled 'any constable to stop, search and detain any person reasonably suspected of being in possession of stolen property'. They 'snatched' workmen carrying wood or paint home that had been 'left over'. These 'dirty dogs', as Daley calls them, booked happy drunks as 'drunk and disorderly'. Though they stopped everyone with a parcel, only occasionally did they catch thieves carrying stolen property. Daley nevertheless recognises that some of the things they did were necessary: if they did not clean up the mess, other people would have had to do so.[46]

While it has not the compelling authenticity of the concrete details of Daley's account, a very similar version of policing at street level is given by James McClure of his time as a police constable in Liverpool.

> At Rose Hill, they'd call in and ask the man on duty to phone somebody for them ... if it was an official they were phoning, they felt the bobby would do it better. They'd pay the tuppence or whatever, and he'd give them a receipt for it. There was a constant stream of late-night callers to look at the station clock to set their alarms. There was another constant stream of late night callers for gas shillings, and certain bridewell sergeants would keep a special bag of them ... First aid was another thing; kids falling down and cutting their knees, dog bites ... They would come in to settle arguments—abstract things that had nothing to do with the police: who won the cup the year before the war? They used the police station as their general information centre.[47]

Most books about the police are by officers who achieved high rank or were involved with major crimes. The few first-hand accounts by lowly constables cannot be dismissed as valueless simply because they must be lying when their autobiographies explicitly state, and in all sorts of indirect ways suggest, that crimes were an English rarity before the 1950s, just as the official statistics say they were.

In *The Failure of Britain's Police* one of the authors refers to a cousin of his, handicapped in speech and posture from childhood as a result of contracting poliomyelitis. As a teenager, this cousin worked as an odd-job boy in the Sunderland Corporation Transport Department. One of his jobs on a Monday was to carry the weekend's tram and bus takings, much of it copper and silver, over to Barclay's bank in the town ... in the tram. In the foyer he enjoyed the opportunity to mingle with the friendly young girls from the department stores round about, like Blackett's and Binns—the privileged shop assistants whose perk it was to get out of the shop for a few minutes to walk round to the bank with cloth bags full of Saturday's takings in their hands.

It was long before being robbed or attacked entered his or anybody else's head. On the rare occasions that he was pestered as a 'cripple', the culprits were immediately put in order by passers-by, or other people around on a social occasion, or by the sight of 'a poliss'. Once he simply limped into the Central Fire Station to protect himself from something little worse than banter, and his verbal tormentors fled as the town's burly firemen piled out to deal with them.[48]

Perhaps, after all, the exponents of the view that crime was as prevalent or more prevalent in those days are themselves wrong, that the statistics, Daley and the reminiscences of his contemporaries are right, and that the falsehood is the view that in 2003 'the risk of becoming a victim of crime remains at a historic low level'.[49]

Recorded crime

Recorded crime rose after the Great War. But in 1919 there were still fewer than 90,000 recorded crimes. The figure rose to 208,000 in 1932 and to 304,000 in 1939. This was for the time a massive rise. The explanations seemed to be obvious—the poverty and unemployment of the Depression, the collapse of staple industries that were the *raison d'être* of the communities that depended on them, and the aftermath of one world war coalescing with the threat of a second. But this did not ameliorate the concern about crime among a public that had known only low crime rates, and could have no premonition of how high the crime rates would rise in the future.

3

Conscience and Community Controls in England from the Nineteen-Sixties

In its election campaign of 1997 the Labour Party chanced upon a slogan that resonated with the electorate's current concerns: tough on crime, tough on the causes of crime. Civitas has undertaken special studies of the treatment of the criminal after he has committed his crime, been apprehended and convicted.[1] The present volume is about preventing crimes being committed in the first place, and especially about the role of the police in securing and maintaining a low crime rate.

The causes of any individual committing a particular criminal act—or any other act whatsoever—are infinitely complex. What any person does, however trivial, at the given point of time, is the result of all the unbroken interactions between his original genetic endowment and the successive situations he has confronted. The product of each moment of interaction is the individual's 'personality' at that moment—that is, the individual's readiness to act in his or her way to any new or existing situation.

John Doe's and Jane Roe's different personalities will always make them perceive, evaluate and react characteristically to the given inter-personal, cultural and physical circumstances in which they find themselves, and will always lead them to an act of conduct that will be the inevitable result of the unbroken chain of cause and effect that constitutes their own life history up to that point.

'Blame' and 'stigma' and 'the punishment he deserves' are not, therefore, unpleasant consequences in a person's life that can be justified in cosmic terms. At a given moment of interaction they are simply unpleasant elements that are either present in or absent from the situation to which he will react as his personality directs.

While each person is unique in some respects, he or she is like other people in many respects. Genetically one is a member of the whole human race, sharing characteristically human ways of responding to many given inter-personal, cultural and physical environmental stimuli.

He or she shares, not with the whole human race, but with many other people, the same or similar material and cultural circumstances. Depending on the society, work is either hard or easy and the standards of economic consumption are either high or low. Each society and each social group within a society is by definition an environment of norms of conduct, adherence to which increase the likelihood of promised rewards, and infractions of which increase the likelihood of suffering pre-announced hardships. At the level of the state some of these norms of conduct and the consequences of violating them are dealt with by the criminal law.

Prevention by socialisation

Whatever the causes of crime, prevention by what sociologists call 'socialisation' (as distinct from 'social control') is designed to make a person mentally resistant to those causes, in the same way that a strong body resists an infection to which a weak body would succumb.[2]

Prevention by socialisation means successfully inculcating the sense that certain acts are undoubtedly 'wrong'; that they are properly prohibited; that people should be prevented from committing them; and that if they do commit them, they should be dealt with in a way that will stop them from committing them again. It means creating—to use the old formula from Juvenal's *Satires*, repeated for centuries throughout Europe as an educational objective—a *mens sana in corpore sano*, a sound, not a clever, mind in a healthy body.[3]

In this country, parents in a relationship of life-long monogamy bringing up their own children, neighbours, clubs, the churches and the schools were for a long period the principal instruments for the inculcation of these strong, uniform judgements of right and wrong.

Religion

Marx's friend Engels is full of frustrated admiration for the success of religion in 'civilising' the English working class, or, pejoratively, 'gentling the masses'.[4] Writing in 1892, he contrasted the law-abiding English working man with the revolutionary proletarian of France and Germany. The French and German capitalists, Engels said, were now silently dropping their disastrous free thought. One by one they were 'turning pious in their outward behaviour, spoke well of the Church, its dogmas and rites, and even conformed to the latter as far as could not be helped'. In doing so, they were imitating what British capitalists had been doing for 50 years. 'Regardless of the sneers of his Continental compeers' British capitalists had spent thousands and tens of thousands in self-imposed taxes, year after year, upon the evangelisation of the lower orders, while the sophisticated continentals had come to grief with their materialism. The English middle class, 'good men of business as they were, saw farther than the German professors'. The practical result was the signal triumph, Engels wrote, of the creation of the 'respectable' English working class.

'*Die Religion muß dem Volk erhalten werden*—religion must be kept alive for the people'. Now, more than ever, 'the people must be kept in order by moral means, and *the first and foremost of all moral means of action upon the masses is and remains—religion'*. At last it had dawned on the 'sophisticated continentals' that law and order depended on the inculcation of a moral code and of motivations to adhere to its injunctions. 'Now it was the turn of the British bourgeois to sneer and say, "Why, you fools, I could have told you that two hundred years ago!" '[5]

In 1925 Trotsky found that the English working class was still hopelessly religious and respectable.[6] A pamphlet on Christian citizenship could casually remark in the 1920s that such things as theft and drunkenness were no long serious problems in an England that had seen the 'benefits of generations of advancing Christian civilisation'.[7]

Education

If we consider the role of the schools in inculcating a clear distinction between right and wrong and the motivations of guilt and shame to secure good behaviour, Charlotte Brontë's account of Lowood charity school in the 1840s, and of its 80 orphan-girl pupils under the strict but never harsh superintendence of Miss Miller, is a strong reminder of the power of socialisation, given a supporting general culture, to maintain 'good behaviour' even under appalling conditions.[8] The Royal Commission of 1858 said that 'a good set of schools civilises a whole neighbourhood'. The 'religious and moral influence' of the public elementary schools was very great, and 'greater than their intellectual influence'.[9] W.E. Foster, in introducing his 1870 Education Bill, spoke of the school as a defence against crime and against other dangers. Speaking of the 1867 enfranchisement of urban working men he said, 'Now that we have given them political power, we must not wait any longer to give them education.'[10] We must 'educate our masters', he said, to be capable of being good citizens.

In *The Silent Social Revolution*, published in 1937, G.A.N. Lowndes wrote that the most patent of the benefits delivered by a sound and universal system of public education were sobriety, orderliness and stability.[11] The contribution that the public education system in England had actually made to these things, as well as to 'cleanliness' and 'self-respect', 'must always, perhaps, seem to outweigh all other gains'.[12] A visitor to any English elementary school in the mid-1930s, he wrote, would observe the 'economy and efficiency of the discipline', would note its atmosphere of 'orderliness and precision' and would carry away 'an indelible impression' of 'good manners and politeness'. Lest these things should be taken for granted in 1935, Lowndes said, it would be well to remind the visitor that barely 50 years before 'the attendance officer who wished to penetrate one of these slums from which some of the children still come had to take a police officer with him'.[13]

The most influential Reader on educational sociology in the early 1960s was *Education, Economy and Society*. In that volume, David Glass points out that until well into the twentieth century the English elementary school gave priority to this task of making the population law-abiding, what he called the school's 'civilisation motive', rather than developing each child's own personality and sense of self-esteem.[14]

By definition, revolutionaries of both the left and the right are hostile to the stupidity and cowardice ('false consciousness') of their benighted fellow-citizens, who supinely embrace the values of a society that justice, or true human nature, or the march of history, or the interests of the master race demand be overthrown. But whether, and in what circumstances, willing obedience to the rules of a particular organisation or to the law of the land under a particular régime is desirable is one question. Whether socialisation empirically is an effective means of preventing people violating rules and breaking the law is quite another.

The English state elementary school in the 1930s was organised to produce loyal, serviceable and law-abiding citizens. Abhorrence of crime was embedded in that general culture of respect for rules. Reading Lowndes's favourable accounts of these schools, it is difficult to believe that his book was a standard text at the London School of Economics as late as 1951. By 1958 public schoolboys like Paul Johnson were consciously searching for something that would stimulate and justify a 'sense of outrage'—by his own account desperately hard to find in 1950s' England.[15] By 1960 the *New Left Review* (created through an amalgamation of the journal of radical academics in the north of England, the *New Reasoner*, and Oxbridge's *Universities and Left Review*) was explicitly committed to unearthing 'frustration and nausea' wherever it might be found, and developing discontent.[16] The achievements of English cultural institutions in producing a law-abiding working class were no longer applauded by the social affairs intelligentsia. They were successfully redefined as the root cause of England 's 'arrested development'.[17]

The family

Primary prevention of crime thus means combating all its causes by building abhorrence for activities that are defined as criminal by the law of the land into the personalities of a society's population. Inculcating into the personalities of children anti-crime perceptions, evaluations and emotional reactions through religion, the schools and the family were historically the principal means of keeping the crime rate low.

Such means are hardly available today. Reinstating nineteenth-century religious attitudes to crime and criminals is not on the agenda of any but the—in modern terms—most eccentric religious sects. While not ignoring law-abidingness, modern pedagogy is strongly committed to the development of the pupil's capacity to find out what is right for himself, rather than transmitting what custom and law dictate.

Though the weakening of the institution of life-long monogamy expresses itself more directly in many other forms (cohabitation, unmarried parenthood, sexual promiscuity and so forth), the divorce figures provide its most easily available and accurately quantifiable annual index. Fifty years ago there were about 30,000 divorces a year in England and Wales. The trend was downwards in the 1950s. But in the late 1950s and early 1960s influential public opinion was successful in its advocacy of easier divorce, not the least influential being the Church of England with its pro-divorce report, *Putting Asunder*.[18]

Figure 3.1
In the 1950s and early 1960s there were about 30,000 divorces a year
Decrees made absolute in England and Wales

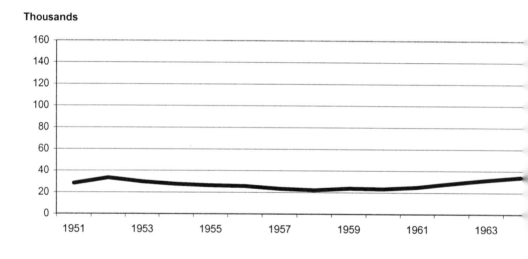

Source: *Annual Abstract of Statistics*

Divorce doubled in the decade, and then quickly doubled again after the provisions of the Divorce Reform Act came into effect in 1969.

Figure 3.2
In the 1960s divorces rise under the existing law
They double under the new law
Decrees made absolute in England and Wales

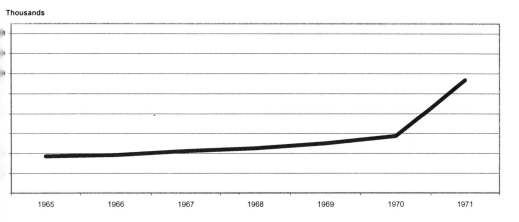

Source: *Annual Abstract of Statistics*

In the 1970s and 1980s the annual number of divorces continued to rise, with the effect that a relationship of life-long duration gradually ceased to be considered the commitment made in marriage.

Figure 3.3
In the 1970s and 1980s divorces continue to rise
Decrees made absolute in England and Wales

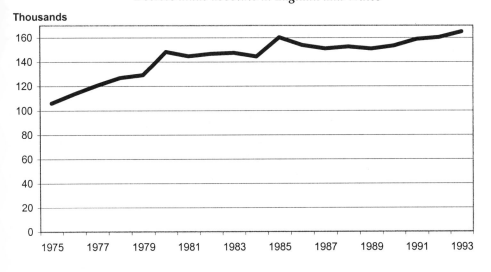

Source: *Annual Abstract of Statistics*

Of couples married in 1951, three per cent divorced in the first ten years of marriage. Among couples marrying in 1991, 41 per cent divorced in the first ten years of marriage. The number of divorces, though remaining at a historically high level, fell in the late 1990s, as marriage itself gradually ceased to be considered the pre-condition of socially approved sexual intercourse, conception and the upbringing of children in the home.

Figure 3.4
From 1993 about 150,000 divorces a year
Decrees made absolute in England and Wales

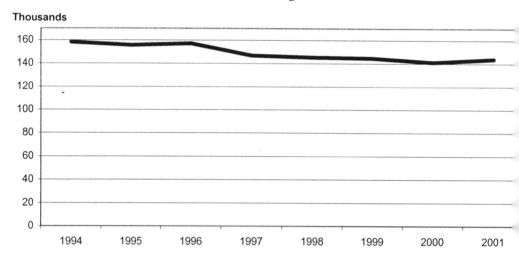

Source: Annual Abstract of Statistics

In 2002, when there were 4,000 more divorces made absolute than in 2001, 149,335 children under the age of 16 in Great Britain experienced their parents' divorce.[19]

Persistent and vocal lobbies representing the sexual or gender interests of their constituencies oppose the maintenance, much less the restoration, of any customary or legal privileges and restrictions aimed at maximising the chances that a child will be brought up to be obedient to its permanently married biological parents as they act as society's transmission belt of culture. The 1994 *Concise Oxford Dictionary of Sociology* has an entry on 'moral statistics'. These are defined in the dictionary as 'numerical data that are generally held to be indicative of social pathology'. The list of examples includes divorce, illegitimacy and abortion.[20] The entry is highly anachronistic, for by 1994 it would have been difficult to find anyone teaching sociology in English schools or institutions of further or higher education who would have said (whatever they thought) that any of these things were in any way 'pathological'. The very term 'illegitimacy' was obsolete and offensive. Ten years later little social stigma attached itself even in the general population to any of these things.

Prevention by removing 'want'

When the phrase was introduced as a party promise in 1997, therefore, 'being tough on the causes of crime' did not mean strengthening cultural barriers to crime. By then, 'moralising' and 'judgementalism' were powerful terms of disapprobation. The causes of crime were assumed to be poverty, unemployment, poor housing, broken homes, inequalities of opportunity based on class or colour prejudices, the lack of constructive activities for the young and other traditional subjects of left-wing reform. As Clement Attlee wrote in his days in Limehouse before the Great War: 'Surely some day we'll make an ending/Of all this wretched state of want...' Secondary prevention meant removing these causes. In place of crime and strife, 'society' would then fulfil its 'highest need' of 'fraternity and love'.[21]

Housing

In 1951, only seven million households out of a total of 13 million in England and Wales—52 per cent—enjoyed in their homes the exclusive use of piped water, a stove, a kitchen sink, a water closet, and a bath plumbed to even a cold water supply. ('Households' of more than one person were nearly all married families.) Just under 1.8 million households shared their water tap with at least one other household, and 740,000 households had no piped water at all. In many cases the tap was outside the dwelling, in the back yard. Thirteen per cent of households (we'll call them families) shared a water closet with at least one other family. Many of these water closets were outside the dwelling. Eight per cent of families still had nothing but dry closets, the contents of which had to be shovelled out onto carts. Thirty-seven per cent of families—4.9 million—had no fixed bath, and at best used a tin bath filled with water heated in the family's cooking pans.[22]

More than 3.6 million people lived overcrowded at more than 1.5 persons a room, and more than 900,000 of them lived at an overcrowding rate of more than two persons a room.

These families knew very well that people better-off than themselves had hot and cold water on tap within their homes, internal water closets, bathrooms and the chance of enjoying some domestic space of their own. To the extent that the size of the known gap between rich and poor is an incentive to commit crimes, the incentive was, by present-day standards, enormous.

By 2001 the Census no longer published figures on households sharing or lacking altogether such amenities as tapped cold water and a water closet. For a time the Census gave figures on households without an internal water closet, but by 2001 this too had ceased to be a housing issue. The total number of households in England and Wales in 2001 was 21,660,000. Only 104,120 of them were without the sole use of a toilet and either a plumbed bath or a shower.[23] In the very poorest households, those with a 'usual gross weekly household income of £100 or less', 98 per cent possessed a television set, 94 per cent a telephone, 88 per cent central heating, and 87 per cent a deep freeze or fridge/freezer.[24]

The figures for people living at a density of more than two persons a room were no longer given. Fewer than 120,000 people in a population of 52 million lived at a density of more than 1.5 persons per room. The 2001 Census enumerated 943 persons sleeping rough—the 'absolute home-less'—who were bedded down on Census night in streets, doorways, parks, bus shelters and buildings or other places not designed for habita-tion.[25]

In 1951 the population of England and Wales was 44 million. The population of males aged 14-19 was 1,335,000. There were 520,000 recorded crimes.

In 2001 the population of England and Wales was 52 million. The population of males aged 14-19 was 1,644,000. There were 5,100,000 recorded crimes.

Since 1951, therefore, on the conventional measures that had been thought most significant at the time, housing had immeasurably improved. The total population had increased by only 19 per cent. The population of male youths who contribute most to the crime rate had increased by only 23 per cent. But crime had increased by 881 per cent.

Claims on the physical necessities of life

If we take an average member of a comparatively badly-off section of the community, an employed single female with a dependent child, her net income on female average earnings meant that in 1971 she had to work 14 minutes to earn an 800 gram loaf of bread. By 1998 it took her only five minutes. A pint of milk took her eight minutes' work in 1971, and only three minutes in 1998. A dozen eggs took 32 minutes in 1971 and only 14 minutes in 1998. A kilogram of cod fillets took an hour and 30 minutes in 1971, in 1998 just 59 minutes.[26] In the 1990s alone, the UK's gross domestic product—the material standard of living—increased in real terms from £668,000 million in 1993 to £863,000 million in 2003 (an increase of 29 per cent).[27]

If the opposite were not so often stated or implied when 'poverty' is adduced as a cause of crime in Britain, and the reduction in 'poverty' as a means of reducing crime, it would seem to be redundant to point out that in the history of the world, and in comparison with the most people alive in the world today, to be able to secure a large loaf, a pint of milk, a dozen eggs and a kilo of cod for an hour and 20 minutes' work (or the somewhat less favourable equivalent in terms of the proportion of minimum state benefits), and for the standard of living to rise by a quarter or a third in a decade, is an astonishing expression of material prosperity. It is difficult to predict, therefore, in the context of contemporary English society, the scale of the additional increments of material prosperity, as distinct from cultural changes, that would be necessary to reduce crime to the levels of even 20 years ago.

Figure 3.5
Expansion of the educational opportunities in the 1960s
Full-time and part-time students, Great Britain, 1951 to 1972

Thousands

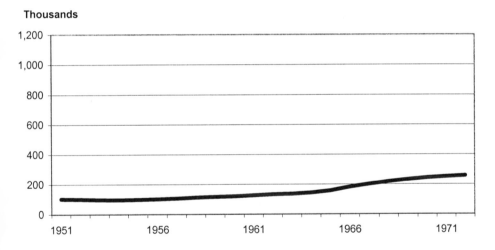

Source: Annual Abstract of Statistics

Educational opportunities

Improvement in educational opportunities since 1951—to choose the same arbitrary date as for housing—are enormous. If we consider higher education, in 1951 all the colleges of London University—the London School of Economics, Imperial, Kings, University College, Birkbeck and the rest—taught a total of only 18,400 full-time students. There were fewer than 8,000 full-time students at Cambridge. Durham, including what is now the University of Newcastle, had only 4,300 full-time students, Birmingham 3,300, Leeds 3,200, Bristol 2,500.[28] The expansion began in the 1960s, when the recommendations of the Robbins Report were implemented by the Wilson government.[29] More than doubling the population of university students was considered at the time an astonishing and unrepeatable feat. It was frequently referred to as the 'Robbins' revolution'. The growth of an independent youth culture, the use of illicit drugs, sexual permissiveness, anti-authority attitudes and, at the end of the decade, violent student unrest, all with consequences for attitudes to the police and to law and order in the general population, were attributed to it.

Universities continued to expand throughout the 1970s and 1980s, the number of students almost doubling again by 1992. There was then a transformation when, under the Further and Higher Education Act of 1992, certain polytechnics and other institutions were redesignated as universities.

Figure 3.6
University expansion accelerates in the late 1980s and leaps in the 1990s
Full-time and part-time students, UK, 1973 to 1998

Thousands

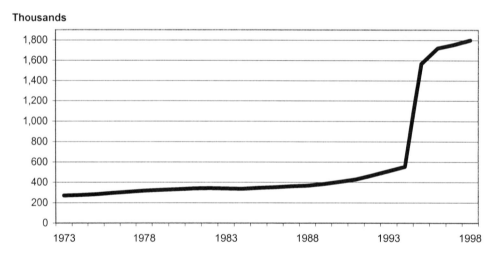

Source: Annual Abstract of Statistics

Expenditure on higher, further and continuing education rose from under £6 billion to nearly £10 billion. In 1990-91 23 per cent of 18-19 year olds were in higher education. By 1997-98 this had risen to 34 per cent. Among young people from 'unskilled' households, the increase was much greater, from six per cent to 14 per cent.[30]

By 2001, within a total population of 2,100,000 full- and part-time university students overseas and UK students, there were 1,100,000 who were full-time students resident in the UK. In 1951 there were 79,000 full-

and part-time male students in higher education. In 2001 there were 939,800. The transformation was even greater for women's educational opportunities. In 1951 there were 22,600 full- and part-time female students in higher education. In 2001 there were 1,128,000.[31]

Obviously the *opportunities* for young people to undertake a university education had vastly increased. What effect that had upon the crime rates, and why, is problematic in all sorts of ways. It is not problematic in one respect. The coincidence of the expansion of educational opportunities and the growth of crime shows that expanding educational opportunities was not a simple answer to crime.

The scale of the changes in education since 1951 makes it difficult to be confident either that new knowledge is now available to predict what further educational improvements would help to bring down crime; or that the knowledge would be ideologically acceptable (would it be acceptable if, for example, it were to be established that it was the changed content of syllabuses and the changed philosophy of discipline in the schools that had contributed to the rise in crime?); or, were the knowledge both available and ideologically acceptable, that the necessary resources would be forthcoming to implement policies based on that knowledge. At best, the effects on crime of changes in the scale of educational provision, and/or the culture of those teaching and those being taught in schools, colleges and universities, is uncertain and long term.

Prevention by reducing inequality

These points are indeed so obvious that some of those who continue to see the causes of crime in such things as bad housing, deficiencies in purchasing power or lack of educational opportunities have switched the argument from material poverty and educational *provision* to income and educational *inequalities*.

The theory that crime is generated by the poor and is reduced as they become rich may be valid in the sense that in some combination of circumstances the relationship would hold. The same is true of the theory that the more equal a society is, the fewer resentful people there are, and therefore the less crime and anti-social behaviour is generated by them.

But, again like the theory that crime is reduced by material prosperity, the scale of the changes implied are difficult to predict, beyond the certainty that they would be large and of uncertain effect. In the context of contemporary English society, how much redistribution of income, accomplished through what mechanisms, would lead to how many fewer crimes? The problem, which is complex and ideologically charged, is dealt with at some length in Norman Dennis's *The Invention of Permanent Poverty*.[32]

When crime was rising rapidly in the 1980s, it happens that *British Social Attitudes*, an intermittent series of snap-shot studies of British society, examined inequality in a way that throws direct light on the question of whether crime was rising because inequality was growing. Whatever the objective facts of class may have been, the British population perceived itself as becoming more equal, the only thing that counted so far as their motivation to conduct was concerned. Each respondent was asked to say what his or her own parents' class had been, and what the respondent's own class was. Eight per cent said that their parents' class had been 'poor', but only three per cent of the respondents said they were in the 'poor' class. Fifty-nine per cent said their parents were working class, but only 48 per cent said they themselves were working class. The respondents from these two classes had moved up, in their own perception, to higher classes. Ten per cent said that their parents belonged to the upper-working class, but nearly double that proportion, 19 per cent, said that they themselves belonged to the upper-working class. Eighteen per cent said their parents were middle class, but 25 per cent said that they themselves were middle class.[33]

The exponents of the theory that crime is caused by the fact of inequality, or by growing inequality, can then only save their theory by maintaining that the ever-larger number of crimes stems from the ever-smaller number of people who for whatever reason do least well under conditions of improved opportunity and a higher standard of living. Their gloomy message, if true, is that the more things improve for the greatest number of people, resentment of residual inequality will generate more criminal and anti-social behaviour from the people who for whatever reason do not enjoy, or will not take advantage of, the improvements, or in the language of the inequality theorists are 'excluded' from them. That is the only way the criminological theory of 'inequality' can explain the surging crime rates of the past 40 years.

In the specific and important field of education the picture is clear. Not only have opportunities been expanded overall. Substantial efforts have also been made over the past 50 years to diminish inequalities of opportunity. We have before us as we write the list of courses available in the city of Sunderland to anyone not at school, and the conditions of entry to the courses. There are day courses and evening courses on French, German, Russian and Spanish for beginners and more advanced students; learning bridge; criminal law; watercolours; the history of witchcraft; assertiveness training; the Teacher Training Certificate; the BA in Education; family trees; courses on access to nursing, social work and teacher training; GCSE courses, AS courses, City and Guilds courses, AAT courses. There are many different computer courses. There are philosophy; aromatherapy; positive parenting—the lists go on and on.[34]

Free child care for children aged three or four months to four years is on offer at three of the college centres, and a subsidy of £3 an hour for childminding expenses at a fourth. There are no entry qualifications for the vast majority of the courses. There are provisions for school leavers with special needs and for graduates taking new subjects. Many of the courses are completely free of charge. No one (and no one whose 'partner') is in receipt of Jobseekers Allowance, Income Support, Working Tax Credit, Pension Credit, Housing Benefit or Council Tax Benefit has to pay course or examination fees, though there is a cap on the number of courses he or she can take at any one time without having to pay. Higher National Certificate students pay no fees if they are on any means-tested benefit, or if their gross income is less than £14,200 a year.

Taking a course on the environment has included free boat trips on the River Wear and in Sunderland harbour. Taking a course in computing has involved a coach trip to a Manchester shopping centre (with computer teaching on the journey) and a free lunch. Vouchers for free meals and for free prize draws have been issued as incentives to students to attend regularly.

The college derives its 'mission statement', 'strategic plan' and 'charter' from its 'statement of values'. According to the statement of values, equality of opportunity is a 'basic right'. Equality of opportunity is also a requirement of the 'law of the land', under Acts listed in the statement, that prohibit discrimination based on disability or ethnic or racial consider-ations, and under Acts and the Code of Practice on Measures to Combat Sexual Harassment that prohibit sexual discrimination. The college's 'policy for equal opportunities' is 'driven' by these values. The policy commits the college to widening participation and promoting access 'to all'. A code of practice protecting the right of every student to study without fear of harassment or victimisation is part of the policy. The College Charter 'ensures equality of opportunity' by supporting students from 'under-represented and disadvantaged groups'. Equal opportunities 'will be implicit in all aspects of college life'. The Student Handbook provides information that explains how a student may exercise equal-opportunities rights.[35] Direct experience by one of us of different courses in college centres over several years has been only of amiable mixtures of old and young, men and women, high achievers and low achievers, working class and middle class.

While equality of income has never been tried in this country as a cure for crime, it is difficult to fault these arrangements for equality of educa-tional opportunity, though more, of course, can be envisaged and accomplished. Yet crime rose while more and more of these arrangements were made. Such is the grip of the theory that crime is owing to poverty or inequality or both, however, that the *Sunday Times* could still see fit to publish a letter explaining anti-social conduct in 2003 by the fact that some young people not only 'knew' that mainstream education had little positive to offer them; they also 'knew' that they were *excluded* by 'mainstream provision and culture'—that the blame lay entirely with the system.[36]

The benefits of improvements in the standard of goods and services such as education can be seen at every hand every day. But the vast majority of people have not become law-abiding as a result of these improvements. They were already law abiding, and as law abiding as their predecessors. The vast majority of people are considerate and helpful to others, including strangers. The desirability of the advances in housing, educational opportunity, income levels—and the countless details of such things as detergents and razors that have made everyday life so much more pleasant—are not to the slightest degree in question.

By the most decisive criterion of all, the effect on the survival of a society's population, they have wrought great improvements in countless lives. In 1961 the average 20-year-old woman in Britain could expect to live until she was 76. (Her grandmother or great-grandmother who had been 20 in 1901 would have died when she was only 64.) The average 20-year-old woman in 2001 could expect to live until she was 81. The average 60-year-old woman in 1961 could expect to live until she was 79. The average 60-year woman in 2001 could expect to live until she was 83.[37]

In the period from 1951, the number of dwellings defective in structure or deficient in amenities had been reduced.[38] The number of children leaving education at an early age was reduced. The number of people in poverty had been reduced. The number of unemployed fluctuated without ever reaching the heights of the pre-war period. All sorts of other traditional 'causes of crime' were reduced. But crime increased. All these changes greatly benefited the vast majority of people. But, by the early 1990s, a minority had been responsible for raising crime and certain public forms of petty anti-social behaviour to heights demonstrably far in excess the 1951 figures, figures that were already high compared with earlier in the century.

One traditional 'cause of crime' that was not reduced was the number of broken homes. But the notion that the broken home was relevant to crime faded into the background from the 1960s onward. Unusually, it is possible to identify rather precisely when broken homes as a cause of crime disappeared from respectable public discourse. *Faith in the City* was published in 1985 as a major statement of the position of the Church of England on social problems. As part of the *Faith in the City* study, clergy had been asked to assess a range of fourteen social problems in their areas. The problem scoring highest nationally and joint-third highest in the areas with most problems, the urban priority areas, was 'the incidence of family breakdown and other family problems'. Burglary was the worst problem and vandalism the joint-third worst problem in urban priority areas.[39] The indicators of 'deprivation' used by *Faith in the City* to identify the urban priority areas were unemployment, old people living alone, ethnicity, overcrowded homes, homes lacking basic amenities—and single-parent families.[40]

But unlike each of the other five items, neither in the text nor in any of the 61 recommendations was there any further mention of 'single-parent families' as a problem to be tackled. One of the commissioners, a vicar who was also a Labour politician, gave a lecture on *Faith in the City* at Sunderland Civic Centre. When questioned, he said that he had acted on the lessons he had learned as a commissioner. What had he done? He had removed the word 'Family' from the 'Family Services' notice outside his church.

Prevention by the police

Since the middle of the twentieth century, and especially since the 1960s, the prevention of crime by the socialisation of the child within the family of its two married parents, and by the schools and churches unashamedly engaged in moralising their pupils and congregations, has encountered great and largely successful opposition. Improved material conditions and increases in expenditure on education have coincided with steep rises in crime. Various efforts by the state and voluntary organisations to prevent crime and control the criminal, some old and some innovative, are more or less effective and expensive. Some are or will prove productive, some counterproductive; here we are in the position of the entrepreneur who knew he was wasting half of the money he spent on advertising—he just did not know which half.

The effects of police supervision, by contrast, are predictable, immediate and more or less proportionate to expenditure. But prevention by police surveillance of the potential criminal, too, has declined drastically since 1951. As Peter Coad, the Director of the Criminal Justice Association argued in August 2003, the number of crimes being committed had put it beyond the capacity of the police to act to prevent crimes being committed in the first place.[41]

In the year ending March 2002, 130,000 police officers had had to deal with five million recorded crimes that had already been committed (as recently as the year ending March 2000 there had been only 124,000 police officers). While attempts at family, educational and religious reform continue, and while experiments take place with new government measures for the control of crime and anti-social behaviour, policing remains an immediately effective check on criminality.

As Peter Coad also pointed out, programmes such as 'cognitive behavioural therapy in the community' will be of dubious value unless offenders are motivated to reform. The motivation to reform is weak when the chances of being connected with the commission of any particular crime is low and moves ever lower. In 1948, 43 per cent of robberies had been cleared up by the police. In 1978, 30 per cent had been cleared up. In 1988, 23 per cent had been cleared up. In the year April 2001 to March 2002 only 17 per cent were cleared up.

There were 18,600 police-recorded robberies in Lambeth in the four years 1999 to 2003. Only 1,300 were cleared up—seven per cent. The average robber in Lambeth commits 14 robberies before he even becomes an official suspect, never mind before he is found guilty in a court of law. 'Three strikes and you're out' for him means, therefore, 'forty-three strikes-plus and you're out', which he is likely to count as pretty good odds in his favour.[42]

In Book II of Plato's *Republic*, Glaucon relates the myth of Gyges, a seventh-century Lydian king. When Gyges was still one of the shepherds tending the king's flock, an earthquake opened a crevasse in the field, and uncovered a brazen horse. Inside the horse Gyges found a man's naked corpse. There was a ring on one of its fingers. Gyges took the ring, and found that when its collet was turned into his palm he became invisible. Using his invisibility when it suited him, he secured a place at court as a king's envoy. He seduced the queen, and with her help and his own invisibility, he killed the king. As the new king he committed all sorts of unattributable atrocities.[43] Glaucon's argument is that the 'unjust man', and even the 'just man', will act to fulfil his own desires at the expense of others if he can do so undetected. The primary role of the police officer is not to detect crime after it has been committed. It is to deprive the potential criminal of his ring of Gyges.

That is not to say or imply, or to be quoted as saying or implying, that all crime and anti-social behaviour either can be, or ought to be completely eliminated by police officers in unlimited numbers, exercising however much, and whatever kind of surveillance they see fit to undertake. On the contrary, in the light of American experience, especially that of New York, but also of English experience, especially at Hartlepool, effective policing that is aimed at *increasing* freedom by dealing with those who interfere with the freedom of others for their own selfish purposes, seems to depend very precisely on what has come to be known as 'broken windows' theory. This will be dealt with in connection with the study of the American police.

4

The Idea of Increasing Crime and Disorder Dismissed as Moral Panic and Exaggerated Fears

The infrastructure of the railway network or of the National Health Service can be neglected, and their performance will decline. That is a commonplace idea. The same applies to the institutional, cultural, moral and policing infrastructure of law and order. But the process of dilapidation of rolling stock or hospital equipment is obvious and tangible. The process of dilapidation of a culture of law and order is diffuse and invisible. What is more, it is easier in this case to be mistaken about or to misrepresent the true state of affairs. One of the principal reasons that crime and disorder were not tackled in England by the institutions of socialisation, community control and the police was that it was simply denied that any deterioration of the culture of law and order in England in the 40 or so years from the 1960s to the 2000s was occurring. The academically popular and influential thesis was that crime had not increased, and law and order had not deteriorated. The ignorant and timid public just imagined it had.

Moral Panic

There are three versions of the moral panic argument. One version is that the crime rate in the past was low. It is still low today. Today compared with the past there is simply a higher rate of moral panic about an unchanged real situation. The second version is that crime is high today, but it was just as high in the past. Again, the difference is not how much crime there is, but in how much more moral panic there is about the same facts. According to this moral panic theory, the present is unjustifiably vilified as being more crime ridden than the past, with 'modern life' represented in some way as a 'degeneration' from a 'golden age' of low crime 'that never existed'. The third version is that crime was higher in the past than it is today. Crime has declined; but the fear of crime has increased. There is more panic but with even less cause for it.

The low/low thesis comes to the fore when the evidence of the crime rate 1857-1957 is under close scrutiny, and is therefore difficult to assess as anything but a low rate of crime. The high/high thesis comes to the fore when the current crime rate is under scrutiny, and it is therefore difficult to

51

deny that there is a real chance of returning to your home to find it has been burgled, or to your bicycle to find it has been stolen.

The best-known attempt to make the case from contemporaneous descriptions that crime has not increased or indeed significantly fluctuated in this country over the past century, and all that had changed was people's propensity to fall into a moral panic, is Geoffrey Pearson's book *Hooligan: a history of respectable fears*. It was reprinted several times as an Open University set book throughout the 1980s and into the 1990s. In the misperceptions of the public mind, but only in the public mind, Pearson argues, 'generation by generation, crime and disorder increase by leaps and bounds'.[1]

The clear argument of *Hooligan* is that crime has not increased since the 1950s. The belief that it had increased was purely the product of the 'moral' panic of 'respectable' people. 'Panic' is obviously pejorative. By the time Pearson was writing, so were 'moral' and 'respectable'.

It is not clear, however, whether he is arguing that crime was high in the nineteenth century and the first half of the twentieth century. Even though all his examples on inspection show that the 1850-1950 period was one of low crime, Pearson fluctuates between the low/low thesis and the high/high thesis. The low-crime facts of the past keep intruding into his narrative. But to imply that 1850-1950 was relatively crime free is to 'glorify the past', and to bring 'the forces of reaction' to the fore.[2] His thesis, therefore, is mainly but not consistently high/high.

He heaps example upon example of crime and anti-social behaviour in the past. It is easy to gain the impression from Pearson that football hooliganism was as high before the 1970s as it was for 20 or 30 years after the 1970s, and that Burford's *Among the Thugs*,[3] compelling reportage from the centre of the 1980s football mob, could have been written to describe football hooliganism at any time in the twentieth century.[4]

The moral panic theory in its most important application purports to show that at the end of the twentieth century there was concern about a rise in crime, and that no such rise in crime had in fact taken place. Incidents are referred to and percentages quoted that purport to show that crime was *high* in the earlier periods, but for one reason or another was not recorded in official statistics.

But when they deal with periods in the nineteenth century or in the first half of the twentieth century when concerns about crime were raised, i.e. earlier moral panics, apparently unbeknown to themselves they adduce, as illustrations of *high* crime rates, evidence that demonstrates that crime rates were *low*.

The crime of 'garrotting' is a good example of this. 'Garrotting' is often quoted in moral-panic circles as proof that nineteenth century England was brutally lawless. In fact there were two 'garrotting' panics, one in 1856 and the other in 1863, affecting very few people, confined to London and soon brought under control. Pearson himself supplies only two examples of 'garrotting'. Both of them seem to modern eyes to be run-of-the-mill street robberies:

> Here is one example of what the new crime amounted to: 'Suddenly set on by two men, who seized him by the throat and threw him to the ground, while the other thrust a quantity of mud in his mouth'. (*The Daily News*, 15 December 1862.) Here is another case, which took place in the Caledonia (*sic*) Road: 'An elderly woman ... seized by the shawl, and dashed upon the pavement. There was a good deal of ill-treatment, which ended in robbery'. (*The Times*, 28 November 1862.)[5]

Pearson's text itself adequately shows that garrotting was rare. He approves of Jennifer Davis's contention that there was no significant increase in violent crime at all in the winter of 1862/63. There was on the one hand an increase of arrests owing to increased police vigilance. On the other there was a groundless panic 'orchestrated into a powerful lobby of reaction' against the humane reforms that were being undertaken within the penal system. The 'Garrotter's Act' of 1863 reintroduced flogging (it had been abolished in 1861) and was thus a historic landmark of reaction: furthermore it was quickly followed by measures to toughen prison discipline and to introduce a minimum penalty of five years of penal servitude for second offenders. The reformative principle was on the retreat.[6] According to Pearson and Davis, the reintroduction of flogging did not defeat garrotting, because garrotting had never increased to be defeated.

Pearson quotes *The Times*: 'Whole sections of a peaceable city community were on the verge of arming themselves against sudden attack'. The article makes clear that there had been a panic in the winter of 1862/63. But it makes it equally clear that it was *over* by the summer of 1863 at the time when the passage quoted by Pearson was written. The 'peaceable city community' had reasserted its control over London.[7] The garrotting robberies of 1856 were attributed by *The Times* to 'the half-hundred Italian ruffians now rollicking about Whitechapel and Stepney'. Happily, *The Times* report concluded, this unusual crime could be dealt with 'very summarily indeed', by 'getting rid' of the few known perpetrators.[8]

In spite of all this, 'garrotting' in nineteenth-century London is frequently quoted as evidence of a high rate of dreadful crimes in the Victorian period, and it is not unusual to hear Pearson's book being cited as evidence for this.

In 1933 'pulling down the shutters of an empty kiosk and stealing cigarettes and sweets' was referred to in Parliament as a 'trivial' crime.[9] Pearson concludes from this that:

> it is evident that certain kinds of common theft, damage and injury were regarded as wholly commonplace in pre-war years and hardly worth a moment's thought. Pulling

down the shutters of an empty shop or kiosk, we should remind ourselves, is what would
today in the aftermath of Brixton and Toxteth be described as 'looting'.

It is by no means self-evident that 'pulling down the shutters of an empty
kiosk' and 'stealing sweets and cigarettes' would now give rise to so very
much alarm. But this comment by an MP is regarded by Pearson as proof
that the equally rampant street robbery, burglary and looting were 'viewed
leniently' in the interwar period compared with today.

He quotes three sets headlines from the 1930s. The implication is that
they show that levels of crime were high in those days also. One of the
headlines reads, 'DARING RAIDS BY BAG SNATCHERS. WIDOW BADLY INJURED
AND ROBBED'. Another of the headlines reads, 'WOMAN INJURED BY VIOLENT
BAG-SNATCHER'. The report says that she was 'thrown to the ground and
bruised'; it was 'a brutal assault upon a helpless woman'. To support his
thesis that people in the 1930s experienced violent crime on the same scale
as today but had not reached today's level of panic about it, Pearson takes
these three cases, not from one evening's provincial newspaper, which
would be an easy thing to do today, but from a national mass-circulation
Sunday newspaper over a period of five years.[10]

Pearson argues in his 1983 book that the Edwardian and interwar
periods were as violent as or more violent than the late twentieth century.
Yet the statistics show that there were only 122 felonious woundings and
other acts endangering life in 1927. (Between 1900 and 1927 the national
figure for felonious woundings and other acts endangering life had more
than halved.) Between 1969 and 1978, the period immediately preceding
Pearson's research for his book, the figure *rose* by 1,800, i.e. by seven times
the total for 1900, and by 15 times the total for 1927.

Pearson also makes much of the fact that 'shop raids' increased by 70 per
cent in the Metropolitan Police District between 1925 and 1929. In fact it
was a 70 per cent increase from 135 to 230. In 1975 there were 303 *armed*
raids. By 1982 the figure for armed raids had risen to 679. During the
period 1977-80 the figure for offences where firearms were reported to have
been used in the Metropolitan Police District increased by seven times the
1929 figure of all shop raids, whether with or without firearms.

The case of street robbery is particularly important for his thesis, he says,
'because this is commonly the most sensitive area for registering public
concern about crime and violence'. There is 'ample evidence', he writes, of
'sharp increases in crimes of this nature' in the interwar period.

The 'ample evidence' he adduces is an increase of 90 per cent in the
number of 'bag snatches' in London between 1925 and 1929. The fact that
there was 'an insubstantial public reaction' to these figures at the time
shows that substantial public reactions at the end of the twentieth century
to much the same thing reflected merely a higher propensity in the later

period for respectable people to panic about their personal safety and the security of their property.[11]

The rise was 90 per cent. Pearson does not say what the actual numbers were in the source to which he explicitly refers. The numbers were an increase from 66 bag snatches in the whole of London in 1925 to 127 in 1929.[12] No numbers could show more decisively that London in the 1920s was a low-crime city compared with London today. In the whole of the 'high' year of 1929 there were 127 snatches. In the first half of 2003 the average number of snatches *each month* was 1,678.

Figure 4.1
Snatches in London
Year totals 1925 and 1929 and monthly average 2003

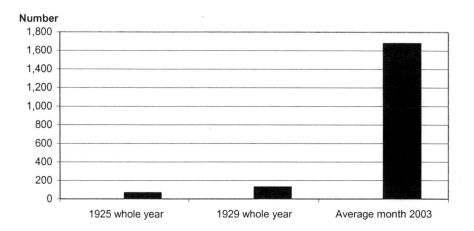

Source: *Criminal Statistics England and Wales* and
http://www.met.police.uk/crimestatistics/index.htm

In addition there was an average of 3,368 robberies each month of personal property which involved violence or the threat of violence.[13] The average monthly figure for snatches in Lambeth alone was 126—by coincidence almost exactly the figure of 127 for the whole of the year for the whole of London that Pearson quotes as evidence of a crime surge in the 1920s—which, according to him, the crime-hardened people of 1920s London greeted with stoic indifference, instead of falling into a moral panic like their irrational descendants.

None of the three possible 'moral panic' theses, therefore, apply even to Pearson's own data, as distinct from his interpretation of them. There has not been a situation (a) of high crime in the earlier period and high crime in the later period, with more moral panic in the later period. There has not been a situation (b) of low crime in the earlier period with low crime in the later period, with more moral panic in the later period. There has not been a situation (c) of high crime in the earlier period and low crime in the later period, with more moral panic in the later period. Contrary to what Pearson and the other exponents of the 'moral panic' theory say, there has been clearly a situation of low crime in the earlier period, and high crime in the later period.

Throughout the 1970s, 1980s and into the early 1990s, the consensual opinion of the conforming social-affairs intelligentsia in education, politics and the media of communication was that the popular view, that crime was increasing, was an illusion. The unenlightened public and the popular press were mocked for reacting not to a real situation, but to the 'images of deviance' that 'respectable' people perennially conjure up out of their irrational fears.[14]

If there was no problem of crime, then there was no need to consider how to solve it. From the 1960s, therefore, not only was the cultural and institutional infrastructure of law and order decaying; the conforming social-affairs intelligentsia was adamant that no one should so much as acknowledge that any decay was taking place.

At least in part this was because the academic, political and media intelligentsia lived in residential areas that were affected far less by the growth in crime than were 'the communities of our dreadful estates'. They could complacently indulge *their* fantasies about such crime as there was being excusable or commendable as the first noble stirrings of violent revolution or the freelance redistribution of income and wealth from the rich to the poor.

The exaggerated fear of crime

Crimes in their own localities have tended to bring, but have by no means fully brought, the 'moral panic' theorists to a chastened silence. 'Moral panic' now appears in the more modest guise of the 'disproportionate fear of crime'.

Human beings do appear to be programmed to be alert to threats. In most areas of life, the saliency given to threats is praised as a highly functional trait, and incorporated into public policy as 'the precautionary principle'. The state requires large sums of money to be spent, for example, in reducing further the statistically small chance of any particular passenger being killed or injured in a railway accident.

As late as the year 2000 the Home Office still applied the 'precautionary principle' to the public's reaction to crime. In 1999 32 per cent of the British Crime Survey's respondents said that it was 'very likely' that something would be stolen from their car in the following 12 months. Twenty-nine per cent said they expected to have their car stolen in the next year. Twenty per cent said they were likely to have their home burgled in the next year; 13 per cent were 'very worried' or 'fairly worried' 'most of the time' about their home being burgled. Ten per cent said they were very likely to be mugged or attacked by a stranger in the next year. Six per cent said that the fear of crime 'greatly' affected their lives. Eight per cent said that they never or rarely walked in the local area after dark, 'at least in part' because of the fear of crime. In the case of women aged 60 or over, the proportion rose to 19 per cent.

The Home Office document reporting these findings in 2000 said that although not as high a proportion as 29 per cent would have their car stolen, and so forth, it was sensible to overestimate risks, and in particular instances individuals faced real risks that were higher than the average risks.[15]

But then the theory of the 'disproportionate fear of crime' began to appear in official statements. Crime was being conquered by the government and the police. The public was simply being backward in not recognising this. The functional trait of giving high saliency to threats was now, in the field of crime, represented as a defect of the aged, the timid and the ill-informed. According to the Home Office's volume on police-recorded crime and the findings of the British Crime Survey, *Crime in England and Wales 2002/2003*, about twice the proportion of over-16s who read the national tabloids as those who read the national broadsheets were very worried about being mugged. Worry about crime was 'associated with' newspaper readership.[16]

But worry about crime is also 'associated with' the fact of crime. In the four years 1999-2003, there were 18,563 robberies in Lambeth. There were 1,040 robberies in Richmond.[17] One wonders how many *Guardian* readers in Lambeth were protected from the illusion that their locality was unsafe, and how many readers of the *Daily Mail* in Richmond cowered at home rather than venture out onto the main shopping streets of the town. One also wonder how many of the Home Office officials who wrote and approved the statement that worry about crime is associated with newspaper readership, were themselves *Guardian* readers in places like Richmond and how many *Daily Mail* readers in places like Lambeth.

The Home Office published a calculation in the late 1990s that showed that since 1918 crime had risen by a fairly steady five per cent a year.[18]

Using the arithmetical numbers, a graph shows the line accelerating rapidly upwards. But substituting the arithmetical numbers with the logs of the numbers, the graph shows no change in the gradient; it shows a gently upward sloping straight line. The Home Office's straight line of the 'fairly steady increase' is purely a statistical artefact of extremely small existential significance.

Ignoring the crucial fact that crime had not risen at a rate of five per cent a year before 1918, but had remained remarkably steady since the figures were first collected in 1857 at about 100,000 crimes, this was immediately added to the 'moral panic' range of arguments. Crime was rising at five per cent in the 1960s, 1970s and 1980s; but it had always risen at that modest rate; therefore there was no new problem to concern ourselves about—except the irrational growth in the fear of crime.

But a five per cent rise in the number of crimes of 50,000 on the previous year's 1,000,000 has a vastly different impact on how people can lead their lives, and what they rightly feel about the security of their person and their home, compared with a five per cent rise in the number of crimes of 5,000 on the previous year's 100,000. The fact that there were already 1,000,000 crimes and that there are now 50,000 extra crimes are what effects people's lives, not in the slightest degree the fact that it is a percentage rise that has been normal since some arbitrary date in the past.

In a statement extraordinary in the enormity of its compressed misrepresentation of the facts, one of the Home Office's statistical bulletins commented in January 2003 that 'the risk of being a victim of crime remains historically low, around the same as the first BCS in 1982'.[19]

The same claim, in almost the same words, was repeated in April 2003. 'The risk of becoming a victim remains historically low, about the same as the first British Crime Survey results of 1981'—as if the crime rate in 1981, enormously higher than in previous years, too, had been 'historically low'.[20] If 'history' extends further back than 1981, then it is relevant that the police recorded 2,964,000 crimes in 1981. This was about double the number they had recorded in 1971, 1,646,000. That figure of 1,646,000 was itself about double the figure recorded in 1961, 806,000.

The same phrase was used by more than one of the authors who contributed in July 2003 to the Home Office's main annual volume on British Crime Survey crime statistics and the statistics of crimes recorded by the police. 'The risk of becoming a victim of crime over the past two sweeps of the survey is still historically low, around the same level as the first BCS in 1982 (which measured crime in 1981).' In two of the formulations, the fact that crime is *still* low and that it 'remains *historically* low' is demonstrated by an incongruous reference to the very high levels of a very recent year, 1995. 'The risk of becoming a victim of crime remains at an historic low (around 27 per cent) according to the BCS, one-third lower than the risk in 1995 (40 per cent).' 'The risk of becoming a victim of crime is still historically low at 27 per cent, around the same level as 1981, and one-third lower than the risk in 1995 (40 per cent).'[21] The same phrase appears in the 'no. 1 on-line information resource for the crime reduction community', dated 15 September 2002.[22] 'The risk of becoming a victim of crime is still historically low at 27 per cent, around the same level as the first BCS in 1982, and one-third lower than the risk in 1995 (40 per cent).'

The same ideas—that crime is low, that it is historically low (though, incongruously, that there has been a massive change for the better in recent years) and that therefore the 'real' problem is the public's irrational fear of crime rather than crime itself—were expressed in another form in a White Paper in March 2003. The White Paper said or implied that many people mistakenly believe that the level of crime is high. The government's *non sequitur* is that if crime *has declined in recent years*, then it must in some sense have now reached an *historically* low level. 'Since 1997 overall crime has dropped by over a quarter and some crimes, such as burglary and vehicle theft, by a third or more. *Despite this* many people perceive that levels of crime are high.'[23]

But, first, in historical terms the level of crime did remain high. If we take the police-recorded crime figures only up to 1998 (from which time, as we have already pointed out, changes in recording rules have allowed commentators to claim that recorded rises in crime do not reflect real rises) and go no further back than 1955 (when crime numbers first began to rise rapidly): there were 462,300 crimes in England and Wales in 1955; 1,243,500 in 1965; 2,105,600 in 1975; 3,426,400 in 1985; 5,100,200 in 1995; and, using the old counting rules, 4,481,800 in 1998/1999. (The recorded figure for 2002/2003 was 5,899,400.)

The British Crime Survey gave a total of 11 million criminal incidents in 1981. Its figure was 12.3 million in the year covered by its 2002/2003 interviews. It requires a certain boldness of the imagination to cast the comparison of 1981 and 2003 as a 'small' percentage difference in the rate of victimisation, and thus to present 11 million criminal incidents and 12.3 million criminal incidents—an extra 1.3 million criminal incidents—as being 'around the same'.

Secondly, an unknown but probably substantial contribution to the reduction in the bulk crimes of burglary and vehicle crime was that householders and car owners had made it more difficult for criminals to break into their homes and cars. It would be reasonable for them not to feel that there was less *criminality* just because they had foiled the car thief and burglar, any more than the inhabitants of a besieged city would think that the enemy soldiers outside the walls had diminished just because they had been prevented from scaling the improved defences. They had to remain more on the alert and take more precautions against the criminal than in the past (including, for example, restricting their own freedom of movement by not venturing out at night). This state of affairs, the feeling that the threat of crime was still rising, was quite consistent with a sense of there being more crime, even though through their own trouble, inconvenience and vigilance the number of crimes was falling.

Thirdly, the very conspicuous offence of robbery continued its sharp rise right throughout the late 1990s and an even sharper rise in the early 2000s. The British Crime Survey's sample is too small to allow its robbery figures to be used. The Home Office therefore uses only the police recorded figures in analyses of this particular offence.[24] In the absence of an effective culture of law-abidingness and cultural and institutional support for civil responsibility and courage, the number of robberies depends upon the police's control of the street; there is little that the ordinary citizen can do. Only when effective police measures were at last undertaken did the robbery figures decline. A Street Crime Initiative to reduce robberies of personal property and snatch thefts commenced in London in February 2002 and was extended to nine other police forces areas in April 2002. The number of police-recorded robberies were cut back by 14 per cent.

Even so, this valuable police achievement of a reduction of 14 per cent did no more than bring the number of robberies back to the very high numbers they had reached two or three years before. Robberies, which were affected only marginally by the changes in police recording,[25] had risen from 63,072 in 1997 to 121,370 in 2001/2002. The belated intervention of the police resulted in a reduction of the figure in 2001/2002 of 121,370 robberies to the figure in 2002/2003 of 108,045 robberies. But this was still 12,891 *more* than the 95,154 robberies there had been in 2000/2001. In a country that was repeatedly reassured in 2003 that crime 'remained' at 'an historically low level', it was worth bearing in mind the fact that until as late as 1977, the *total* number of robberies was never as high as 12,891.

While the detection rates for robberies increased by two percentage points in the ten areas of the Street Crime Initiative, in the remaining police forces of England and Wales the detection rate fell by three percentage points.

Fourthly, the British Crime Survey took no account of growth in the number of crimes committed against people under the age of 16, or against businesses (e.g. shoplifting) or public sector establishments. It did not include any growth in fraud, or sexual offences. It did not include any growth in so-called 'victimless' crimes; in particular, the rapidly growing number of drug offences.[26]

In spite of these obvious weaknesses of the British Crime Survey as a measure of the growth of overall crime, it was used by the Home Office to make the case not only that overall crime had come down since its peak in the middle of the 1990s (which was true), but that the key date was 1997, when Labour won the general election, and that consequently under Labour, so far as crime was concerned in 2003, all was for the best in the best of all possible worlds.

A plethora of statistics and changes in the basis of their collection and analysis made it increasingly possible and common for governments to publicise the statistics that at the time were most favourable to the case the government wanted to put. Crimes on the government's other set of statistics, crimes recorded by the police, did not decline by a quarter overall between 1997 and 2002/2003. When the inflationary effects of new counting rules were discounted, crime rose from 4.6 million in 1997 to 4.8 million in the year ending March 2003. (The unadjusted figures showed a rise from 4.6 million in 1997 to 5.9 million in the year ending March 2003.)[27]

What is more, even when the inflationary effects of changes in the way the police had been required to record crime were taken into account, police-recorded crime rose by two per cent from 2000/2001 to 2001/2002. At a time when the annual number of crimes was on any calculation about five million, a two per cent rise meant 100,000 more crimes in the year. As late as 1925—in the memory of many people still living—the *total* number of recorded crimes was still only 110,000 a year. As late as 1945 there was a total of only 500,000 recorded crimes a year. Despite the White Paper, it was therefore no wonder that 'many people' made the 'mistake' of continuing to 'perceive that levels of crime were high'.[28] Crime then fell by three per cent from 2001/2002 to 2002/2003, when discounting for the inflationary effect of the National Crime Recording Standard was removed.[29]

The basis of the claim that the crime figures 'remain *low*', '*remain* low' and 'remain *historically* low' is that they were as low in the early twenty-first century as they were in the early 1980s.

The way in which the Home Office calculated the victimisation rate is a little difficult to ascertain. It appears that a crime affecting the whole household (e.g. a burglary or the theft of a vehicle) was counted as one crime, however many adults there were in the household ('household' crimes). Crimes such as robbery or assault were counted against each adult affected ('personal' crimes). The total number of household crimes and personal crimes were then expressed as a percentage of all people in England and Wales aged 16 or older living in private households.[30]

On that basis, and on the basis of the population in private households aged 16 and older given in the Censuses of 1981 and 2001, the victimisation rate was 29.7 per cent in 1981 and 30.3 per cent in 2002/03. On the basis of the mid-year estimates of the population in all types of accommodation in 1981 and 2002, the figures were 28.2 per cent and 29.3 per cent.[31]

An annual crime-victimisation rate of 27, 28, 29 or 30 per cent is not 'low'.

Nor, between 1981 and 2002/03, had the crime victimisation rate 'remained' low. There were 11 million crimes recorded by the BCS in 1981. By 1995 the figure had risen to 19.2 million. It was only later that the figure began to decline to the still historically high figures of 2002/03.

What is more, the victimisation or 'prevalence' rate of 30 per cent in 2002/03 may be an understatement compared with the 30 per cent of 1981. First, the British Crime Survey's 'victimisation rate' is 'the risk of a person aged 16 or over' being a victim of crime. No account is taken, therefore, of the increase of victims of crime under the age of 16. Yet a special analysis of 2,000 cases in the spring and summer of 2001 in nine police areas of one class of offence, personal robbery, reported that nearly a quarter of the victims were under the age of 16. What is more, the study reported that in the previous ten years the number of victims under the age of 16 had increased threefold.[32] A previous study had shown that a quarter of all victims of robberies of personal property were in the 14-17 age group.[33]

Secondly, certain categories of crime have not decreased since the mid-1990s, and remain far above the high figures of 1981. Even though he repeated the misleading word 'remains' low, a Home Office minister in April 2003 was somewhat more circumspect than his officials in that he dropped the word 'historically' low. The risk of being a victim 'remained' at its 'lowest level for 20 years'. But he then committed the particularly egregious error of including robbery.[34] Because of the size of its sample, the British Crime Survey's estimate of robbery alone is subject to a wide margin of error. The robbery estimate in the total population of England and Wales for the year 2000 was within the range of 140,000 as the lowest estimate to 411,000 as the highest estimate.[35] But the British Crime Survey's best estimate for robberies in 1981 was 164,000; in 1987 177,000; in 1991 183,000; and in 1993 237,000. The best estimate for the year 2000 was above all these figures, 276,000.

The figures for robberies amalgamated with personal thefts or with snatch thefts were published by the British Crime Survey for the whole period from 1981. In 1981 there had been 248,000 victims of robbery and personal theft.[36] In 2001/2002 there were 441,000 victims of robbery and snatch theft ('mugging'). As late as 1997 the figure was lower—423,000. It is impossible on the basis of the published data to make a valid claim that they were at their 'lowest level for 20 years'.

The 'victimisation rate' is the 'risk of being the victim or one or more crimes'. Account has therefore to be taken of possible changes in the distribution of crimes since 1981. If each victim in 1981 had suffered only a single crime, the victimisation rate for the amount of crime committed would be as high as it could be. If by 2001/2002 there was twice as much crime, but all the extra crime fell on people who had already been a crime victim at least once, then because the criterion is 'one or more crimes' the victimisation rate would be the same in 2001/2002 as it had been in 1981. By taking it to the extreme, it is easy to see the importance of this point. If all the crimes committed were committed against a single individual, then no matter how many more crimes there were, there would still be only one victim 'of one or more crimes'.

By looking at the proportion of respondents who have been victims of two or more crimes and of three or more crimes, the British Crime Survey takes this difficulty partly into account. It studies the incidence rate (the total number of offences), the prevalence rate (the proportion of the population victimised once or more) and the rate of repeat victimisation.[37] A high rate of repeat victimisation in 2002/2003 was found in cases of domestic violence. Nearly a quarter (23 per cent) had been victims three or more times in the year. Sixteen per cent of victims of non-vehicle vandalism had been victimised three or more times in the year. (At the other end of the scale, two per cent of victims of mugging had been mugged three or more times, and one per cent of victims of car thieves.)[38]

It may have been expected that the rate of repeat victimisation would have been rising, and therefore the prevalence rate would have been understating the incidence rate. The rich are able to protect themselves from rising crime more effectively than the poor. They can acquire cars that are increasingly difficult to steal or break into. They can install more elaborate security devices on their premises. They can move into safer residential areas. In recent years, however, the opposite appears to have been happening, with crimes spreading themselves more evenly over the population.[39]

The crimes that have immediate impact on the emotional lives of victims, such as robbery and burglary (as distinct from, say, much more costly commercial and insurance frauds) affect the poor disproportionately. In 2001/2002 nearly three times the proportion of unskilled respondents (18 per cent) compared with professional respondents (seven per cent) said that they were very likely or fairly likely to be mugged in the following 12 months.[40] More than twice the proportion of black respondents as white respondents in the British Crime Survey's report on crime in 2000 were worried about burglary in their area, 37 per cent compared with 18 per cent. Almost twice as many black respondents as white respondents were worried having their car stolen, 37 per cent compared with 20 per cent. Exactly twice the proportion were worried about muggings in their area, 32 per cent compared with 16 per cent. The level of worry about being mugged was still higher among Asians, 38 per cent.[41]

The unequal impact on the poor of disorder (as distinct from crime) can be seen at a glance from the proportion of British Crime Survey respondents living in different kinds of area who reported that there was a high level of disorder in their own neighbourhood. The criteria were: (i) teenagers hanging around, (ii) vandalism, (iii) racial attacks, (iv) drug dealing and (v) people being drunk or rowdy. The proportion of respondents giving their own immediate locality a score of eight or more on these five measures (out of a possible worst score of 15) was clearly highest in the poorest areas. The proportion was 54 per cent in multi-ethnic, low-income neighbourhoods, 44 per cent in the worst council estates, and even in the best housing estates the proportion was as high as 35 per cent. By contrast, in prosperous professional, metropolitan neighbourhoods the proportion was 18 per cent. It was only 11 per cent in the areas of affluent executives with families.[42]

Figure 4.2
Within a given type of area, percentages perceiving own immediate neighbourhood as disorderly
British Crime Survey respondents 2001/2002

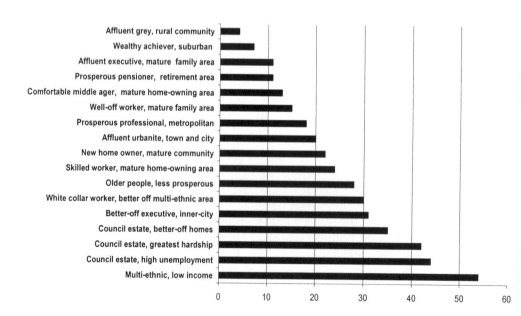

Source: Home Office Statistical Bulletin 07/02

Contrasting all council estates with all non-council areas, 52 per cent of respondents on council estates gave their own locality a score of eight or more so far as vandalism was concerned, while the proportion was 30 per cent in non-council areas. (A score of eight or more equated with 'a very or fairly big problem in their area'.) The proportion perceiving drug dealing or drug misuse as a very or fairly big problem in their area was 47 per cent on council estates, and only about half that in non-council areas, 27 per cent. The figures for rubbish and litter were almost the same, 47 per cent as contrasted with the 28 per cent.[43]

If or to the extent that the fear of crime is indeed exaggerated, the figures above directly contradict the 'moral panic' theory that it is respectable society (meaning the well-off) that does the exaggerating. These data show that if or to the extent that the fear of crime is exaggerated, it is the poor who do the exaggerating, not the rich. As we pointed out above (p. 57), the 'fear of crime' theory has, indeed, tended to be adapted to take account of this fact—the exaggerated fear of crime of the poor is owing to the fact, it is alleged, that they constitute the readership of the hysterical popular press. But it is also significant that when 'better off executives' live in the inner city, that is, in high-crime areas, they too have a great fear of crime. This suggests that their fears, like those of the poor, if somewhat exaggerated—something true of all threat situations—vary in proportion to the real dangers they face.

The theory that the disproportionate fear of crime was a problem as well as crime itself (or, sometimes, that the fear of crime was *the* problem rather than crime itself, now that the government, it was claimed, had reduced crime so much) was contradicted by the British Crime Survey's own data. These showed that the public was becoming more blasé towards crime rather than more fearful of it. In spite of muggings more than doubling between 1983 and 2001/2002, from 208,000 to 441,000, the proportion of British Crime Survey respondents saying that they were 'very worried' about being mugged fell from 20 per cent to 15 per cent.[44] The proportion of the public believing that the national crime rate was a lot higher than two years before, again contrary to the 'moral panic' doctrine, with a little lag realistically declined as the overall crime rate declined in the 1990s. Though it remained at historically very high levels (to adapt the Home Office's phrase), the overall crime rate began to come down after 1992. In 1996 54 per cent of the population said that the crime rate was not a lot higher than it had been in 1994. By 2001, 75 per cent said the crime rate was not a lot higher than it had been in 1999.[45]

But where the situations had actually deteriorated, those of street crime and all categories of disorder, the problem *was* perceived by the public to have deteriorated in the 1990s. Only 14 per cent of all respondents saw drug use and dealing as being a very or fairly big problem in their localities in 1992. In 2002 the proportion had more than doubled to 32 per cent. Teenagers hanging around was perceived as a problem in their neighbour-hood by 20 per cent of respondents in 1992. In 2002 the proportion was 33 per cent. The figure for vandalism and other deliberate destruction of property had risen from 26 per cent to 35 per cent. The figure for respon-dents perceiving racial attacks and harassment as being a very or fairly big problem in their own locality had nearly tripled from three per cent to eight per cent.[46] A question about 'being insulted or pestered in public places' was not asked until 1994. This figure rose by six percentage points from 26 per cent in 1994 to 32 per cent in 2001, falling back by one percentage point to 31 per cent in 2001/2002.

In spite of the 'exaggerated fear of crime' theory, it was perfectly reasonable for such a proportion of the population to 'fear' in this way that they might be included among the victims, to take precautions and to seek protection.

The fact that crime is in fact high in poorer areas, where fears are highest, is confirmed by the figures shown below on the differential impact of robbery in different areas of London. Over the four years 1999/2000 to 2002/2003 there were 18 robberies in poor Lambeth for every one robbery in prosperous Richmond.

Figure 4.3
Eighteen robberies in Lambeth for every one in Richmond
Number of London robberies in the four years 1999/2000 to 2002/2003

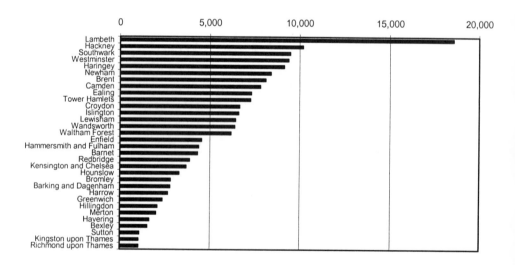

Source: http://www.met.police.uk/crimestatistics/index.htm

Any version of either the moral-panic theory or the theory of the exaggerated fear of crime is serviceable to people who for one reason or another want to deceive the public, and perhaps themselves, into believing that crime is no more of a problem today than it was in the past—politicians and pressure groups, for example, who deny or will not face the fact that their family, policing, educational, drugs, religious, planning or welfare policies have caused an upsurge in crime. If there has been no upsurge in crime, there is no case for them to answer. They denigrate the cultural achievements of previous generations in order to conceal the cultural disasters of their own.

The error and the folly have not lain, therefore, with a benighted public that has succumbed to unrealistic fears of crime, or has been stampeded into a moral panic by a sensationalising gutter press. The error and folly has lain with ideologically driven academics, and the broadsheet, radio and television journalists who depended on their 'findings'. Together they propagated the morally complacent falsehood that crime was not rising—and they thus blocked for more than a generation any effective policing response to the problems of law and order. *Si monumentum requiris, circumspice.*

5

Police Powers and Numbers in Response
to Rising Disorder and Crime

When the Royal Commission on the Police 1960 reported, the only priorities it was concerned with were, first, preventing crimes occurring at all, the traditional role of the police, and, secondly, the deplorable necessity of detecting crimes that had occurred, where prevention had failed. The commissioners expressed concern that, for a variety of reasons that they gave, prevention was losing out to detection as the top police priority.

The Royal Commission observed that there was 'a great deal more crime in this country today than there was before the war'. That was obvious to everyone: it was a commonplace, the commissioners said. They referred to parts of the country that had been hitherto relatively free of crime but were now experiencing it.[1]

The commissioners pointed out that in England and Wales crimes of violence had risen from 2,700 in 1938 to 12,100 in 1958. (By 2002/2003 even the 12,000 crimes of violence would come to seem unbelievably few, for then there were then not 12,000 but 991,000 crimes of violence.) They were concerned at the reversal of the fall in crime in the early 1950s. That fall had been in line with widespread expectations that the country was 'getting back to normal' as a very low crime society now that the Depression and the Second World War were over.

They argued that of course there were reasons for the new tendency for crime to be rising. These reasons had to be identified and addressed. But in the meantime, '*whatever* the cause, or causes, of this upsurge of crime, it is imperative that it should be checked before it gets completely out of hand'. The belief was gaining hold in some quarters that the risks to the criminal were being reduced, making crime more attractive: and 'the criminal statistics of the past few years lend strength to that belief'.[2]

The Metropolitan Police Commissioner told the commissioners that although 'the man on the beat', and only the man on the beat, could *prevent* such crimes as car theft, the number of men on beat duty was being reduced. In the face of the worsening deficiency of police strength in comparison to the number of crimes, it was unfortunate that preference was being given instead to detection. The CID branches were being kept fully manned, but not the uniformed force.[3]

The loss of priority to prevention was identified as a central problem by the Royal Commission. Fewer men on the beat meant that the police were less successful in preventing crime. This in turn called for a greater concentration on the detection of crimes committed. But this prevented the reinforcement of the preventive uniformed branch. More crimes were then committed. More resources were siphoned off for detection. The police's preventive arm was further weakened. There were more crimes that had to be detected, and so on. 'Here is a vicious circle.'[4]

The Royal Commission also recognised the importance of changes taking place in English culture as an explanation of the growth of crime: 'the decline in religious observance, a general lowering of moral standards, a restless, turbulent age', and so on. Yet 'over and over' the commissioners still found that the policeman was expected to set an example of 'old-fashioned virtues'. As the cultural scene shifted, the policeman remained a stable element.

(In fiction, the chaotic, bizarre personal lives of the officers at Sun Hill police station depicted in the television series *The Bill* provided an astonishing contrast in the early twenty-first century with the television depiction of police life at about the time of the Royal Commission of 1960, *Dixon of Dock Green*. Though *Dixon of Dock Green* was probably a much more accurate picture of everyday police life in the 1950s than *The Bill* was of everyday police life in the 2000s, life does tend to imitate art.)

But precisely because the 'Dixon'-type policeman was a 'stablising', 'old fashioned' and 'virtuous' figure, the emerging cultural conditions could easily foster a climate of opinion hostile to him, and the commissioners foresaw that this clash would make his task increasingly difficult.[5]

There was a growing, generalised 'defiance of established authority'. At one end of the social scale, 'classes of society' that 20 or 30 years before 'were rarely involved with the police' were now finding themselves, as motor car ownership became common, the subjects of police control.[6] They now had their own reasons to be critical of the police, and to be sympathetic to criticisms of them. At the other end of the scale, associated with a less police-friendly middle class, the commissioners found that police officers were subject to a good deal more annoyance, abuse and defiance as they tried to deal with 'young hooligans' or 'young thugs'.

One chief constable told the commissioners that his officers now said, naturally, 'Why should I put up with this?' 'They go to court and they are accused of all sorts of things and they say: "Why should I put up with all this, when there is a chap in the factory getting £5 a week more than I am?"'[7]

In 1960, just as the cultural revolution was beginning in England, there had been 744,000 crimes for the 72,000 police officers to deal with. By 1977 there were 2,636,000 crimes for the 107,000 police officers to deal with—that is, an additional 35,000 officers, and almost exactly an additional two million crimes.[8]

The growing gap between the number of crimes and the number of police officers to deal with them led to demands that the police be granted more powers, so that they were not so hampered by restraints of the criminal justice system. The old restraints had been suitable for the control of a more law-abiding and co-operative population by a police force that was large in relation to the number of crimes. They were now unnecessarily favourable to offenders. The police also looked to see what existing but underused legal powers might be available for them to use.

But the police were opposed by 'effective' public opinion (that is, the public opinion that has access to the influential media). Academia and the broadsheet media propagated the view that crime was not rising. The police, by unnecessarily abusing existing powers and illegally exceeding their powers, were endangering individual liberties and damaging 'community relations'. In the 1960s the police were opposed by student radicals, with the broad support of the students generally, in demonstrations against the war in Vietnam. The heroes of British university student politicians were successful foreign revolutionaries like Che Guevara and Mao Tse-Tung, and revolutionary or nihilistic intellectuals of the left like Marcuse and Sartre. Relations between the police and young people deteriorated because of the growing popularity of the recreational use of illicit drugs. Relations with young men deteriorated as the police tried to control the situation in neighbourhoods where the rise in crime was particularly marked.

The year 1968 marked the high point of anti-establishment and therefore anti-police student politics, but 'the spirit of sixty-eight' lived on through the 1970s, 1980s and beyond. In the 1980s there were two principal crises of policing. One was the urban riots of 1981. The other was the miners' strike of 1984-85. The policing problem in 1984-85 stemmed from the strategy adopted by the miners' leader, Arthur Scargill. He had failed in previous ballots to secure support for a national strike. Having won the support of his Yorkshire miners for a strike, therefore, he used the new possibilities of motorways, cheap and comfortable coach travel and car ownership to mobilise large bodies of 'flying pickets' to close mines and other facilities in areas that had not had a ballot for a strike.

Anti-war demonstrators and strikers, urban rioters and drug users had this common characteristic: they all demanded the right not to be policed. The Peelite principle that 'the police are the public and the public are the police', which had assumed a unity of interest of both in the police upholding the law of the land as it stood at the time, was transmogrified into the claim that the unity of police and public required that if and to the extent particular 'communities' or sections of the population did not approve of the law of the land, then it ought not to be imposed on them. 'Community policing' came to mean 'community non-policing'.

In the 'battle of the Saltey gates' during the miners' strike of 1972 the police had to succumb to the demands of the massed flying pickets of the miners, reinforced by pickets from other unions. In the same year violent pickets wrecked building sites and terrorised workmen ('Kill the Lump! Kill, kill, kill!') on building sites in Shrewsbury and Telford.

In February 1974, faced with the prospect of another miners' strike, the Prime Minister, Edward Heath, called a general election on the issue of 'who runs Britain?' He was defeated.

In 1974 more people were killed in political violence than in all the previous years of the twentieth century taken together, 45 by terrorist bombs. Twelve of the bomb deaths were caused by an IRA bomb on a coach on the M62. Twenty-one people were killed when a public house was bombed in Birmingham, and another five in a public house bombing in Guildford. Kevin Gateley, the forty-sixth victim, was the first man to be killed in a political demonstration in England, Scotland or Wales since 1919. He had fallen to the ground in the middle of a disorderly demonstrating crowd and been trampled to death.[9] In August 1974 there was violence over the police's attempt to control drug use at the Windsor Park Free Festival, when 70 police officers and 46 members of the public were injured. In October 1975 the IRA recommenced its bombing campaign, mainly attacking restaurants in the west end of London. In November, two hostages were held by the IRA in a five-day siege in Balcombe Street, London. In March 1976 'Right to Work' marchers injured 41 police officers at West Hendon, and in August 250 people were injured (120 of them police officers) at the Notting Hill Carnival. In June 1977 mass picketing in support of the strikers at the Grunwick film processing laboratory began, and, by the middle of July, 243 police officers had been injured. In August, Socialist Workers Party demonstrators attacked a National Front march at Lewisham and then switched their attack to the police. In the same month 58 officers guarding a National Front by-election meeting in Ladywood, Birmingham, were injured by Socialist Workers Party demonstrators, and 170 were injured while they were policing the Notting Hill Carnival.[10]

Meanwhile, from the battle of the Saltley gates in 1972 to the Notting Hill Carnival disturbances of 1977, the number of recorded crimes had risen by a million from 1,646,000 to 2,637,000.

In the face of the police's difficulties in bringing down crime and controlling social disorder in the new cultural circumstances of the 1970s, the Labour government announced in 1977 its intention to set up a Royal Commission. The Royal Commission on Criminal Procedure, under the chairmanship of Sir Cyril Philips, began its work in February 1978. Its recommendations resulted in the Police and Criminal Evidence Act of 1984 (known as PACE), which came into operation on 1 January 1986.

The overall effect of the Act was to weaken the powers of the police *vis à vis* suspects and therefore to weaken the position of victims *vis à vis* those among the suspects who were in fact the perpetrators of the crimes. From 1977, when the Royal Commission was set up by the Callaghan government, to 1986, the first year of the operation of PACE, crimes had risen from 2.6 million to 3.5 million. The strength of the police rose from 107,000 to 120,000. The number of special constables fell from 19,000 to 16,000, but civilians were being employed in increasing numbers. By 2002 there would be 58,000 civilian staff and 2,000 traffic wardens, as well as 12,000 special constables as support for police officers.

Stop and search

Opponents of the way the police used stop and search secured a victory in the year the Philips Commission reported, 1981.[11] The growth in burglary, street crime and drugs offences in the 1960s and 1970s led some police forces to intensify the use of section 4 of the Vagrancy Act of 1824—the so-called 'sus law' for stop-and-search operations. The sus law became the focus of indignation in the permissive atmosphere of the 1970s, and section 4 was repealed in 1981.

The year 1981 was important, too, because of the riots that gave rise to the criticisms levelled at the police by Lord Scarman. The prelude to the Brixton riots was a stop-and-search operation, 'Swamp 81'. In his report on the riots, Lord Scarman absolved the police as an institution (but not individual officers) from the racism that was attributed to the institution (but not to individual officers) by Sir William Macpherson two decades later.[12] But Scarman condemned Swamp 81 as 'a serious mistake'.[13]

The original incident that occasioned the riot was a stop-and-search of a taxi driver in Atlantic Road, Brixton, by two young officers in plain clothes. In spite of a gathering hostile crowd, the officers continued with the search. Scarman said to one of the two officers concerned, 'If you are getting unfriendly reactions from the crowd ... are you serving the cause of public peace better by continuing or not continuing?' The officer replied, 'I think I would be failing my public duty if I was ever intimidated by a crowd in exercising my authority'.

Well-publicised hostility to stop and search (especially to its differential impact on black compared with white young men),[14] the Royal Commission's report and the Scarman Report, all formed the background of the Police and Criminal Evidence Bill:

> On the one hand, the growing crime rate gave force to the arguments of those who said that the police were hampered by the restraints of the criminal justice system. On the other hand, there were those who argued that the police were abusing their existing powers, and thus endangering individual liberties and putting community relations in danger. ... The power and eloquence of the rival advocates of these two positions caused the Police and Criminal Evidence Bill to consume an unprecedented amount of parliamentary time.[15]

The terms of discourse were generally 'the community' versus the 'suspect', not the 'victim' versus the 'perpetrator'. The terms 'suspect' and 'community' were useful propaganda weapons against the police. 'Suspect' covered the innocent as well as the guilty.

What a 'community' wants and does not want was a question incapable of being answered objectively. The right of the inhabitants of some locality or the adherents of some particular culture within the state, not to be policed if it did not want to be, was powerfully endorsed by Scarman. The evidence that a 'community' did not want to be policed in some way or another was the readiness of that 'community' to engage in acts of violence against private and public property, if it were policed in the unwanted manner, and against the police.

Even vaguer, perhaps, than the concept of a community in this connection, and therefore even more useful in anti-police agitation in the 1980s, was the idea of 'community relations'. The police had not to act in such a way as to damage them.

PACE provided a national statutory framework for the restricted exercise of stop-and-search powers. The police's powers of stop and search were clarified but not strengthened. A code of practice was introduced that was designed to protect subjects of stop and search from the inappropriate use of police powers. The code specified how stop-and-search powers could be exercised. Violations of the code by a police officer were given disciplinary and in certain cases criminal weight. Under the code, it was no longer sufficient for a police officer to have reasonable suspicion that a person was carrying stolen property or a prohibited article. It could not consist merely of the fact that a person fell into a particular social group. Suspicion now had to have an objective basis. The officer had to make a written record of the stop and search, and the person stopped had a right to a copy of the record.

An early academic assessment of the likely effects of PACE asserted that in black communities the 'underlying bonds' that existed between the police and young white working-class males were lacking. Young blacks, the study said, saw the police as 'dedicated to upholding the social order as it now exists, an order from which many of them feel alienated'. 'In the sensitive area of community relations', the effect of PACE and its code of stop and search would be beneficial if it made the police withdraw from the 'confrontational attitudes' that had led up to the riots of 1981.[16]

Historically in British police practice, 'upholding the social order' as it existed had meant upholding it until new laws and regulations made by a democratically replaceable government changed it in some respect or another. The fifth of the Peelite principles was that the police should be rigidly unpolitical. They were unpolitical only when they upheld the current law of the land as it stood, 'without regard to the justice or injustice of the substance of individual laws'. The justice and injustice of individual laws was a matter for Parliament to consider and act upon, not the police.

Questioning suspects

In dealing with the powers of the police to question suspects, as when it dealt with other police powers, PACE either codified and thus confirmed existing powers, or restricted them.[17] There was very little increase in the powers of the depleted police forces in any direction.

Before PACE, cases of the police detaining a suspect without charge for more than 48 hours were rare. Softley's, and Barnes and Webster's investigations for the Philips Commission 1978-81 found *no* such cases.[18] Seventy-five per cent of cases were dealt with within six hours before being charged or released, and 95 per cent were dealt with within 24 hours.[19] In the serious cases that made up the remainder, the length of time was determined in individual cases by the High Court through a writ of *habeas corpus*.

Under PACE, people suspected of having committed a non-arrestable offence could be detained for only 24 hours while the police carried out their inquiries.[20] In the case of arrestable offences, under PACE, the suspect held while police carried out their inquiries had to be released after 36 hours, unless at an *inter pares* hearing a magistrates' court issued a warrant of further detention. PACE gave detainees the right to eight hours' rest, free from interview, in every 24 hour period.

On 17 September 1983 fighting broke out at Cookham, Berkshire, between factions of Hell's Angels. Two men were killed and seven seriously wounded by firearms, axes, knives and acid. Fifty-eight members of Hell's Angels were arrested. Among the weapons discovered were a sawn-off shotgun, a pistol, four axes, 36 knives and numerous metal stakes. There were no witnesses, and the Hell's Angels refused to answer police questions.

It took 36 detectives three days to gather sufficient evidence to charge 26 of the 58. If PACE had been in operation at that time, would a magistrates' court, faced with the information the police were able to provide, and hearing the arguments of an astute defence lawyer, have agreed to issue a warrant of extended detention? 'Even if the magistrates had been willing to do so', Chief Constable Buck asks, 'what damage would have been done to the police case by the requirement to "declare their hand" at this stage of the investigation?'[21]

The Royal Commission on Criminal Procedure considered the fact that the old right of legal advice under Judges' Rules and judicial decisions was rarely sought, and if sought, was often refused by the police.[22] Under PACE, the detainee had to be informed both orally and in writing that he had the right to legal advice. If the detainee did ask for legal advice, then no interview could be conducted until he or she had received it.[23] This was a move in the direction of United States practice, where in 1964 and 1966 the newly powerful civil rights movement and the libertarian movement, through decisions of the Supreme Court in the celebrated cases of *Escobedo v Illinois* and *Miranda v Arizona*, had secured the rights of suspects to have counsel present during a police interrogation (their 'Miranda' rights).

Police establishments and strength were not increased sufficiently, however, to enable police forces to incorporate these reforms into their good practice. Police resources, therefore, had to be withdrawn from both the prevention and detection of crime.

Admissible evidence

PACE also dealt with the admissibility of police evidence in court. One of the most important libertarian measures that protected suspects and people accused of crimes in the United States was the exclusionary rule that prevented evidence illegally seized by the police from being used against defendants in state courts.[24]

There had been scandals from time to time in England about abuses in police investigatory practices. But there were none that suggested that there existed in England the deep-seated problems both in the police and the courts revealed in the United States from the time of the Wickersham Commission in the 1930s.[25]

Before PACE, judges in England had wide discretion in admitting or excluding police evidence.[26] Section 78 of PACE dealt with the exclusion of unfair evidence. 'In any proceedings the court may refuse to allow evidence on which the prosecution proposes to rely to be given if it appears to the court that, having regard to all the circumstances, including the circumstances in which the evidence was obtained, the admission of the evidence would have such an adverse effect on the fairness of the proceedings that the court ought not to admit it.'

Up to the 1960s, the cultural conception in England of a 'fair trial' was based on the following beliefs. Someone had or had not committed a particular act. That particular act was or was not a crime. The prior existence or absence of the fact of the act having been committed, and the fact that it was or was not a crime, was not affected in the slightest by any result of any trial. The guilty person knew that he was guilty. But an innocent person could be thought by others to be guilty. It could be that in good faith or bad faith the victim or the police had accused the wrong person. To protect the innocent—decisively not to protect the guilty—the benefit of the doubt had to be given to all suspects. Given the system's procedures to protect the innocent, the perpetrator could dissemble, and attempt to gain for himself or herself the benefit to which only the innocent suspect was entitled. In no sense was the system in place in order to give scope to what lying and dissembling could achieve. A trial was a highly imperfect procedure for establishing the truth. The benefit of the doubt had therefore to be given to the defendant. The acquittal of a guilty suspect was unfortunate. But in no sense was the guilty person 'entitled' to his or her acquittal. The acquittal of someone who was guilty was a by-product of measures that justly protected someone who was innocent. It had to be tolerated because, if the innocent were not to be unjustly condemned, it was unavoidable.

In the 1960s the conception of 'the fair trial' began to alter in a way that was favourable to the perpetrator of a crime. A person was not *just presumed to be* innocent until proven guilty, as a convenient and highly benign fiction. He *was* innocent until he was proven guilty—a proposition that is of course nonsensical in the case of a guilty man.

The newly emerging cultural conception went further. Criminals, including users of illicit drugs, were entitled to be protected by the state from the consequences of their own actions. In some notorious cases the perpetrators' entitlement to the state's protection from their own actions came to be deemed greater than their victims' entitlement to the state's protection from the criminal's actions. The criminal or drug-taker or vandal had proved by his or her behaviour (about which it was reprehensible to be judgemental) that his 'need' was the greater.[27]

According to one of its leading members, many of the recommendations of the Philips Commission 1978-81 followed the suggestions of his organisation, JUSTICE, the lawyers' organisation.[28] But the Commission did not accept JUSTICE's case that there should be a rule that rigidly excluded illegally obtained evidence. 'It would be contrary to the interests of justice to exclude relevant evidence solely because it was obtained following a breach in the rules. Breaches are more suitably dealt with by police complaints and disciplinary procedures or separate criminal or civil proceedings ... It would be a deviation from the original criminal trial to use it [the trial of the criminal] as an instrument for disciplining the police.'[29] But at the Committee Stage in the House of Lords the absolute exclusion rule was nevertheless proposed—by Lord Scarman.

Initially 'the Scarman amendment', as it was called, was supported by other judicial members of the House, including Lord Denning. But by the time the amendment was reintroduced at the Report Stage, Lord Denning had discussed the matter with the Chief Justice of the US Supreme Court, who told him about the dreadful effects of the absolute exclusionary rule in the United States. The Scarman amendment—JUSTICE's—was therefore greatly diluted in the light of Lord Denning's information.

Under section 78 of PACE a judge was still free to accept, for example, the evidence of a police officer who had made a minor mistake in applying for a search warrant but who as a result of the search discovered a store of explosives and machine guns. Under the Scarman amendment that would not have been possible. At the other end of the scale, the court had the power, as ever, to exclude police evidence where, say, the police had a grudge against a citizen, obtained a warrant by fraud, broke down his door, tore up his floor boards and prosecuted him for some cannabis they found stored there.[30]

Had the absolute exclusionary rule been incorporated into PACE, the results in England might have been the same obvious shock to the criminal justice system that the United States experienced, and which led New York from the early 1990s to begin the countrywide process of redressing the balance between suspect on the one hand and the community/victim/ police on the other in favour of the latter. The Germans suffered two such shocks to the system that prevented them ever descending into the spiral of crime and disorder of post-1955 England: the breakdown of law and order in 1945, and the surge in crime in Berlin following the opening of the frontier of the old Federal Republic to the east. That crime was a substantial and greatly expanded problem in England remained until the early twenty-first century plausibly deniable by the dominant opinion makers of the social affairs intelligentsia.

Police numbers

The number of police officers in England and Wales in any given year cannot be exactly stated. Different forces counted their numbers in different ways. Sometimes the figures were for police officers on ordinary duty, at other times police officers overall, or police officer strength, or police officer establishment, or police officers appointed under one Act or another. Only in the early 2000s did the Home Office make a determined effort to standardise the way in which 'headcounts', 'full-time equivalents', 'numbers of staff available for duty', 'numbers actively on duty' and so on were recorded and reported by all forces covered by the 1996 Police Act.[31]

But the trend over time is less affected by local differences in what appears in the statistics as 'a police officer', and by whether the number relates to the average for the year, or on a particular date in the year. Whatever the method of counting, *the magnitude of the rise or fall* in the national numbers will be registered with some accuracy.

There were 120,000 police officers in 1981, and this number had grown to 130,000 by 31 March 2002. This meant very little improvement in the ratio of population per police officer. It was 408 persons per police officer in 1981; it was 401 persons per police officer in 2002.

Table 5.1
Ratio of population to number of police officers

Year	Population (millions)	Police Strength	Population per officer
1981	49	120,000	408
2000 (31 March)	52	124,170	419
2002 (31 March)	52	129,603	401

The police had to wait yet another year before the ratio of population to officers improved significantly. On 31 March 2003 it was 389.

Emphasis was constantly laid by people speaking on behalf of the government and the Home Office on the fact that police forces were at record strengths. The Chief Inspector of Constabulary, for example, wrote—of course correctly—that 'the number of police officers in England and Wales is now at the highest ever'.[32]

But the essential ratio is not population per officer. It is *crimes per officer*. In 1961 81,000 police officers had to deal officially with well under one million recorded crimes. In 1981 120,000 police officers had to deal with three million recorded crimes.

From 1997, when New Labour formed the government, to 2002/2003, the number of police officers went up from 127,000 to 134,000—a five per cent increase.

Offences rose by 186 per cent. About a quarter of this rise (23 per cent) was owing to changes in police recording rules. But in connection with the relationship between police resources and the demands on them it would not have mattered if all rise had been owing to changes in recording practices. This was the number of crimes the police *had to deal with*. In numbers, violent crimes rose from 347,000 in 1997 to 992,000 in 2002/03. The number of recorded drug offences rose from 23,000 to 141,000.

Table 5.2
Number of crimes each police officer has to deal with

Year	Crimes (thousands)	Police Officers (thousands)	Crimes per police officer
1921	103	57	2
1931	159	59	3
1961	807	81	11
1971	1,646	97	17
1981	2,964	120	23
1991	5,276	127	40
2001/2002	5,525	126	44
2002/2003	5,899	134	44

The English attempt to combat rising crime and disorder by technology had failed disastrously. And these figures show that statements in the late 1990s and early 2000s that the police were responding to public demand and putting officers back on the beat could refer to nothing but token gestures. With 5.9 million recorded crimes to deal with—even if all recording changes are subtracted, with 4.8 million crimes—any meaningful systems of beat policing on pre-1960s models was simply physically impossible.

6

Failure of Prevention is Followed by Failure of Detection—and Failure in Confidence in the Police and Criminal Justice System

Shortly after the passage into law of Sir Robert Peel's Bill for Improving the Police In and Near the Metropolis on 19 June 1829, every member of the new Metropolitan Police was issued with the force's General Instructions. Accompanying these instructions were nine principles of policing.

The first of the nine was that the police existed 'to prevent crime and disorder', rather than to detect crime that had been committed or repress disorder that was in progress. The last of the nine was that the test of police efficiency was 'the absence of crime and disorder, and not the visible evidence of police action in dealing with them'. No detail is given of author or date, but they were issued with the authority of the joint commissioners, Charles Rowan and Richard Mayne, and it is quite likely that they wrote them. They are the 'Peelite' principles of policing. Mayne stayed on as commissioner until 1868—a period in office of 40 years, during which time his principles were adopted by all the new police forces being set up throughout the country.

The Nine Principles of Peelite Policing

1. The basic mission for which the police exist is to prevent crime and disorder.

2. The ability of the police to perform their duties is dependent upon public approval of police actions.

3. Police must secure the willing co-operation of the public in voluntary observance of the law to be able to secure and maintain the respect of the public.

4. The degree of co-operation of the public that can be secured diminishes proportionately to the necessity of the use of physical force.

5. Police seek and preserve public favour not by catering to public opinion but by constantly demonstrating absolute impartial service to the law.

6. Police use physical force to the extent necessary to secure observance of the law or to restore order only when the exercise of persuasion, advice and warning is found to be insufficient.

7. Police, at all times, should maintain a relationship with the public that gives reality to the historic tradition that the police are the public and the public are the police; the police being only members of the public who are paid to give full-time attention to duties which are incumbent on every citizen in the interests of community welfare and existence.

8. Police should always direct their action strictly towards their functions and never appear to usurp the powers of the judiciary.

9. The test of police efficiency is the absence of crime and disorder, not the visible evidence of police action in dealing with it.

The role of the police officer, then, was not detection. Together with his fellow-citizens, his role was to prevent crimes occurring. Principle 7 said that England's 'historic tradition' was that the police were nothing more than 'members of the public who are paid to give full-time attention to duties which are incumbent on every citizen in the interests of community welfare and existence'. It was the duty of every member of the public to prevent crime and disorder. That aspect of citzenship just happened to be, in the case of the police officer, his full-time job.

The community would create law-abiding citizens through the work of parliament, literature, the press, the municipal and county authorities, the church, the schools, the family, the neighbourhood, the workplace. Where culture failed, then the certainty of public knowledge, disapproval, and informal and formal adverse consequences would make up the deficit in controlling potential doers of a consensually defined 'wrong' that was serious enough for the community to suppress, among the most serious being those dealt with in the criminal code.

In assessing the Peelite principle of prevention by the creation of law-abiding citizens, it is essential to bear in mind that this was not an abstract matter of citizens obeying the laws of any state, or of being influenced by any body of literature, or of being brought up in any type of family, or of being a member of any church or sect. It was the concrete matter of these complex and multifarious things as they existed, with their histories and cultures, among the English at that time, including a strong ideology at all levels of society of 'English liberty', the 'free-born Englishman' and so on, a phenomenon remarked on throughout the world at that time.

Where these failed to create the law-abiding citizen, then the police officer would be simply a full-time element in the complex situation of community knowledge and willingness to act that dissuaded the potential criminal from actually committing a crime. The potential criminal was to be deterred from committing any crimes by the high likelihood that if he did so he would be caught.

The primacy of prevention and the identity of the duty of citizen with the duty of police officer were reaffirmed one hundred years later by the Royal Commission on Police Powers and Procedures of 1929. The commissioners made it clear that the office and powers of the constable were basically controlled by the Common Law of England, whatever 'extraneous' duties were placed on the police by statute, and that the Common Law of England required that authority should be exercised only with the 'broad consent and active co-operation of all law-abiding people'.

> The police of this country have never been recognised, either in law or by tradition, as a force distinct from the general body of citizens. Despite the imposition of many extraneous duties on the police by legislation or administrative action, the principle remains that a policeman, in the view of the Common Law, is only 'a person paid to perform, as a matter of duty, acts which if he were so minded he might have done voluntarily'. Indeed the policeman possesses few powers not enjoyed by the ordinary citizen, and public opinion, expressed in Parliament and elsewhere, has been very jealous of any attempts to give increased authority to the police. This attitude is due, we believe, not to any distrust of the police as a body [as distinct from individual bad policemen] but to an instinctive feeling that, as a matter of principle, they should have as few powers as possible not possessed by the ordinary citizen, and that their authority should rest on the broad basis of consent and active co-operation of all law-abiding people. ... A proper and mutual understanding between the police and the public is essential to the maintenance of law and order.[1]

In this passage, then, the Royal Commission restated the Peelite principle that 'the police are the public and the public are the police'.[2]

As the power faded of the institutions and culture of the general community—through the family, neighbours, popular entertainment, education, religion and so on—to create law-abiding citizens, the emphasis was put on the police detecting those who had committed crimes. For any crime to be counted as detected, the following conditions had to be met: (i) a notifiable offence had to be committed and recorded; (ii) a suspect had to be identified and interviewed, or at least told that the crime had been cleared up as result of his being suspected; (iii) evidence was sufficient to charge the suspect; (iv) the victim had been informed that the crime had been cleared up. A detected crime was then cleared up by the police by their either (i) charging or issuing a summons against the suspect; (ii) issuing a caution, reprimand or final warning to the offender; (iii) having an offence taken into consideration in court; or (iv) counting the offence as cleared up but taking no further action because of any of a number of listed reasons, including the suspect being under the age of criminal responsibility, the death or illness of the suspect, or a decision by the police or (when the organisation came into existence) the Crown Prosecution Service that no useful purpose would be served by proceeding.[3]

Figure 6.1
Decline in proportion of crimes cleared up,
England and Wales 1938 to 2002/2003

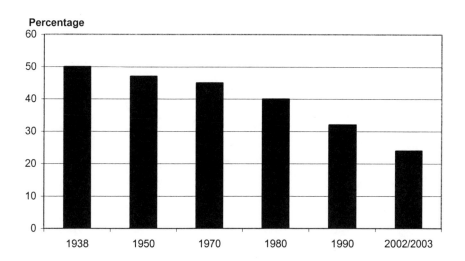

Source: *Criminal Statistics* and *Crime in England and Wales*

But in the period during which the police was turned into a detecting force rather than a preventing force in the circumstances of a deteriorating culture of law and order, the success of the police in detecting and clearing up crimes diminished. Of the 280,000 crimes recorded by the police in 1938, 50 per cent of them were detected. Of the 5.9 million crimes recorded by the police in 2002/2003, 24 per cent were detected. Thus 4.5 million recorded crimes were committed in 2002/2003 without even a suspect being uncovered, much less an offender being convicted, much less a convicted offender being made to bear some legal consequence of his criminal actions.   There must be a detection before there is a clear-up of any description. In contrast to the figure of 4.5 million undetected crimes in the single year 2003/2003, there were not as many as 4.5 million crimes in total in all of the 22 interwar and early war years from 1919 to 1941 taken together.

Figure 6.2
Decline in proportion of crimes cleared up
England and Wales 1980 to 2002/2003

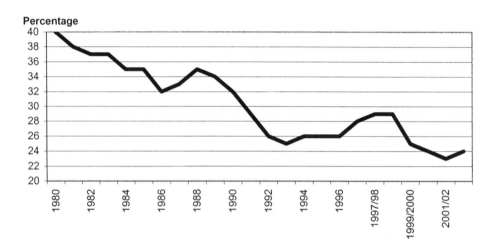

Source: *Criminal Statistics* and *Crime in England and Wales*

In 2003 detections were described as the 'cornerstone' of the government policy of 'narrowing the justice gap'. The government wanted to increase the number of offenders brought to justice, and no offender could be brought to justice without his having been detected.[4] But without the resources adequate to the cultural situation, the new attempt by the police to secure law and order by a high level of detection would prove, like prevention (to use of Chief Superintendent Michael Pike's phrase) 'the pursuit of the impossible'.[5]

There is a high detection and clear-up rate for some offences. The suspect in sexual offences is often able to identify the offender. In the area of drug crime, the crime of possession is only known to the police when the offender has already been detected—i.e. when someone has been found in possession of a prohibited substance. Robbery, burglary and criminal damage are much less likely to be detected and cleared up. In 2002/2003 the clear-up rate for drug offences was 96 per cent and for violence against the person 62 per cent. At the other end of the scale, for robbery the clear-up rate was 18 per cent, for criminal damage 13 per cent, and for burglary only 12 per cent.

In nearly all offence groups, the overall detection rate in London in 2002/2003 was far below the national average. The overall detection rate was 14 per cent compared with 24 per cent nationally. The detection rate for violence against the person was 24 per cent compared with 54 per cent nationally. The robbery detection rate was 13 per cent compared with 18 per cent nationally. Only the burglary clear-up rate was better than the national average, 13 per cent compared with 12 per cent. The overall detection rate in London dropped from 25 per cent in 1997/1998, to 22 per cent in 1998/1999, to 16 per cent in 1999/2000, to 15 per cent in 2000/2001, to 14 per cent in 2001/2001 and 2002/2003.[6]

Changes in the basis of the statistics in recent years have become a rich source of excuse and obfuscation. The changes in rules affecting detection are much discussed. In fact, up to 2003 at any rate, these changes made little difference to the overall statistics. New rules introduced in 1998 about what counted as a crime had the effect of slightly raising the overall detection rate by one per cent. But new rules introduced in 1999 about what counted as a detection had the effect of then lowering the overall detection rate by one per cent. The National Criminal Record Standard, introduced not later than April 2003, was expected to have the effect of worsening the detection rate, by increasing the proportion in the mix of reported crime of less serious crimes, where there was a low detection rate.[7]

Thus, overall, less than one quarter of the crimes reached the first stage of the criminal justice process, that of the identification of a suspect when the evidence was sufficient to charge him. Necessarily, then, fewer than 24 per cent of crimes were dealt with in court proceedings, fewer still ended in the conviction of the suspect, and fewer again ended in a penalty being paid by the perpetrator. The number of detections per officer in 2002/2003 was eleven.[8]

Given the strength of English culture in the nineteenth and twentieth centuries, crime was prevented for the first hundred years of the existence of the Peelite police and then contained for another 20 years or so. But from the 1960s, while the police force expanded only slowly, crime grew rapidly, and the police's capacity to prevent crime was diminished. Reacting to calls for assistance when a crime had been committed, and detecting and apprehending a suspect, replaced primary prevention as the police's priority. Here too, given the number of police officers and their technical resources in proportion to the number of crimes, and given all other aspects of the changed culture of the British, the police had lost ground.

In 1984 *British Social Attitudes* published the results of a survey in which respondents were asked about the prospects for law and order in Britain. Fifty per cent of the respondents said that it was very or quite likely that within the following ten years the police would find it impossible to protect people's personal safety on the streets.[9]

Since their inception in 1982, the British Crime Surveys have asked respondents whether they thought their local police did a 'very good' job. Between the British Crime Survey of 1982 and that of 1984, the year of the findings of *British Social Attitudes*, the proportion of respondents saying that the local police did a very good job had already declined from 43 per cent to 34 per cent. By 1988 the figure was down to 25 per cent. It then remained at about that level until the British Crime Survey of 2000, when it fell to 19 per cent. In the British Crime Survey of 2001/2002 it had declined to 14 per cent—one third of the figure of 1982.

If those who thought that the police did a 'fairly' good job were included, the decline was from 92 per cent thinking their local police did at least a fairly good job in 1982 to 75 per cent in 2001/2002. Among people with a household income of £30,000 or more, among professional and managerial respondents, and among Chinese respondents, the figure was 80 per cent. Among black respondents the level of satisfaction with their local police was also above average, 77 per cent. But among the unskilled the proportion was below average at 72 per cent, and in council areas the proportion was only 66 per cent. Among victims of crime it was 67 per cent.[10]

The first of the 'Key Findings' listed in the Home Office Statistical Bulletin that reported these facts was that 'three-quarters of people in the 2001/2002 BCS interviews felt that the police in their local area did a good job. Levels of confidence in the police remained virtually unchanged throughout the 1990s, but have fallen since the 1998 BCS'. The steep fall from the early 1980s in the proportion thinking that the local police did a good job was shown in a figure, but mentioned neither in the text nor the key findings.[11]

Victims who contacted the police were asked if they were satisfied with the police response. The basis of the figures from 1996 onwards was altered from that of previous years. Using the comparable figures, the proportion very satisfied with the way the police handled their case fell from 28 per cent in 1996 to 24 per cent in 2001/2002.[12] (The figure in 2002/2003 was 25 per cent.[13])

Fifty-eight per cent of all victims were at least 'fairly satisfied', but this proportion fell to 51 per cent of victims on housing estates. The proportion of victims very or fairly satisfied with the way the police handled their case varied from a high of 69 per cent in the case of victims of domestic violence to a low of 45 per cent in the case of victims of mugging.[14]

In a table that mixes policing objectives with policing techniques in a single set of what police priorities should be, the priority most frequently given first place by respondents was that of 'responding to emergency calls' (39 per cent). The second was 'detecting and arresting offenders' (31 per cent). 'Preventing crime by their presence', the key Peelite objective, was not offered even as a possibility. The third was the technique of 'patrolling on foot' (16 per cent). The technique of 'patrolling in cars' was regarded as the most important aspect of police work by only two per cent of the respondents. In 2001/2002 burglary was the most frequently chosen crime that the police should primarily target (by 55 per cent of respondents). The next most frequently chosen was drug dealing (by 52 per cent of the respondents). Police action against drug taking was the chief priority preferred by 20 per cent of the respondents.[15]

Figure 6.3
Percentage of respondents saying agency is doing a 'good' or 'excellent' job England and Wales 2001/2002

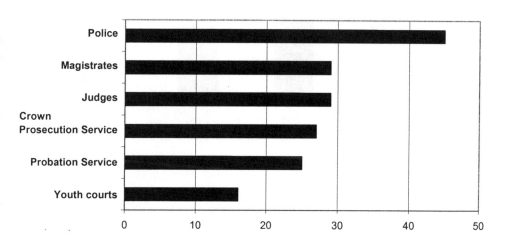

Source: HOSB 01/03

In assessing their *local* police, British Crime Survey respondents were asked to characterise them as 'very good' or 'fairly good'. In assessing the police generally as part of the criminal justice system, they were asked to characterise them as 'excellent' or 'good'. In 2001/2002, 47 per cent of respondents said that the police did a 'good' or an 'excellent' job. This was a far higher approval rate than any of the other components of the criminal justice system: the magistrates, the Crown Prosecution Service, judges and the youth courts.[16]

But whereas the other components of the criminal justice system at least held steady in their position of low public esteem in the 1990s and early 2000s—the judges indeed improving from 20 per cent in the 1996 BCS to 29 per cent in 2001/2002—the esteem in which the police were held by the public declined sharply.

Figure 6.4
Decline in confidence in the police
Respondents saying that the police do a good or excellent job
England and Wales 1994 to 2001/2002

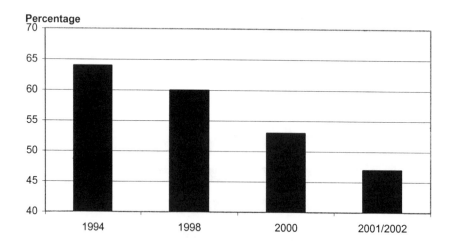

Source: HOSB 01/03

Those that felt at least 'fairly' confident—not a ringing endorsement—that the criminal justice system as a whole, including the police, was effective in reducing crime fell from 36 per cent in 2001/2002 to 31 per cent in 2002/2003.

A *Daily Telegraph* poll in September 2003 reported that the proportion of respondents 'very' satisfied with their own experience of the police and the experience of the police of people they knew was only six per cent. Fewer than half the respondents (48 per cent) were even as much as 'fairly' satisfied.[17]

The percentage reporting that the criminal justice system treated *suspects* as distinct from *law-abiding citizens* or *victims* fairly was by far the highest for all the aspects of the criminal justice system measured, 77 per cent in 2002/2003. In a society that was widely assumed to be 'institutionally racist', the figure for black or black British respondents who thought the system treated suspects fairly was, nevertheless, 66 per cent, and for Asian or Asian British 74 per cent. 'Fairness to suspects' was the only measure out of six where confidence in the criminal justice system increased between 2001/2002 and 2002/2003.

No other achievement of the criminal justice system inspired as many as 40 per cent of the respondents with a level of confidence even as modest as 'fairly' confident. Those who were at least fairly confident that the criminal justice system met the needs of the criminal's *victims* fell from 34 per cent to 30 per cent.

Figure 6.5
Criminals, victims and crime-fighting in the criminal justice system
England and Wales 2002/2003

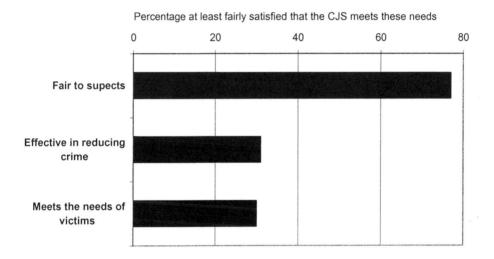

Percentage at least fairly satisfied that the CJS meets these needs

Source: HOSB 05/03

In its assessment of these figures, there was a slight hint in the Home Office's 'however' that because 77 per cent believed the system was fair to the perpetrators of crime, this somehow compensated for the 70 per cent who believed that the system was not fair to the victims of crime, and for the 69 per cent who were not even 'fairly' confident that the system was effective in reducing crime.[18] Yet even among those respondents who themselves had ever been in court accused of a crime, 69 per cent thought that the system was fair to suspects, but only 25 per cent of them thought either that it was effective in reducing crime, or that it met the needs of victims.[19]

The primary prevention of crime, and, where that fails, the secondary prevention of crime—deterrence—by the detection and conviction of criminals, remain for the public the essence of any policing function. Peelite policing put prevention far ahead of detection, but in any list of policing priorities, the prevention and detection of crime are out on their own, far above any other desirable aim or activity, such as the welfare of the perpetrator, or a particular composition of the police force, or 'preserving public favour by catering to public opinion'. Lists of priorities can sometimes function to clarify an organisation's core purposes and its permitted means of achieving them. Sometimes, however, they can conceal an organisation's failure to achieve its core purposes. An under-resourced organisation in a hostile environment that is facing insuperable difficulties in doing what its is expected to do can be tempted to succumb to the more-readily achievable priorities of pressure groups. Then, as long as the organisation is giving prominence to their efforts to comply with their demands, its most vociferous, and therefore, from the organisation's point of view, the most dangerous and damaging critics are kept at bay.

Part II

Germany

7

The Historical Roots of German Policing

The freeborn English in their self-policing communities, myth or reality, were for long a version of history that was not only a source of English pride, but also a source of foreign admiration. For Voltaire in the eighteenth century, English liberty was not a claim that had to be established. It was a fact, and it only remained to account for it. *La Liberté est née en Angleterre des querelles des tyrans.* Liberty was born in England from the quarrels of tyrants.[1] Because of the historical good fortune of civic consensus, policing was perceived in England as a matter principally of preventing crime and petty nuisance, not of controlling political subversion or social unrest.

The German myth or reality of law and order, by contrast, had been that of the police suppressing disorder against the régime. The national and international image of the German police as a protector of the powers-that-be (*zivile Ordnungsmacht*) seemed for considerable periods not to apply to the British police at all.

That the contrasting images of the German police and the British police in the past did to some extent reflect reality is shown by the fact that, while the London police force was set up in 1829 to prevent crime, the Berlin police force was set up in 1848 explicitly to combat civil unrest.

The nature of the celebration of the 50th anniversary of the Berlin police force in 1898 could hardly be imagined as an expression of British culture at the time. Paul Schmidt, a Prussian police captain, gives this account of the occasion:

> In 1848, a difficult year, the Berlin police was set up as a provisional body of men by our Prussian King, Frederick William IV. In 1898 it was able to look back on the many changes of the half-a-century that had elapsed since then. On 13 June 1898 the King of Prussia, German Kaiser, celebrated the jubilee in a military manner, as was fitting given the nature of the force.

> In the presence of His Majesty, 2,140 constables and 168 sergeants, together with their superior officers, and 238 plain-clothes constables and sergeants of the criminal investigation department and their superior officers, sang in chorus:

> *Though everyone opposes you*
> *Still will we be your shield.*
> *Our thankfulness shall never fail*
> *For the blessings that you yield.*

93

We will remain for ever true
Both to the Throne and Altar.
Just like the sturdy men of old
No storm can make us falter.[2]

Then a thousand-throated roar swept through the palace: 'God bless, God protect and God preserve our Emperor, our King, our Lord and all his royal House!'[3]

Schmidt's account of the ten years from the golden to the diamond jubilee of the Prussian police force deals exclusively with political and trade union disorders. Crime is hardly mentioned. In this celebratory volume he expresses his utmost contempt for street demonstrators. 'In January of this year, 1908, we yet again had to deal with disorderly conduct (*krawallartigen Vorgängen*) in the streets. The excuse for hooliganism on this occasion were demands for the so-called "right to vote". But we were present in sufficient numbers, and we dispersed the shrieking mob without actually having to attack it.'[4]

When the German ambassador to China was murdered, William's oration to the departing troops was to go to China and behave as the Huns had behaved (*sich wie die Hunnen zu benehmen*).

> You shall be an example to the Chinamen of breeding and discipline, but also of restraint and self-control. ... You shall inflict revenge. ... No pardon will be granted. ... You will take no prisoners. ... Just as a thousand years ago, the Huns under their leader King Etzel make such a name for themselves that it still resounds today, so may the name of Germany be made known in China in such a manner that never again will any Chinaman dare so much as to look askance (*auch nur scheel anzusehen*) at any German.[5]

According to Prince Phillip of Eulenburg, William's political stance was that domestic opposition was a personal insult. William is reported as saying in 1899 that until the leaders of the Social Democrats had all been dragged out of Reichstag by soldiers and shot dead, no improvements were possible.[6] During a tramworkers' strike in 1900 he sent a telegram to the commandant of the Berlin troops saying that he expected that when the troops intervened, at least 500 people should be shot down (*zur Strecke gebracht werden*). In 1903, when considering how Germany should prepare itself for the coming revolution, he said that he would eventually see that all Social Democrats were shot down, but not before they had plundered the Jews and the parvenues. Thus he would be revenged for the humiliation inflicted on the Prussian monarchy by the revolutionaries of 1848—the revolutionaries whom the Berlin police had been constituted in 1848 to defeat.[7]

According to Tonis Hundold (another senior police officer but in his case an important influence as police reformer in the Federal Republic), the Prussian tradition of the authoritarian police officer acting against the subject as a coercive institution in the hands of the authorities (*eine obrigkeitsgefügige Zwangsinstitution gegen den Untertan*) was one of Germany's most essential characteristics (*ein typisches Wesenmerkmal der deutschen Geschichte*)—as a fact and not as a myth.[8]

Up to the time of the French Revolution and beyond, the *Polizey-Söldner*, the police-mercenary, was the servant of whichever duke, arch-duke or prince hired him, no matter how petty the ruler's sovereign territory or how arbitrary and violent his power. With benevolent exceptions, the rulers of the scores of German states exercised their authority without legal restraints, though in such a way as to create generally in Germany a long-lasting culture of passive willingness to obey orders (*das Volk in einer «Muß-wohl-so-Sein» Vorstellung lange obrigkeitshörig gehalten wurde*).[9] *Befehl ist Befehl.* Orders is orders.

In the eighteenth century the absolute rulers, affected by the ideas of the Enlightenment, used their authority with more respect for the law and the welfare of their subjects. But their subjects were still subjects, with very limited rights. The police idea remained that of imposing the will of the authoritarian ruler, enlightened or not, on the underlying population. When the Enlightenment culminated in the French Revolution, the German potentates developed a system of mutual spying, widespread denunciation (*alle durch alle*) and arbitrary imprisonment without trial to protect their thrones.[10]

Hundold says that, with rare exceptions, liberty was not fought for in Germany. The milestones of freedom, he writes, were set up in England. He lists Magna Carta, the Petition of Right of 1628, the Habeas Corpus Act of 1679 (the Act freed the old practices of the law from all difficulties and exceptions), and the Declaration of Rights and the Bill of Rights of 1688 and 1689. America and France had followed with their own contributions to English-style policing through the claims made for freedom and law in the American War of Independence and the French Revolution.

A German contribution was not made until two more generations had passed, when the German revolutionaries at Frankfurt produced a constitution in 1849. Hundold drily observes: the constitution of the German liberals would have protected the rights of the individual and set limits to the powers of the state and the police—had it not been stillborn. He writes that 'in comparison with our democratic neighbours' German culture was characterised by the absolutism of the executive with the police as its coercive instrument.

When the German state under Bismarck became the first 'welfare state', it only gave German authoritarianism, in Hundold's phrase, more scope for infantilising the citizen and keeping him tied to the state's apron strings.[11] It was not until 1882, with the *Kreuzberg* judgement, that the right of any police officer to give any order, with penalties for disobeying it, was restricted to situations when the avoidance of danger justified the order.[12]

By the end of the nineteenth century and for the first two decades of the twentieth, under the Prussian-dominated German Empire, both the obedience of the German citizen to authority and the strict formal rectitude of the German police were legendary. In 1914, young adults, living in Germany, of nations with whom Germany was about to go to war, were advised to go home and join their own fighting forces. The German police, where necessary, stored their belongings. When they were called for in 1919, nothing had been interfered with, much less stolen. *Alles in Ordnung!*

The shock of civil violence in the revolutionary turmoil of 1918 and 1919 had persuaded leading politicians of all the parliamentary parties, and also broad categories of the electorate, that the liberty of the individual sought for through well-intended forms of democracy was impossible without self-regulation based on general agreement on what constituted 'good behaviour'. Good behaviour had been too narrowly conceived in Germany as 'deference to authority'. Deference to authority had been successful in producing a law-abiding population in Prussia and then in the Prussian-dominated German Empire (even among the members of the large pre-war Social Democratic party, who in doctrine and rhetoric set themselves outside official Germany as a state within a state).

As part of its effort to democratise the whole of the state machine, the Weimar Republic tried to modernise the police force in accordance with the advanced ideas of the time. Coercion from above through the use of the police was not acceptable to the elements of society that now wielded power. They demanded a social order in which the content of the laws and their enforcement were at least intended to be consensual on the English model, 'the police are the public and the public are the police'.

It was on that basis that the minister responsible for reforming the Prussian police, Carl Severing, aimed at providing a police service that was under the control neither of the executive nor of professional police officers, but of the democratically elected and dismissible Prussian parliament. The other German police forces, under the control of their own state authorities, were reformed in their own way, or remained unreformed.

Severing's reforms were hindered by the existing culture of the Prussian force. It was still military in its structure and as strongly state-authoritarian (*obrigkeitsstaatlich*) in its outlook as it had been under the Kaiser. Recruitment was still a matter of employing men who had served as non-commissioned officers—who then tended to treat private citizens in the street as they had been used to treating private soldiers under their control in the German army.

But the Prussian police reforms at the time of the Weimar Republic in principle, if less in practice, did assimilate the Prussian police to the English police, and laid down English rules of civility, restraint and helpfulness. The formal regulations, however, met with a great deal of personally felt opposition among those who had to put them into operation: the militarily trained police officers themselves and the bureaucrats of the police administration whose first priority was not the welfare of the citizen but the interests of the Prussian state and of Germany.

In spite of all the shortcomings of the attempts at reform, the Weimar Republic had at least started on the track of creating a civilian force that would be capable of acting on behalf of the ordinary citizen. The Weimar period, for Hundold, was particularly benign in its influence on policing because it did succeed in establishing in practice the English institution of the local police station and the beat foot-patrol officer, the 'good old beat system' (*die guten alten Polizeireviere*). In Hundold's view, in the ultimate development of the German police in a pluralistic democracy, these measures were exemplary in organisation, in the motivation of the police reformers concerned, and in the success of their preventive function.

During the Weimar period, these local police stations with their beat officers gradually changed public attitudes to the police, who came to be seen as the source of security and order in town life (*zum Hort der Sicherheit und Ordnung im bürgerlichen Dasein*), and as the approachable representatives of necessary, moderate state power in their localities (*zur Repräsentation der staatlichen, aber schon gemäßigten Macht*). The system of local police station and the officer on foot patrol began in the towns, but it slowly spread into country areas, and there, too, steadily raised people's trust in the police.

The political unrest unleashed in Germany by the economic crises of the 1920s threatened to bring down the pluralistic democratic order of the Republic—as indeed it did bring it down in the 1930s. But in the 1920s the police succeeded in part in keeping extremist unrest and violence under control. In Hundold's view, the success—and failure—of the police in those times persuaded many Germans that an effective police force was a necessity for a pluralistic democracy, and police forces as such were not the discardable relic of the oppressive authoritarian régimes of the past. '*Especially* a pluralistic democracy cannot do without a strong and efficient police force.' (*Gerade ein demokratisches, freiheitliches Staatswesen nicht auf eine starke und gut funktionierende Polizei verzichten kann.*)[13]

But these impressive achievements of the Weimar police concealed the fact, Hundold says, that the political and civic culture of Germany in the 1920s interfered with the growth of a civilian police force. A large proportion of the German population, and many members of the army and the administration, remained politically immature and sheep-like (*unreif und unmündig*) They were soon to pay the heavy price in the traumatic form of the Nazi tyranny.

From 1933 to 1945, the worst German traditions of arbitrary police coercion on behalf of the ruling authorities were embodied in the Nazi secret state police, the Gestapo. The National Socialist German Workers' Party, the Nazis, had been elected into power in a pluralistic democracy, but the Nazis had promptly abolished the really essential feature of pluralistic democracy, namely, the power of the electorate to vote the government out of power. The ordinary police continued to maintain internal law and order in a society in which millions of its citizens and citizens of conquered territories were being exterminated.

After the war ended in 1945, law and order temporarily broke down. Vandalism in parks was a problem in Western cities at the end of the twentieth century: but in 1945 the Tiergarten—Berlin's Hyde Park—was stripped of every tree and bush by West Berliners helping themselves in their bomb-ruined city to desperately needed fuel.

8

The Culture of Totalitarian Law and Order and Policing in East Berlin and East Germany

Between the 1950s, when East Germany—the German Democratic Republic (GDR)—was founded, and 1989, the time of the re-absorbing of its territory into a reunified Germany solely on West German terms, the crime rate in East Berlin remained at a very low level compared with that of West Berlin—and of course compared with the rapidly mounting rates that Britain began to experience after about 1955. The figures show the trends of population and crime in East and West Berlin from 1975 to the last year when the two parts of the city were separate political entities, 1989.

In 1975 the population of East Berlin was 1.1 million; there were 11,700 crimes recorded by the police. By 1989 the population of East Berlin had increased to 1.3 million; there were fewer crimes recorded by the police than in 1975, 10,600. Of course, the defects of official statistics that afflict the figures for England and Wales afflict these figures also. But no source of information, either from supporters or opponents of the GDR, either from internal sources or foreign observers, either from official or academic sources, deny that 'ordinary' crimes (theft, robbery, private violence etc.), were infrequently committed in the GDR itself. As with the figures for England and Wales, proof that the figures were *defective* is no proof at all the figures were *high*. Even were the official figures to be shown to be unusable, then evidence would have to be produced from elsewhere before any statement on the actual frequency of crimes could be made. Both élite and popular reports, and popular memories, give broad support the evidence of the official figures.

With the same caveat and argument, West Berlin's crime rate, though distinctly higher than East Berlin's, remained lower than that of other major cities of the West.[1]

In 1975 the population of West Berlin was 2.0 million, twice East Berlin's population of 1.1 million. There were 188,600 police-recorded crimes, sixteen times East Berlin's 11,700 crimes. By 1989 the population of West Berlin had increased by 100,000 to 2.1 million. There were 105,500 more crimes than in 1975.

Figure 8.1
East Berlin population and crime, 1975 to 1989

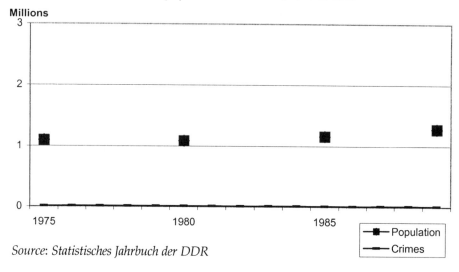

Source: *Statistisches Jahrbuch der DDR*

Figure 8.2
West Berlin population and crime, 1975 to 1989

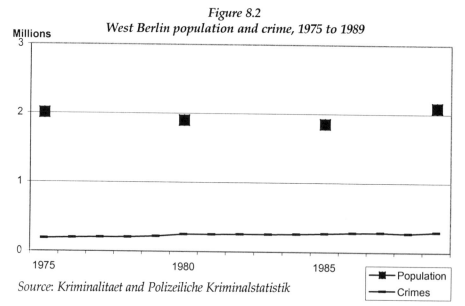

Source: *Kriminalitaet and Polizeiliche Kriminalstatistik*

Nothing shows the low crime rate of East Berlin and East Germany more strikingly that the fact that, in the course of the period 1955 to 1989, the number of crimes in *the whole of East Germany* including East Berlin fell to a figure that was well below that of *West Berlin taken alone*. In West Berlin there had been 70,000 crimes in 1955, and this number had increased to 294,000 by 1989. In all of East Germany, the decadal annual average was 157,000 in 1955, and this number had decreased to 117,000 by 1989.[2]

Figure 8.3
Crime in West Berlin alone and the in the whole of East Germany, 1955 to 1989

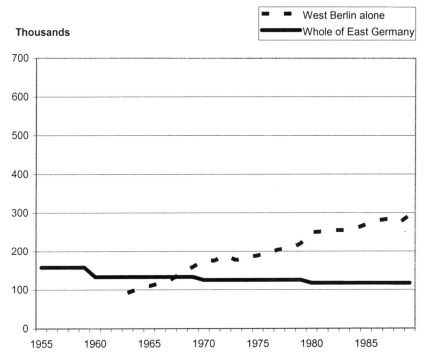

Source: *Jahresbericht, Kriminalitaet, Polizeiliche Kriminalstatistik* and *Statistisches Jahrbuch*

The number of young people getting into trouble with the police in the whole of East Germany fell from 19,000 in 1980 to fewer than half that number, 8,400, in 1989.[3]

Figure 8.4
Number of suspects halved: German Democratic Republic, 1980 to 1989

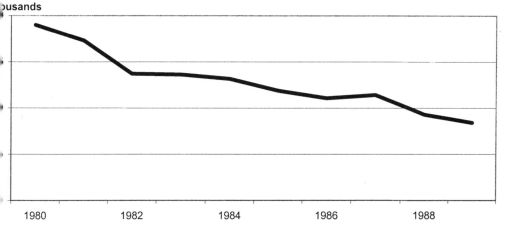

Source: *Statistisches Jahrbuch der DDR*

The crime rate in West Berlin did increase distinctly following the cultural revolution of the 1960s, but not as rapidly as elsewhere in the West. Weimar Berlin in the 1920s had been the standard-bearer of what came to be known in the 1960s as the permissive society. When permissiveness did begin its conquest of the West, East Berlin was, of course, tightly sealed off from what was seen in East Germany as Western decadence. But West Berlin's geographical isolation partly sealed that section of the city too from the criminal fall-out of outside cultural influences. 'From the building of the Berlin Wall in 1961 until 1988, crime in West Berlin was to a large extent enclosed within its own borders. The Wall immobilised criminals, who could cross neither the Wall with East Berlin nor the frontier with the rest of East Germany in either direction.' Robberies remained at a level of about 400 a year until 1968—the chart shows the yearly figures from 1963.[4]

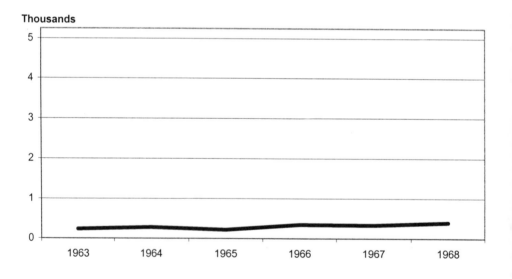

Figure 8.5
Robberies under 400 a year until 1968
West Berlin, 1963 to 1968

Source: *Jahresbericht, Kriminalitaet and Polizeiliche Kriminalstatistik*

After 1968 there was a sharp upturn (though the numbers remained small relative to those reached by this time in cities like London and New York).[5]

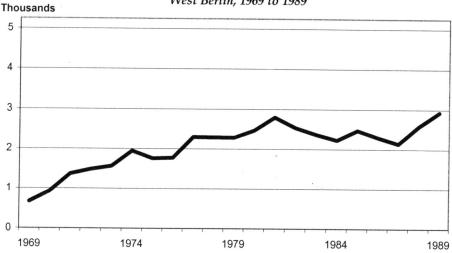

Figure 8.6
Robberies rise to 3,000 a year after 1968
West Berlin, 1969 to 1989

Source: *Kriminalitaet and Polizeiliche Kriminalstatistik*

Associated both with the anti-police sentiments generated in the period of student unrest in the 1960s and with the strain on police manpower in the face of rising crime, the situation improved for the criminal, in that his risk of being brought to book for his crime declined. In the 1960s the detection rate for robbery in West Berlin in most years was well above 50 per cent.[6]

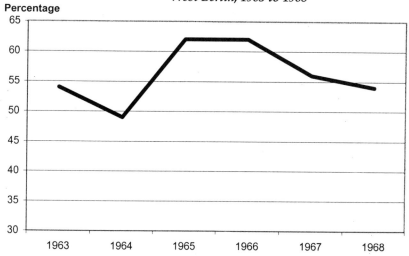

Figure 8.7
Half of all robberies cleared up until 1968
West Berlin, 1963 to 1968

Source: *Kriminalitaet and Polizeiliche Kriminalstatistik*

After the 1970s the detection rate was never that high, and in two years it fell as low as 33 per cent.[7]

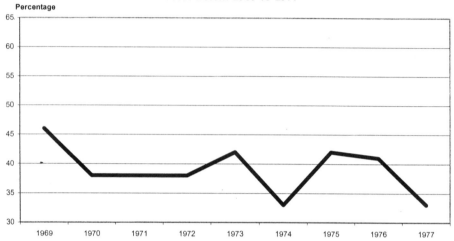

Figure 8.8
Detection rate falls as low as 33 per cent after 1968
West Berlin 1969 to 1977

Source: *Kriminalitaet* and *Polizeiliche Kriminalstatistik*

Policing and culture in the German Democratic Republic and East Berlin

The low crime rate in the German Democratic Republic was partly the result of endless indoctrination in schools, in entertainment and in the media. But it was also due to strict policing.

In the German Democratic Republic outside East Berlin, the German People's Police (*die Deutsche Volkspolizei*) was centralised under the sole control of the government—that is, of the ruling communist party (the *Sozialistische Einheitspartei Deutschlands [SED]*).[8]

But until the reunification of Germany in 1990, the four Allied Commanders held ultimate power over the police, the Soviets in East Berlin and the British, Americans and French in West Berlin. Under the direction of the East Berlin police headquarters (*das Präsidium der Deutschen Volkspolizei*), were eight police command districts (*die Deutsche Volkspolizei Inspektionen*), each covering one of East Berlin's local government areas. Each command area had from six to eight police Precincts (*die Polizeireviere*). Each Precinct was then divided into policing zones. The People's Police included the 'crime prevention' officers (*die Schutzpolizei*); the 'crime detection' officers (*die Kriminalpolizei*); the police who controlled passports and registration (*das Paß- und Meldungswesen*); the *Transportpolizei*; and the paramilitary emergency police (*die Bereitschaftspolizei*).

According to the central office for political training and press information, the People's Police was the particular instrument of power of the
revolutionary working class (*das Machtinstrument der revolutionären
Arbeiterklasse*).[9] The ideologically defined task of the People's Police from
the moment of its foundation was to combat the subversion of the
communist régime.[10] Shortly before the régime collapsed in 1988 an official
account of the character and functions of the People's Police was provided
by three serving senior police officers.[11] This proud self-portrait (as the
writers obviously perceived it) gives a clear account of the distinctive,
though short-lived, roots in German culture of *regular* (not secret) East
German policing, so different from the cultural roots of regular English
policing.

The People's Police had been consciously established to protect the
existing political régime—in this case the communist régime of the Soviet
zone of Berlin, and then of the German Democratic Republic. 'Lenin's most
important lesson was the need for a body of armed men under the
leadership of the party of the working class. In order to put this lesson into
practice, the Communist Party of Germany (KPD) instructed numerous
battle-hardened and tested comrades (*kamperfahrene und bewährte Genossen*)
to undertake work in the police force, especially in positions of
leadership.'[12]

According to Meiniger, Fechter and Heyser, the orders and regulations
issued on 25 May 1945 by General Besarin, the Soviet Commandant of East
Berlin, were the birth certificates (*Geburtsurkunden*) of the People's Police
and the death certificate for the old police apparatus, which was 'totally
liquidated'. No fewer than 200 of the communists who were prisoners in
the Brandenburg-Görden gaol joined the People's Police, and within a few
months of the end of the war, 80 per cent of the force were 'by origin'
industrial workers and agricultural labourers.

'The People's Police was born in the first hours after the defeat of
fascism. The first members of the People's Police, especially those in
leadership positions, were veterans of the International Brigade, steeled in
the war for Spanish freedom, and other antifascists. They shouldered the
task of guarding the new régime at a time when fascist elements hoped to
make use of chaos, in order to spread fear and uncertainty—and above all
to destroy any burgeoning trust.'[13]

Together with officers of the Soviet army, these antifascists aroused in
the young workers and working lads from the country the spirit of
proletarian internationalism (*der Geist des proletarischen Internationalismus*).
They 'handed on experience that was a thousand times more valuable than
the most perfect police expertise'—although it had to be emphasised,

Meiniger and his co-authors are quick to add, that recruits soon received professional instruction in the newly built police training colleges.[14]

It was obvious to everybody, the writers say, that the new régime needed order, and that only those people who had defied fascism and who were truly devoted to the cause of the working class could provide that order. This instrument of power (*das Machtorgan des Volkes*), the People's Police, was, they write, essential to give strength the working class. All previous class wars (*Klassenkämpfe*) had shown that the ruling classes use every means of violence in order to protect its interests. When they are deprived of the means of violence, the ruling classes try to interfere with the growth of the new order through sabotage, rumours and chaos.[15]

This, of course, was the pure Jacobin milk of the French Revolution, to which English culture had remained relatively immune. It had been passed down to the European left by Marx and Lenin, and to both the European left and right through the doctrinaire mentality of the paternalistic bureaucrat. Any faction is criminal, Saint-Just declared, because it neutralises the power of public virtue; any opposition is perverse, because it ignorantly or maliciously interferes with the welfare plans of the expert public official:

> No government can preserve the rights of the citizens without severity, but the difference between a free system and a tyrannical régime is that in the former severity is employed against the minority opposed to the general good ... while in the latter the severity of the state power is directed against the unfortunates who have delivered themselves to the service of injustice.[16]

In East Germany policing was also the task of the officers of the secret state police. In Nazi Berlin that is what the organisation had been bluntly called the *Geheimstaatspolizei*, the Gestapo. In communist Berlin it did not even have the name 'police' in its title. It was called the state security service, the *Staatssicherheitsdienst*, the Stasi. Andrej Paczowski, using the Stasi archives, wrote in 1999 that the picture of the Stasi as the 'eyes and ears' and 'shield and sword' of the communist régime was exactly right. The Stasi was an instrument of constant and detailed surveillance, and it dealt ruthlessly with any opposition that it considered it had discovered. 'In a totalitarian society, no less in its communist than in its other forms, surveillance and terror are the two distinguishing features of the a security apparatus.'[17] But in East Berlin and East Germany generally the protection of the régime from political subversion was not solely the work of the secret state police. It was explicitly a function of the regular police too.

The presumption of guilt or innocence is a flexible principle. There is a continuum. At the one extreme, a suspect is routinely treated as objectively guilty unless he can prove his innocence. At the other extreme, there is the firm assumption that if a court of law has failed to find him guilty, he could not, as matter of fact, have committed the act of which he had been accused. Both the limiting poles are purely theoretical concepts. In the most oppressive of arbitrary régimes, when whole categories of the population are rounded up, there are other categories who remain free. In real life, in the most liberal of régimes there is some trace of a presumption of guilt, some suspension of the assumption of unquestioned innocence, necessarily implied by the very category of 'suspect'. In the most liberal of régimes, too, while the line between the legal fiction of innocence and the fact of innocence can become very blurred in people's minds, rarely is the distinction completely lost. All régimes, in real life, are located at some point along the continuum, and show historical shifts, large or small, towards one pole or the other.

Since Peel's day, the culture of the British police has always included strong elements of respect for civil rights, minimum intervention, the use of minimum force and a commitment to the notion that a person is innocent until he or she is found guilty in a court of law. As the numbers of the British police weakened in relation to the volume of crime and disorder in the 1960s and beyond, these elements were reinforced. The British police assimilated itself to the 'hands-off' ideology of the lobbies protecting the civil rights of suspects and offenders. It assimilated itself also to the 'non-judgemental' ideology of social work that emphasised the role of the social causes of crime and the inappropriateness as well as the ineffectiveness of police work in relation to those social causes. Both sets of ideas were attractive to senior police officers who needed to justify their mounting ineffectiveness to themselves and to the public.

By contrast, the culture of the People's Police up to the collapse of East Germany at the end of 1989 remained Wilhelminian in its approach to crime and to apolitical anti-social disorder. The People's Police located itself much nearer the 'assumption of guilt' pole than did the British police.

When the civil rights of the suspect and non-judgementalism are paramount, the police officer can only intervene when some legal offence appears to have been committed, and then pass the 'innocent' suspect on to the courts. The People's Police officer, however, in the role of preventer of crime and disorder, was brutally old-fashioned in his or her judgements on anyone who looked as if they were getting up to mischief, or might get up to mischief. People's Police officers were primarily the agents of law-abiding citizens, and only secondarily the protectors of the rights of 'rootless elements' (*Entwurzelten*) and 'reprobates' (*Gestrauchelten*).

The same principle was applied by the People's Police to others who 'chose to place themselves outside the social order', such as adolescent youths who became criminals whether or not that was all they could do 'to survive'. Identifying and remedying the causes of delinquency, a task fraught with uncertainties, was mainly the long-term role of other agencies of society, hardly at all the role of the police. Until those causes of criminality and apolitical disorder were removed, the clear and finite role of the police was to prevent criminals committing the crimes they were motivated to commit, and stopping disorderly elements disturbing the peace, even if legally they were not committing any offence.[18]

To back up the regular police in their task of controlling petty crime and nuisance, under a decree issued in April 1982 anyone who was 18 or older, who had the necessary political and moral qualities, and who wanted to support the regular police in carrying out the duties the state required of them, could become a voluntary helper (*freiwilliger Helfer*).[19] The job of the voluntary helper was to be the person to whom someone in the neighbourhood could turn if there was any noise nuisance or damage to their neighourhood's amenities, and either stop them himself or herself, or contact the regular police. When voluntary helpers received information about a suspect in a case of crime or petty disorder, their task was to make a record of it and pass it on to the beat police officer (*zuständiger Abschnittsbevollmächtige*), or if necessary to a criminal investigation detective. Two of the things that voluntary helpers prevented in their neighbourhoods was damage to public property and rowdyism—the official German term is a comment on the reputation of the British by the 1980s, for it is the British word 'rowdy' that is used—*rowdyhaftes Verhalten*. Any citizen who violated socialist rectitude (*sozialistische Ordnung*) could receive a lecture on good behaviour from the voluntary helper.

In 1979 the Ministry of the Interior produced instructions on the responsibility of the People's Police for ensuring that towns and villages were kept clean and free from vandalism.[20] The fully developed socialist state, the instructions said, is characterised by the extension of good behaviour into more and more areas of social life and the conduct of individuals. The preservation of orderliness, cleanliness and high standards of hygiene stood at the centre of police work. Clean and cared-for neighbourhoods were both a condition and expression of the socialist way of life. Young people 'acting out of stupidity, indiscipline, shallowness or indifference' damaged neighbourhood amenities and parks.[21] Whoever or whatever was to blame for the young people's present ignorance, boredom, superficiality or resentment, and whoever and whatever in the long term was being done and had to be done to combat these evils, in the here and now the People's Police had to step in firmly and stop them spoiling other people's reasonable enjoyment of their neighbourhoods.

In 1977 the Central Committee of the East German Communist Party demanded that good 'ways of thinking and acting' should be fostered by the mass membership of the party. These ways of thinking and acting were listed as a good attitude to work, a high sense of social responsibility, creativity, productivity mindedness, thrift, conscious self-discipline, community spirit and intolerance of faults and abuses.[22]

Political officers attached to the People's Police and the police helpers were already responsible for 'supervising' the 'moral development' of the residents in their area.[23] But in 1979 instructions were produced by the Ministry of the Interior that placed upon the regular police themselves the moralising tasks set out in 1977 in the decision of the Central Committee of the SED.[24] The instructions referred to the development of the 'socialist personality'.[25] The development of the socialist personality meant the heightening of the sense of law-abidingness, and was an important ideological basis for the fight against bourgeois, revisionist and other non-Leninist conduct.[26] The Ministry made it clear that this was not just exhortation. How well they met this obligation to foster in the population the virtues of the socialist personality would be closely bound up with how officers were trained for senior positions and therefore with the nature of the qualifications for promotion.[27]

Berliners from the nineteenth century and early twentieth century would have recognised in the communist police culture the delineaments of their own. Like the Berlin police in 1848, the People's Police had been founded to protect the powers-that-be. If the official statistics of the Prussian and East German authorities respectively are to be believed, the crime rate had been low in Prussian Berlin, and it was low in East-German Berlin. In Berlin in 1911, a rapidly expanding city of 3.7 million, the police had to deal with only 232 cases of robbery. In the year of defeat and revolution, 1918, there were only 274 cases of robbery. In the middle of the Great War, in 1916, there were only 110.[28] Of course, the same authorities on criminology who dismiss the low crime figures of this period in England, dismiss also the low crime figures of this period in Prussia—even though by discarding these figures they have no statistical evidence of their own to support their claim that crime was as high as it is was by the end of the twentieth century. Yet, in the absence of all figures, there are the same sort of non-statistical indications that we found for England that crime was low. In *The Riddle of the Sands*, referred to above, an intruder appears at night on an apparently unoccupied yacht lying on a beach on one of the Frisian Islands. In 1903 the possibility that it was a burglar is dismissed out of hand by the English, anti-German, hero of the novel. 'They're not like that in Germany.'[29] Any evidence to the contrary, statistical or non-statistical, is, in terms of the cliché, conspicuous by its absence.

The police in Prussian Berlin dealt with 'rootless' elements. The police in East Berlin dealt with 'rootless' elements. In 1918 the 'general security police' (*Allgemeine Sicherheitspolizei*) in Prussian Berlin took into custody 232 male and 29 female beggars. They took into custody 407 homeless men, 137 homeless women and 12 homeless children. The police in Prussian Berlin dealt with immoral conduct. The police in East Berlin dealt with immoral conduct. In 1918, no men and no children, but 10,254 women were arrested for offences against the morality code (*übertreten der sittenpolizeilichen Vorschriften*). Twenty-three men and 13 women were taken into custody for causing a public nuisance (*grober Unfug*). The police in Prussian Berlin were numerous in comparison with the number of crimes. In 1908 the Royal Berlin Constabulary numbered 6,382, of whom 5,206 were uniformed foot-patrol constables (*Schutzmänner zu Fuß*).[30] They were a highly visible, preventive police. This was also the case in communist East Berlin.

The image of the People's Police projected by its official authors as late as 1988 was that of a force that for 40 years had been synonymous with trust, solidarity, protection and cooperation with the people (*Vertrauen, Verbundenheit, Schutz* and *Zusammenarbeit mit den Bürgern*) because its officers were the first in history that did not repress the majority of population, but were their class comrades.[31]

To some extent, at any rate in retrospect, this official account was accepted by many East Berliners. When East Berlin did not catch up economically with West at nearly the rate that had been hoped, *Ostalgie* became a favourite topic of journalistic comment—nostalgia for the benefits that the East had forgone for a Western promise that had not in all respects materialised. Not the least of these benefits forgone were communist East Berlin's low rates of crime and of English-type '*Rowdyismus*'.

After the Second World War 'Germany', as a consensual community with a unified sense of what law and order the ordinary citizen should automatically support, for so long a taken-for-granted feature of the policing basis of British society, was once more rendered problematical. Two different cultures developed in two parts of the country, communist and anti-communist, both in East Berlin and on the island of non-communist culture in West Berlin.

Germany's division into a Soviet zone of occupation and three western zones occupied by the British, French and Americans laid the groundwork for a 40-year development of two distinct societies, with different law and order and policing régimes and police/citizen cultures, fenced off against one another, with patrols, watchtowers, checks on every car, lorry and train passing from east to west, and automatic machine guns pointing inward to shoot any disloyal East German citizen who might attempt to defect to the West. Berlin itself, of course, was divided by a lethally guarded high wall. What 'Germany' was in territorial terms was again drastically revised.

The erection of the Berlin Wall and the closing of the frontier in 1961 was an attempt by East Germany to stem the outward flood of its citizens who preferred the 'western way of life', with its individual liberties and economic abundance. During the period 1949-61, an annual average of almost a quarter of million people fled from East to West Germany, amounting to a total of 2.7 million of East Germany's population of only 16 million.[32]

The relations between the two separate German states went through three phases. In the first phase each refused to recognise the existence of the other as a state. The second stage was one of partial reconciliation. The third was the unconditional incorporation of East Germany into a reunified Germany wholly on West Germany's terms.

The Preamble to the West German Basic Law—the Constitution of the Federal Republic of Germany—stated that the Federal Republic had 'also acted for those Germans for whom it was made impossible to participate', meaning mainly the East Germans on the other side of the Iron Curtain. West Germany's claim was that it was the 'sole representative' of Germany (this was the Federal Republic's *Alleinvertretungsanspruch*). The West Germans were acting on behalf of Germans in the Soviet zone and the Saarland. Article 23 left it open for these other German territories to accede to the Federal Republic.

After attaining *de facto* sovereignty in 1955, the Federal Republic proclaimed the Hallstein Doctrine, which stated that the Federal Republic would cut off diplomatic relations with any country that recognised the communist German Democratic Republic. This doctrine was not abandoned until 1967.

Paradoxically, it was the building of the Wall and the closing of the frontier that eased the way to improved relations between the two states. The effects of the closed frontier on families led to contacts between East and West Germany in order to obtain what were called 'humanitarian alleviations' (*menschliche Erleichterungen*). From 1969 Chancellor Willy Brandt's social-democratic government adopted a policy of trying to bring about change in East Germany through rapprochement. East Germany did allow more West Germans to travel to the east, and after 1986 there was a large increase in West German visitors.

But East Germany was much more careful than West Germany about the dangers of the contamination of its culture with ideas, observations and experiences picked up by their own citizens travelling in the other direction. East Germans found it difficult to obtain permission to go to the West. It was almost impossible for people of working age. The few people who were allowed out had to be thought to be ideologically committed to the communist régime—and often had to have relatives left behind as hostages to their good behaviour while away, and as an incentive for them to return. People's Police officers were not allowed to have contacts any at all with the West. Many People's Police officers did not see western relatives from 1961 to 1989. But while the police in East Berlin were the police of the capital of East Germany, West Berlin was hermetically sealed-off. In his study of the city's two police forces, Andreas Glaeser reports that many officers in the Berlin Police said that they went 'stir crazy' (that they caught 'island madness', *Inselkoller*).[33]

Brandt's *Ostpolitik* was a matter of negotiating treaties regulating communication between the two countries. This led to a gradual *de facto* recognition of the German Democratic Republic by the Federal Republic. Even though 'sole representation' had been the policy engineered by the founding father of the conservative Christian Democratic Union (CDU), Konrad Adenauer, *Ostpolitik* was continued by Chancellor Helmut Kohl's CDU government that came to power in 1982. In 1984 credit worth one billion marks was granted to communist East Germany, and in 1987 the conservative CDU government accorded a fully fledged state reception in the West German capital, Bonn, to Erich Honecker, East Germany's communist leader.

Ostpolitik also led the German Democratic Republic to renounce its claims to be the sole German state. In 1976, the ninth communist party congress revoked all references to German unity in the constitution, in the East German national hymn, and in the party statutes.

In contrast to Poland and Hungary, however, East Germany did not seize the opportunities for internal liberalisation created by Mikhail Gorbachev's glasnost and perestroika. The East German government continued to suppress every sign of protest. The policy of East Germany's splendid communist isolation was taken so far that travel to Poland and Hungary was prohibited—and even *Sputnik* was banned, the magazine of the soviet youth organisation Comsomol.

In the summer of 1989 there was another mass exodus. Several thousand refugees sought protection in the embassies of the Federal German Republic in Budapest, Warsaw and Prague. By far the largest number of refugees from one German culture to the other took advantage of the dismantling of the Iron Curtain on 9 September 1989. In September 1989 alone, more than 25,000 left East Germany for West Germany by way of Hungary and Austria.

In Leipzig on 11 September 1989, and on Mondays thereafter, there were large demonstrations to demand the release of demonstrators who had been arrested. On 4 November about one million East Germans gathered in East Berlin's Alexander Square. They were addressed by members of civil rights movements, well-known intellectuals and leaders of the ruling German communist party (the SED). Even as late as 4 November 1989 in

Alexanderplatz, however, German reunification was not an issue. Neither was it in Leipzig. There should still be two distinct German cultures. The demand was for socialism—communism—'with a human face'.

Nine days later, to everybody's surprise, the Berlin Wall fell. By the end of the first weekend, three million East Germans had visited West Berlin or elsewhere in West Germany. Still there was no public mention of German reunification. Ten days after the border was opened, the prime minister of the German Democratic Republic, Hans Modrow, vaguely brought German unity into play by talk of the German 'community'. This was already the language of *Ostpolitik*, which referred to the German 'community of responsibility' (*Verantwortungsgemeinschaft*). Modrow said it should become a 'treaty community' or (in German somewhat of a contradiction in terms) a 'contract community' (*Vertragsgemeinschaft*).

But then in Leipzig, the banners and chants at the Monday demonstrations proclaiming '*we* are the people' (wir *sind das Volk*) were replaced by banners and chants for German unity, 'we are *one* people' (*wir sind* ein *Volk*). Egon Krenz, the new leader of the GDR elected in October 1989, no longer excluded the confederation of a socialist East Germany that had withdrawn from the Warsaw Pact, and a West Germany that had withdrawn from NATO.

Erich Honecker, along with other leading members of the communist élite, were excluded from the party. Some were put under house arrest. The SED appended to its name the explanatory label, 'the party of *democratic* socialism'.

The four victorious powers of the Second World War still held rights over Germany as a whole. They had to be persuaded that a united Germany would not pose a threat to its neighbours. The United States, the United Kingdom, France and eventually the USSR acceded to German demands for unification. On 19 April 1990 the newly constituted government of the German Democratic Republic declared its intention to use the Federal Republic's constitution to seek accession. That was the end of East Germany, and of the distinctive law and order culture and policing ideology of the People's Police and the Stasi.

9

The Culture of Policing by Consent in West Germany and West Berlin before Reunification

A fter the Second World War, Britain rested on its laurels, and took law and order and its preventive, civilian police force for granted. But their own experiences forced Germans in the pluralistic Federal Republic, once Germany had been defeated, to look again at the answers Germany had given to fundamental questions of political obligation—Germany's political and policing culture—so that 'never again could the immature politics of citizens and leaders bring down such disaster on Germany and the world'. (*Nicht wieder dürfen staatsbürgerliche Unmündigkeit und politische Unreife solch ein Unheil über Deutschland und die Welt bringen.*)[1]

West Germany

These questions were sharpened in the pluralistic west of Germany, the Federal Republic, by the fact that the old German police traditions, of the 'command state' and the subordinate citizen, continued unbroken in what had been the Soviet zone of Germany, and what became the German Democratic Republic.[2] The ethos and organisation of the state security police and the People's Police, explicitly now the expression of the armed might of the working class as exercised by the communist vanguard, was unchanged. The master was new. The servant's task was the same: to crush all opposition.

But—again unlike in Britain, where the police did not have an overt or felt problem of preserving the fundamental political order of parliamentary democracy until the 1970s—internal challenges to the pluralistic régime meant that West German police recruits were taught, fully in the German tradition, to explicitly and consciously think of themselves as committed defenders of the existing régime. 'The German police'—the police of the Federal Republic—'should always go back to the first principles of a *civilised* society (*eines* kultivierten *Volkes*).' It was not enough to be simply efficient. The police must be efficient in achieving the value objectives (*Wertzielen*) of a morally sound society (*einer gesitteten Gesellschaft*).[3]

In the mid-1960s—before the full blast of the student-led cultural revolution was felt in Germany, with its sequel of acts of political terror committed by, for example, the Baader-Meinhoff gang—opposition to the democratic régime of the Federal Republic came from two sides. On the one side there were some people still loyal to Nazism, and there was a considerable portion of the older population who, while reviling tyranny, had not yet overcome their feelings of dependence on an authoritarian state. On the other side there were young people who took the benefits of a pluralistic democracy for granted and yearned for the delights of anarchistic utopias. Lazy boredom and cheap cynicism (*Demokratieverdrossenheit*) eased the way to success for those who did hold strong views and were willing to use illegal violence to get their own way.

In December 1967 the Allensbach Institute of Opinion Research examined the extent and intensity of student unrest in the Federal Republic. Eighty-one per cent of German students were dissatisfied with the existing arrangements (the *Hochschulverfassung*) in their university, and 42 per cent were in favour of demonstrations against them. Of those in favour of demonstrations, seven per cent were in favour of demonstrations in which soft objects were thrown; four per cent were in favour of hard objects being thrown—a mild enough beginning to the student unrest that produced the political violence of what are still called in Germany 'the nineteen sixty-eighters'.

After December 1967 the extreme radical groups increased their appeal to students. Prominent among the radical German students was Rudi Dutschke, who invented the slogan 'the long march through the institutions'. He himself was eventually assassinated. The students of the extreme left found justification for violent opposition to the Federal Republic in its political, economic and cultural totality in the writings of a group of German political philosophers collectively known as the Frankfurt School.

The writers of the Frankfurt School described themselves a Marxists, but a distinctive element in their social and political theory was the rejection of the Marxist notion of an ever increasing mass of misery, poverty and exploitation in the advanced industrial countries of the West. What was *wrong* with the West was that its working class *had* become rich. But in becoming materially rich, and in doing what they did in order to be rich, proletarians had been deprived of their wish and capacity to lead a higher and better life.

They rejected also the usual Marxist rhetoric about the brutality of the agents of the state—mainly the police—in holding back the worker in his quest for the equality he justly sought. Though it was still, in Marx's phrase, nothing but the 'executive committee of the bourgeoisie', what characterised the modern state, they said, was its subtlety. To meet this phenomenon

Marcuse invented the term 'repressive tolerance'. The modern state with its 'tolerant' police permitted freedom of speech because it had ensured that whatever was said by critics came to nothing. Reform therefore required violence—violence not for personal gain or revenge, but because one wants to be a human being (*weil sie Menschen sein wollen*). Law and order (*Gesetz und Ordnung*) 'everywhere and always' serve the interests of the already powerful.

Marcuse gave students the justification to use violence in a society where peaceful demonstrations were permitted—precisely because they *were* permitted: without violence, demonstrations were a sham. He also gave them the justification for using violence against laws made by governments that the electorate could replace, because the electors suffered under the illusion from which the students were free, that by the peaceful use of institutions of society they affected, or could affect if they tried, what happened in government and the economy.[4] Violence was as justified, then, in a society with a government dismissible by the electorate, and where there was freedom of expression and of peaceful demonstration, as it was in a dictatorship where none of these things applied. Germany had escaped terror from above. Marcuse and the Frankfurt School legitimised violence from below. Paradoxically, the political left that supported the East German police state succeeded in demonising the police in the West, and not only in Germany.

In 1968, from a West German perspective, Hundold wrote that the past culture of German policing should not be an unconscious burden of debilitating guilt on the consciences of modern German police officers. They should not be deflected from their duty to apply the laws made by the democratically dismissible parliament. On the contrary, the open recognition and lively memory of police repression and the pressures of violent student radicalism should be a constant reminder that it was the duty of the police officer to be the custodian of the democratically arrived-at laws, and be close to and serve the broad public.

In 1968 the Federal Republic, West Germany, had a population of about 60 million. The West German police strength was 130,000 regular police officers, a ratio of one police officer to every 437 inhabitants. Hundold remained conscious of the internal security aspect of policing. In his opinion the threat to the pluralistic democracy in the Federal Republic was still underrated, just as it had been underrated in the Weimar Republic. The size of police forces in relation to the problems they had to face was a question, therefore, that was raised early in Germany, late in England. The West Germans were also conscious that Weimar had made the fatal mistake of not spending enough money on the police force. The Weimar government had lost control of the streets to the rioting factions of the extreme right and the extreme left.[5]

West Berlin

In the wake of the cultural changes of the 1960s, which included propaganda aimed at the police as aggressors against student and other demonstrations, crime rose in West Berlin in the 1970s, though not at the rate that crime was rising in cities of comparable size in other Western countries.

Figure 9.1
Crime rises in the aftermath of the cultural revolution of the 1960s
West Berlin, 1967 to 1980

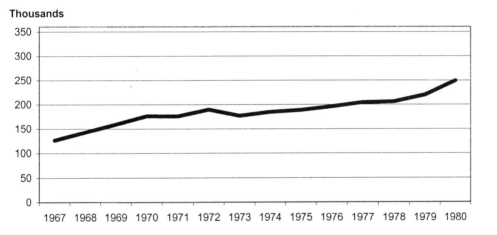

Source: *Jahresbericht, Kriminalitaet* and *Polizeiliche Kriminalstatistik*

In the 1980s, too, though crime rates rose in West Berlin, its cultural milieu and the actions of its police force meant that the increase in the crime rate was not so rapid as it was in England and the United States.

Robberies rose from the low normal levels of about 400 a year in the period before the cultural revolution of the 1960s to 2,500 in 1982. Robberies were then also stabilised in the 1980s at the higher, post-1960s, rate.

But then, in 1989-90, West Berlin suffered the 'shock to the system' that made all public authorities realise that there was a serious crime problem to be confronted. In that, Berlin resembled New York. New York suffered a crime crisis of such proportions that it faced up to it by electing Mayor Giuliani on the basis of his promise to reduce crime.

CULTURES AND CRIMES

Figure 9.2
Crime rises less steeply in the 1980s
West Berlin, 1980 to 1988

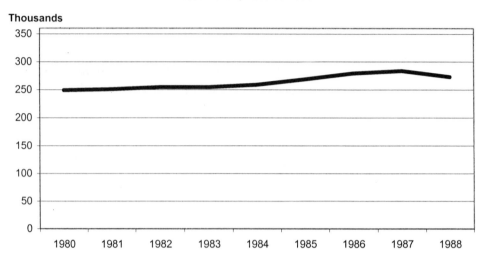

Source: *Jahresbericht, Kriminalitaet* and *Polizeiliche Kriminalstatistik*

Figure 9.3
Robberies under 400 a year until 1968
West Berlin, 1963 to 1968

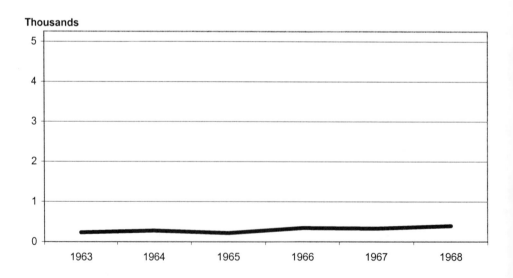

Source: *Jahresbericht, Kriminalitaet* and *Polizeiliche Kriminalstatistik*

Figure 9.4
Robberies rise after 1968
West Berlin, 1969 to 1981

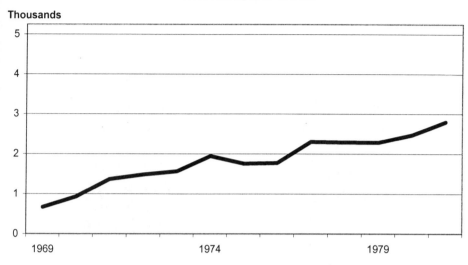

Source: *Kriminalitaet* and *Polizeiliche Kriminalstatistik*

Figure 9.5
Robbery stabilised in the 1980s
West Berlin, 1983 to 1988

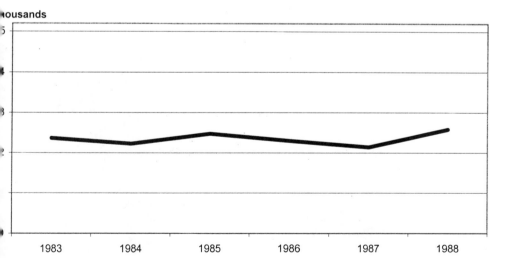

Source: *Polizeiliche Kriminalstatistik*

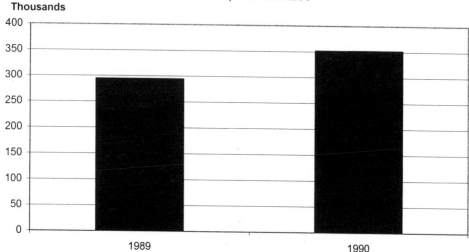

Figure 9.6
Rise in crime in West Berlin when frontier opened
West Berlin, 1989 and 1990

Source: Polizeiliche Kriminalstatistik

Robbery rose from the, for West Berlin, historically high figure of 2,900 in 1989 to 5,000 in the following year.

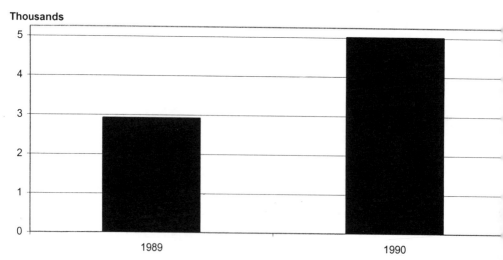

Figure 9.7
Robberies in West Berlin almost double in a single year
West Berlin, 1989 and 1990

Source: Polizeiliche Kriminalstatistik

10

Crime and Policing in a Reunited Berlin

Economic and social union of the two Germanies took effect at the beginning of July 1990. At the end of July the German Federal Republic reintroduced five states to its territory—including the old state at the heart of Prussia and therefore at the heart of the both Bismarck's and Hitler's Second and Third German Empires, Brandenburg. On 23 August 1990 the parliament of the German Democratic Republic voted almost unanimously for incorporation into the Federal Republic. German unity was thus accomplished by the almost complete self-dissolution of the East German communist state, and the wholesale acceptance of the West as a model. East Germany became part of a reunified Germany solely on West German terms. There was no question of West Germany accommodating itself to or arriving at a compromise with the culture of East Germany.

The West German constitution was left intact. The constitutions and laws of the five resurrected states were copies of western models. Almost the whole of West Germany's political, judicial and administrative system was applied to the territory of the former Democratic Republic. The exceptions concerned certain transitory arrangements for pay scales and rents. Another exception was the law on abortion. East German women were able to proceed on the basis of East Germany's liberal abortion laws until a jointly elected Bundestag could promulgate a new all-German law.

Just as the Second World War resulted in the very name of Prussia disappearing from the map, the names of institutions associated with the Democratic Republic were obliterated. The name of the new unified state was that of the former West German state, the Federal Republic of Germany, not just Germany, and not the German Republic. The very word 'former' German Democratic Republic (*ehemalige DDR*) was avoided as politically incorrect, because it preserved the memory of an independent state. New verbal inventions appeared after unification on 3 October 1990. Late in the 1990s the two terms most common in use were the 'accession area' (*Beitrittsgebiet*) and—in spite of the fact that Saxony was an independent kingdom long before there was a state of North Rhine Westphalia—'the new states' (*die neuen Länder*). The East Germans had simply spent '40 years deep in the cave of the Russian bear', and had been brought out blinking in the light. Using a phrase that is an obvious echo of a favourite with

121

communists, 'the dustbin of history' to which their opponents and their ideas were for ever being consigned, Andreas Glaeser wrote that the German Democratic Republic 'disappeared without a trace into the abyss of history'.[1]

The new constitution of the state and city of the united Berlin, approved by referendum in 1995, 'extended the validity of the Berlin constitution of 1950'—that is, West Berlin's constitution was made to apply to East Berlin as well.

A fortiori, there was no negotiation over the organisation and ethos of the police force of the newly unified Berlin. The police culture would be that of the West Berlin police. As far as the employment of the individual members of the East German force was concerned, the West Berlin police authorities simply made an administrative decision to take or reject whomsoever they wanted. The personal and professional record of every former East German police officer was checked as a precondition for continued employment. If any People's Police officer deemed suitable by West Berlin police standards did not want to join on West Berlin's terms he or she was, of course, free to make that choice. The pre-unification name of the West Berlin's police force, the Berlin Police, was applied to the police force of the unified Berlin, with no reference to the People's Police, its structure, its interests or its ethos.[2]

After reunification, the Berlin Police was highly democratic in its relation to parliament. It was also highly local in the large scale in its freedom from Federal control, and in the small scale in the deployment of its uniformed officers.

With a population of only 3.4 million, Berlin was a city-state (*Stadtstaat*) within the Federal Republic of Germany, with its own powerful mayor and its own senate and parliament. The Berlin city-state parliament (*Abgeordneteshaus*) elected Berlin's Minister for the Interior (*Senator für Inneres*). With other state Interior Ministers, he or she attended the Federal conference that tied all the German states (*Länder*) to the Federal level of government. The Federal Minister of the Interior participated in the conference (*Innenministerkonferenz*) but did not chair it. The Berlin parliament also elected the Berlin Police Commissioner (*Polizeipräsident*), who was responsible to it through Berlin's Interior Minister.

The Berlin Police was organised into four administrative departments under the Commissioner, who like a British chief constable was responsible for day to day operational decisions. Two of the departments were directly to do with police work. One dealt with the uniformed police officers (the *Landesschutzpolizeiamt*). The other dealt with the plain clothes criminal investigation officers (the *Landeskriminalamt*).[3]

From 1994 to the early 2000s, Berlin was divided into seven basic command units (*Direktionen*), each covering more than one of Berlin's boroughs. Each command unit had its own central offices specialising in crime, public security and traffic. There were 48 Precincts (*Abschnitte*) in these basic command units. These were responsible for the basic work of the uniformed police officers. The 48 Precincts were then divided into 1,227 'contact areas' (*Kontaktbereichen*), whose officers were responsible for a multitude of tasks in dealing with organisations and acting as 'community helpers' (*Kontaktbereichsbeamte*, the *KoBBs*). The central functions of the uniformed officer in the Precinct and contact area was foot patrol (*Streifendienst*) and rapid vehicle response to calls. The *KoBB*'s duty was to know his milieu well, and be known personally by people in the area he served. The Berlin police authority (whose officers' uniforms are green) remained in the early 2000s very concerned with 'getting more green onto the streets' (*mehr Grün auf die Straße bringen*).[4]

It was distinctive of Berlin policing that the service-oriented foot patrol officers (*Dienstgruppen*) were separated from the rapid-reaction vehicle patrols. This was in accordance with the so-called 'Berlin model' of policing developed in the early 2000s.[5]

Berlin did have a problem of 'multiculturality' in the police force—the clash between the culture of policing in West Berlin as contrasted with East Berlin. By mid-1994 the first screening of ex-East German police officers for their cultural suitability for western-type police work, and especially to weed out Stasi collaborators, had been completed. Shortly afterwards most East German officers were offered tenure.[6]

Andreas Glaeser studied the residual problems of multiculturalism, specifically, in this case, the problems of biculturalism in these highly monocultural circumstances of no concessions being made to the culture of the Democratic Republic. He spent two years in the mid-1990s with the 'Wessies' and 'Ossies' as they worked together in a police station in the south-east suburb of Köpernik. Glaeser also studied a police station in Potsdam, the old capital of the Kings of Prussia and like Köpernik a location redolent of the old Prussian respect for, to adapt the English term to make it more accurately applicable, laws and orders. From October 1994 to August 1996, he interviewed police officers and accompanied them on their daily patrols.

He found hostility between the 'Ossie' and 'Wessie' police officers, based on these cultural differences developed over 40 years of one-party state experience and a pluralistic-party state experience, of a statist society and of a market society. The fact of continuing dissensus was palpable.

There were, Glaeser said, 'walls in the heads' of both the 'Ossies' and the 'Wessies'. Officers from the old East and West forces differed in their understanding of what 'democracy' meant. They disagreed about morality. They differed in the view of the proper relation between the public and private spheres. They differed in their views of what made somebody a 'good worker'. (Each side accused the other of being 'shirkers'.) Since 1949 the content of educational courses, popular literature and entertainment, propaganda, religion, the laws, policies and the German language itself (as witnessed by the divergences that developed between the East and West German versions of the standard Duden dictionaries) had followed their own paths.

In spite of an extensively shared cultural heritage as fellow-Germans, therefore, which made the problem of multiculturalism relatively slight compared with the problem posed by multiculturalism when cultures are widely divergent, their transfer into the ethos of the West Berlin force was experienced by many officers from the People's Police as a 'loss of meaning' of what policing was about. Glaeser detected a hostility that sprang even from one officer's pride in what was familiar to him, and another officer's contempt for what was strange in the layout of streets, the colour, shape and the 'odour of houses' in East or West Berlin.[7]

Beat policing in Berlin and England

Glaeser looked at the police patrols in cars. Officially car patrols were a matter either of being sent out on specific assignments, or of patrolling the streets. Patrolling the streets was a matter either of waiting to be called by radio to a task or of themselves encountering a problem that might require police attention—traffic accidents, helpless people in need of assistance (mainly drunks), suspected stolen vehicles, suicide threats, traffic impediments such as broken water pipes, deceased persons where cause of death was uncertain, and so on. But unofficially patrolling in the police car was not about the search for action. It was also about getting away from action. One of the advantages to the neighbourhood of the patrol officer on foot, the beat policeman, was that he or she found it much harder thus to slope off (to use the old army term) or *sich zu verpissen* (to use their own).

In contrast to England, the institution of the neighbourhood-beat patrol officer was genuinely strengthened in West Berlin the 1970s and in the whole of Berlin in the 1990s.[8] The German police reformers did not lose sight of the admired Peelite conception of the police officer, who *in a pluralistic democracy is welcomed* precisely because he or she is 'in the streets' in order to, and with the necessary power to, secure compliance with rules *agreed upon after due process* by the legitimate authorities.[9]

Whatever the precise form of 'beat policing', and there have been many, it worked only because the police officer had *plenty of time* to chat with the people of the neighbourhood. Only thus could he or she gain intimate knowledge of what was going on there. The beat officer on foot is an established figure in the neighbourhood, not a transient one, and personally available, not an anonymous figure who appears on call. An essential feature of beat policing, both for potential wrong-doers and for law-abiding citizens, was frequent visibility. The inhabitants of the neighbourhood could see that the police were present and cared about what was happening. These effects could be obtained only by the highly labour intensive activity of police officers frequently walking or cycling about their neighbourhood, not just driving through it.

The old beat system in England had meant, in the boroughs that controlled their own police forces, a three-shift system covered the whole 24 hours in the town's central business districts, and day-time foot patrols further out. A police constable patrolling every beat would have a set time in every hour or so when he had to report to his superior officer in person, or from a set public phone box, or from a phone in a police box. He would be visited by his inspector once a shift, and by his sergeant perhaps twice a shift. In the 1960s phone contact began to be replaced by wireless contact.

In the country districts of the English counties the old beat constables were not in constant contact with their sergeant or inspector, but were on duty 24 hours a day. During the day and in the evening these 'detached beat' constables toured their designated area on foot or by cycle. The less experienced constables started their careers in the towns of the county, under stricter supervision.

When the county constables won the eight-hour day, available manpower was cut at a stroke, and from the 1960s patrolling began to be done by panda car. The old beat policeman was still in contact from the car with his usual acquaintances, but new motorised constables could not, of course, build up his rapport with the local community or fund of information about the 'local villains'.

Technology in the form of wireless communication and the police car had seemed at first to be an answer to police manpower shortages and to the mobility of criminals. It rapidly became a pernicious substitute for preventive policing, and an excuse for keeping police numbers low. It was therefore quite wrong, for example, for the BBC to say in news broadcasts in October 2003 that there was a record number of police 'on the streets'; and no matter what type or period of beat policing the BBC may have had in mind, it was the height of absurdity to say that there was a record number of police officers 'on the beat'.[10]

Unlike England's police forces (including London's), in nearly all years Berlin's police numbers were kept at least steady. An exception was 1989, when the uniformed branch dropped to 11,600 from the previous year's figure of 12,500, and the criminal investigation branch dropped to 1,900 from the previous year's figure of 2,100. The total number of officers and civilian staff dropped from 20,800 to 19,100. In 1989 crime jumped, though this was partly owing to the rise in crime that followed the opening of the frontier in November 1989 and continued into the following year. Throughout the 1990s and into the early 2000s, there were generally between 16,000 and 17,000 uniformed officers, and between 3,000 and 4,000 detectives. Civilian staff rose from 800 in 1992 to 1,300 in 2001.[11] These numbers served a city whose population remained stable throughout the 1990s at 3.4 million, the difference between the beginning and the end of the period being a matter of fewer than 50,000 residents.[12]

Police effectiveness in Berlin

As in any large Western city, the crime with which the police had to deal varied greatly from district to district. In 1999 the crime rate per 100,000 population, which was 17,000 overall, varied from 57,000 in Precinct 27 in the Borough of Charlottenburg to under 5,000 in Precinct 11 in the Borough of Reinickendorf.[13]

It also varied greatly and persistently from one ethnic group to another. Taking West Berlin, and then the part of the united Berlin what had been West Berlin, in 1980 the 2,025 Lebanese suspected of crimes amounted to no less then 58 per cent of the total Lebanese population legally resident there. In 1985 the figure was 52 per cent. In 1995 the 939 Lebanese suspects amounted to 23 per cent of the resident Lebanese population. In 1985 15 per cent of the resident Polish population ended up as suspects. In 1990 the figure was 11 per cent, and in 1995 20 per cent.[14] The rates for residents from Finland, Japan, South Korea, Sweden and Holland, by contrast, were consistently under three per cent.[15] Although it would be condemned as 'racial profiling' in British police practice, the Berlin uniformed police used these cultural data to save themselves from spending too much time on preventing crimes that remotely might be committed by law-abiding residents of Berlin.

The persistence of the residues of fear of the police and a culture of obedience to authority; the dreadful memories of Nazi policing; the example of communist policing in the German Democratic Republic; and the two shocks to the system of sudden leaps in the crime rate—the breakdown of civil order after the Second World War and the sharp rise in the crime rate in the early 1990s that was too obvious to be denied or ignored by anybody—had positive effects on policing and the control of crime in the Bonn Federal Republic up to the 1990s, and in the reunited Federal Republic from the 1990s.

Figure 10.1
The rate of growth of crime again brought under control
All Berlin, 1991 to 2001

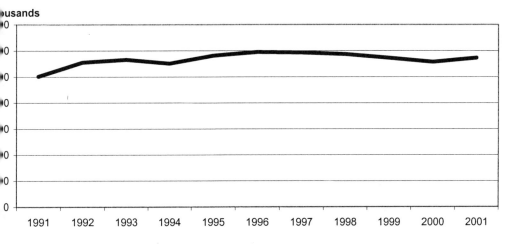

Source: *Polizeiliche Kriminalstatistik*

Figure 10.2
Robberies remain within the 7,000 to 10,000 range
Berlin 1993 to 2002

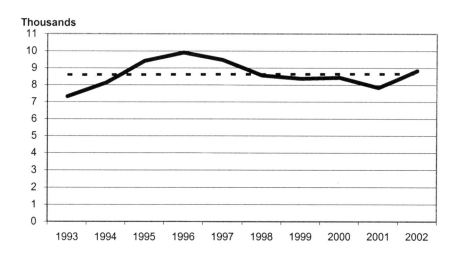

Source: *Statistisches Landeskriminalsamt*

Unlike in England and London in the 1990s, where there was an overall fall in the number of crimes after 1992, but a continuing rise in the number of crimes that symbolised 'loss of police control of the streets', namely robberies, in West Berlin the number of robberies stabilised in the 1990s. The trend line—the dashed line in the figure—is almost horizontal.

Unlike London, too, the detection rate rose from the low levels of the post-1968 period (though not back to the levels of the 1950s).[16]

Figure 10.3
Robbery clear-up rate rises to 40 per cent
All Berlin, 1991 to 2002

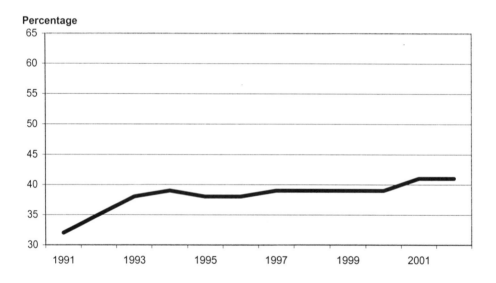

Source: Polizeiliche Kriminalstatistik

In Britain, by contrast, a process of decline was complacently ignored where it was not tendentiously denied, and the immense historical advantages of a consensual social order and a low crime rate leaked slowly away.

Part III

France

11

Policing a Politically Split Society

Figure 11.1
The post-1960s surge in crime in France
Recorded crimes, Metropolitan France, 1949 to 2000

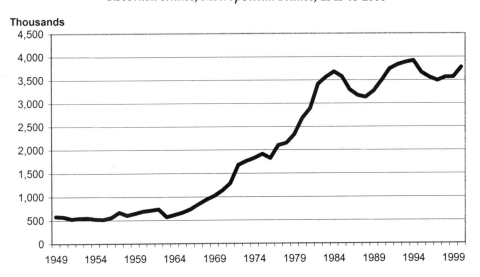

Source: *Aspects de la criminalité constatée en France*

For cultural reasons Berlin, like New York, provided police responses to street crime in the 1990s that neutralised to some extent the crimino-genic effects of the 1960s' revolution in Western world-views of social institutions and personal morality—the counter-culture that became the hegemonic culture of the rest of the century. Paris, like London, failed to do so. Even so, France responded more quickly than England to the law-and-order implications of the 1960s' counter-culture, and stabilised the over-all crime figure a decade earlier than England.[1] The cultural basis for England's response to crime was very different from France's, just as the cultural basis for Berlin's response was very different from the cultural basis for the response of New York.

England rested complacently on the laurels of its historic culture of civic cohesion and the consensual, crime-preventing, civilian policing that its

131

civic cohesion permitted. But France's tradition of 'tough' policing had built up so much resentment among the Marxist, neo-Marxist, Trotskyist, anarchist, libertarian and nihilist leaders and supporters of the 1960s counter-culture that, so to speak, the resultant of the parallelogram of forces was surging street crime in 1990s France as it was in 1990s England.

Although both French and German policing have a stronger tradition of controlling political subversion than has English policing, the policing experience of France differs from that of Germany. The German *Polizey* and its successors (into the mid-twentieth century in West Germany and the late-twentieth century in East Germany) were the instruments of authoritarian and totalitarian régimes, crushing any opposition, however slight. During a brief interlude in 1848/1849 German liberalism, participating in the revolutionary ardour that swept continental Europe, attempted to combat authoritarianism. It failed. It was not until late in the nineteenth century that Germany showed the traits of what Samuel Huntington called a 'torn' country, with the emergence of a powerful communist party. That the tear was impermanent and restricted to small sections of the population was shown by the patriotic solidarity displayed by all sections of the German population in the Great War until near its end. It became a torn country in autumn of 1918 and throughout the era of the Weimar Republic.[2] But from 1933, nearly all the opposition that remained after the propaganda campaigns and the international and domestic successes of the Nazi régime was ruthlessly and with almost universal success eliminated by the secret police and other bodies. This was also the situation in communist East Germany for the 40 years that ended in 1989.

West Germany in the 1960s and 1970s was, to a greater extent than England, 'torn' between, on the one hand, the alternative society of the revolutionary students' 'long march through the institutions' and, on the other, the respectability (*Biedersinn*) of the prosperous West German bourgeoisie and working class that the radical students so much despised.

The violence of West German left-wing groups in the late 1960s and early 1970s—such as the Red Army Faction led by Andreas Baader—found only faint echoes in England. Left-wing dissidents in England did some rioting themselves in the late 1960s and the 1970s. They supported riots carried out by others in the 1980s. That support often took the form of protests against miscarriages of British justice against alleged rioters, i.e. it took the form of an appeal, not to the values the dissidents embraced, but to the dominant culture to act according to its own values.[3]

France, by contrast, was a 'torn' country from 1789, and for most of the time more of a 'torn' country than Germany. France's police had the been admired for efficiency, if not for gentleness, since the time of Louis XIV as a guarantor of the régime against dissidents. From the revolutionary years of the early 1790s the French police became even more of a force to prevent the revolutionary or counter-revolutionary overthrow of the existing social order. Britain's police have been concerned with the 'low' policing of preventing petty crime and anti-social behaviour occurring, France's with by the so-called 'high' policing of combating the illegal and violent subversion of the régime.

Raymond Aron, perhaps the most widely respect commentator on French affairs after the Second World War, contrasted the weakness of a national consensus in France with the strength of the national consensus in Britain and the United States. In a lecture delivered at the Sorbonne in the late 1950s, he said that whatever disputes separated the great parties of those two Anglo-Saxon countries, 'the régimes are taken for granted; the constitutional arrangements are not called into question'. Their modes of settling differences were and unbrokenly had been 'intertwined with national values' from which no large group detached itself.[4]

In Britain, Aron said, social relations were and had been for centuries controlled by the silk thread (*le fil de soie*) of mutual consent to abide, not just by the requirements of the law, but by the rules of good behaviour. Without the silk thread of a shared culture, the disruption of the civil rights of the law-abiding citizen by the illegal encroachments of the criminal, and by the disturber of neighbourhood and domestic tranquillity, could only be prevented by the edge of the sword (*le fil de l'épée*). What is not conciliated by agreement on values has to be crushed by the police.[5]

The Jacobin Reign of Terror from the summer of 1793 to the summer of 1794 was aimed at exterminating those who were or were suspected of seeking to restore the old order. If Robert Peel was the father of the tradition of decentralised, civilian, crime-preventing policing, Joseph Fouché was the father of centralised, armed (*gens d'armes*) and (like the German *Polizey*) social-order policing, the function of which was to preserve the social order of either the left or the right, whichever dominated at the time.

For someone whose policing concentrated on finding and dealing with opponents of the established order, Fouché's own loyalties were remarkably fluid. He began as a Girondin. When the Girondin star waned, he became a Jacobin. As a Jacobin he was responsible for putting down anti-Jacobin unrest in Lyons, and he did so by meting out terrible punishment. Later he acted as a spy for Barras, a member of the new government—the Directory—who had been instrumental in the downfall of Robespierre, and therefore of the Jacobins generally. Barras himself was notorious for his intrigues and corruption.

Fouché was made minister of police in 1799. He closed the Jacobin clubs. He then aided Napoleon's coup d'état of 18 brumaire (9 November 1799). By a decree of 1800, Napoleon set up, in effect, the modern French police. Fouché circulated a petition demanding that Napoleon should be made Emperor, and was rewarded by being appointed minister of the police. Napoleon dismissed Fouché when it was discovered that he was secretly dealing with the British, but by 1814-15 he was again in Napoleon's service. After negotiating with the allies, it was Fouché who handed Napoleon the document requiring his abdication. He was minister of police under Louis XVIII.[6]

Under all régimes, Fouché's police operations were heavily dependent upon a large network of spies and *agents provocateurs*. The quintessential eighteenth-century Englishman, Samuel Johnson, had said: 'The danger of unbounded liberty, and the danger of bounding it, have produced a problem in the science of government which human understanding seems hitherto unable to solve.'[7] For the first 30 years of the nineteenth century, the image of French policing loomed large in the public consciousness of the English. They did not want anything like Fouché's police. Finding a proper balance between the freedom to do as one likes, and the freedom not to suffer from other people doing what they like, appeared to be intractable, and things were left more or less as they were. Between 1780 and 1829, seventeen parliamentary committees investigated the problems of balancing these desiderata: to be free from the control by the state, and to be secure from crime and disorder.

The cultural difference in the matter of policing between continental Europe and England, the prevention of crime as opposed to the suppression of political dissent, was early and precisely pointed up by the *Morning Chronicle*. It said in 1812:

> We have heard much of the admirable effects of the police in Paris. Certainly the police of Paris is most dextrously contrived for the purposes of tyranny, but that it is so very efficacious in the prevention of crimes, we very much question.[8]

The French historian Halévy, writing before the First World War when national cultures were more distinct than they became later in the twentieth century, and their importance therefore more obvious, also highlighted cultural differences in the English and the continental approach to policing in Napoleonic times. 'The national optimism' of the English, he wrote, 'opposed an obstinate resistance to the organisation of a state police throughout the country.' Local communities brought their own criminals and disturbers under control. A little 'vigilantism' went a long way, because there was little crime and anti-social nuisance when the people that might have been tempted into those courses knew that they would almost inevitably suffer the adverse consequences of any bad behaviour. For cultural reasons, too, vigilantism did not descend into a spiral of vendettas. 'Men reckoned on the phlegmatic temperament of the people, and on the rarity of acts of revenge.'[9] As late as 1822 a select committee of parliament decided that freedom from professional policing was the greater of the two benefits.

> It is difficult to reconcile an effective system of police with that perfect freedom of action and exemption from interference which are the great privileges and blessings of society in this country; and Your Committee think that the forfeiture or curtailment of such advantages would be too great a sacrifice for improvements in police ... however desirable in themselves, abstractly considered.[10]

In the July Revolution of 1830 yet another régime was overthrown by revolutionary Paris, that of Charles X, a monarch whose aim was to set aside the results of the revolution and restore the pre-1789 order in France. Britannia can be taken as a symbol of the stability and order within the limits of which people can lead free lives. France's equivalent to Britannia is Marianne. Her most famous portrayal was painted in 1830.[11] It shows her at a Paris barricade, bare breasted, with a gun in one hand and the tricolour in the other, rallying her fellow-revolutionaries.

The national history of coups d'état and revolutions from 1789 to 1830 led Alexis de Tocqueville to study France and the United States in order to discover the reasons for the recurring repressive régimes of the one and the freedom enjoyed by the other.[12] He traces the cause to the profoundly different cultures of the two societies. In dealing with crime and the police, Tocqueville noted that in France the population took no responsibility for law and order. In France, the criminal was seen as the victim of circumstances, and controlling his criminal behaviour was the job of the police. He was 'an unhappy man struggling for his life against the agents of power'. Other people saw themselves as 'merely a spectator of the conflict' between the police officer and the law breaker.

In the United States, by contrast, 'a state police does not exist, and passports are unknown'. The army numbered only 6,000 soldiers. But because there is a civil culture of law and order, 'in no country does crime more rarely elude punishment'. In the 1830s, still predominantly populated by people of English origin, Americans were 'more conversant with ... the principles of true freedom, than the greater part of their European contemporaries'. They had brought with them from England the township system, 'that fruitful gem of free institutions' that was 'deeply rooted in the habits of the English', and with it 'the doctrine of the sovereignty of the people that had been introduced into the bosom of the monarchy by the house of Tudor'. In America, therefore, 'every one conceives himself to be interested in furnishing evidence of the crime, and in seizing the delinquent'. 'The delinquent is looked upon as an enemy of the human race, and the whole of mankind is against him.'[13] Few people, therefore, are willing to pay the heavy price that delinquency would cost them.

Tocqueville contrasts this state of affairs not precisely with France, but with 'some countries in Europe', where the inhabitants, he writes,

> consider themselves as a kind of settlers, indifferent to the fate of the spot which they inhabit. ... The want of interest in his own affairs goes so far, that if his own safety or that of his children is at last endangered ... he folds his arms and waits for the whole nation to come to his aid. ... This man ... does not, more than any other person, love obedience; he cowers, it is true, before the pettiest officer; but he braves the law with the spirit of a conquered foe as soon as its superior force is withdrawn; he perpetually oscillates between servitude and licence.

> When a nation has arrived at this state, it must either change its customs or its laws, or perish; for the source of public virtue is dried up; and though it may contain subjects, it has no citizens. Such communities are the natural prey to foreign conquests; and if they do not disappear wholly from the scene, it is only because they are surrounded by other nations similar or inferior to themselves.

Such nations have fallen prey either to vigorous modern nations, or armies motivated by religious fervour. 'The Turkish tribes ... have accomplished stupendous enterprises, so long as the victories of the Sultan were triumphs of the Mohammedan faith.' It was Europe's good fortune 'in the present age' that militant Islam was 'in rapid decay, because the religion is departing, and despotism only remains'.[14] America itself had little to fear from its neighbours. Canada was not likely ever to attack the United States. 'Serious hostilities may one day be expected to arise' from Mexico. But that would not be before 'a long time to come', Tocqueville says. Mexico had been unable to develop, so far, either an effective thread of silk to prevent its population falling into a state of 'depravity of morals', or an effective edge of steel to put a stop to the depravity.[15]

The social order of the Bourbon Charles X was replaced by that of the Orléanist Louis Philippe. The Orléanist social order was in its turn overthrown in February 1848. Acting entirely on his own initiative, a revolutionary called Marc Caussidière led a group that took possession of the Paris police headquarters. Caussidière, whose background was in revolutionary secret societies, who had been sentenced to 20 years imprisonment in 1834 for his part in riots in Lyons, and who was accused of murdering a policeman, announced he was now head of the Paris police. His authority, he stated, was that he was acting in accordance with a decision of a citizens' committee at the office of *La Réforme* newspaper. He did indeed succeed in being chief of police from February to May 1848.

The nature and failure of Caussidière's police was one of the influences on the Paris police tradition. His first act was to disband all the units of Louis Philippe's police. Membership of the new corps was open to anyone who could show a gaol registration as a political prisoner, or proof of participation on the revolutionaries' side of the barricades, in the February street fighting. All ranks up to that of captain were decided by election by the rank-and-file. The names of the new companies of police all honoured places or people connected with bloody revolution. One was the Montagnard company, honouring the most extreme of the left-wing groups in 1848. The February company was a reference to the February revolution. The name of the Lyonnaise company honoured the Lyons riots of 1834. The name of the Saint-Just company honoured a member of the triumvirate that had organised the Reign of Terror. Describing police headquarters, an observer wrote that 'nothing can give any idea of the spectacle unless it is a camp of drunken and rampant Cossacks'. Caussidière is the first person Marx mentions when, in contrasting him with Danton, he makes his observation that history occurs twice, the first time as tragedy and the second time as farce.[16]

Caussidière was an exponent of what he called 'a police of conciliation' as against a 'police of repression'.[17] Arguments were being put forward in France at this time in favour of a civilian preventive police concentrating on crime and petty disturbances, and not politics. Caussidière might have picked up the terms that were being used by exponents of prevention and protection such as Horace Raisson, a leading contemporary advocate of a 'purely civil police' on the British model.[18] (Some of Raisson's recommendations were adopted in the Paris police reforms of 1854.)

But for Caussidière all this meant was, that he had been against being repressed by the reactionary police, and was now in favour of his police being conciliatory to the most left-wing of the revolutionaries. He was forced to resign in May 1848 because he failed to act against a mob that stormed into the National Assembly. Tocqueville, who was in the National Assembly on 15 May, gives a memorable description of the leader of the insurgents:

> I saw a man go up onto the rostrum, and, though I have never seen him again, the memory of him has filled me with disgust and horror ever since. He had sunken, withered cheeks, white lips, and a sickly, malign, dirty look like a pallid, mouldy corpse; he was wearing no visible linen; an old frock coat covered his emaciated limbs tightly; he looked as if he had lived in a sewer and only just come out. I was told this was Blanqui.[19]

Blanqui's punishment was ten years' solitary confinement. The proletarian insurgents of May and the ineffectiveness of Caussidière's claimed policing by consent intensified the fears of respectable society of an uncontrolled—and unrepressed—lower class.

On 20 May the Paris police force was completely abolished and replaced by a volunteer militia, the Mobile Guard, together with the National Guard and the army. In June 1948, policing returned to being a matter of internal war.[20]

The February Revolution was the *beautiful* revolution, the revolution of universal sympathy, because the antagonisms slumbered *undeveloped*, harmoniously, side by side ... The *June Revolution* is the *ugly* revolution, the repulsive revolution, because deeds have taken the place of phrases. Order! was the battle cry of Guizot. Order! cried Sébastiani ... Order! shouts Cavaignac ... Order! thundered the grape-shot, as it ripped the body of the proletariat. Woe to June! Woe to June! re-echoes Europe.

'It is well known that the workers ... held in check for five days the army, the Mobile Guard, the Paris National Guard, and the National Guard that streamed in from the provinces. It is well known that the bourgeoisie compensated itself ... by unheard of brutality, massacring over 3,000 prisoners.'[21] The 'bloodbath of helpless prisoners' after the June Days had not been seen since the civil wars that ushered in the downfall of the Roman republic, Engels wrote 40 years later. The bourgeoisie showed for the first time to what 'insane cruelties of revenge' it would be goaded the moment the proletarian took its stand as a separate class. The defeat was the first suffered by the revolutionary side in all the great insurrections of the previous 60 years. In four days of battle, more than 100,000 men took part, and four generals were killed. Cavaignac, the general in charge, had ordered all the regiments along the line of the new railway to converge on Paris, and called up the National Guard from the districts around Paris. That a victorious outcome had been so uncertain was a memory that strengthened the French sense on the one side that the police had to be strong enough to control insurrections and on the other that the police was an enemy that had to be defeated for a revolution to succeed.

Unlike the Chartists in England, who sought improvements to the British constitution, and the trade unionists who sought improvements in their pay and working conditions, the revolutionaries in Paris sought to alter the organisation of society. 'In truth it was not a political struggle, but a class struggle ... a powerful effort of the workers ... by the sword to open up a road towards that imaginary well-being that was shown to them in the distance as a right.'[22]

For the century and half that followed them, the June Days of 1848 provided the French working class with a more satisfying sense of grievance against the forces of law and order than could be mustered by the English working class over the Tolpuddle Martyrs. English radicals could not share this indignation until students applied Marx's horror of repression in Paris in 1848 to the way the London police controlled their own disorderly demonstrations in 1968.

In addition to those killed in the four revolutionary 'June Days', 15,000 were arrested, and 4,000 deported, mainly to Algeria. 'It had left among certain classes of the Parisian workers a deeper hatred than before of the bourgeoisie ... There were two opposing mentalities: the bourgeois and the proletarian.'[23]

There had been another coup d'état in December 1851, when the elected President of the Republic, Napoleon's nephew, overthrew the government and assumed dictatorial powers and suppressed all opposition. The next year he made himself Emperor. In Marx's account—the account accepted by the leaders of the French proletariat for the rest of the nineteenth century and most if not all of the twentieth century—'the centralised state power, with its ... police ... and judicature assumed more and more the character of ... a public force organised for social enslavement, as an engine of class despotism.'[24] In the late 1860s Paris was honeycombed with extremist societies and clubs.[25]

When France was defeated in the Franco-Prussian War of 1870-71, there was another revolutionary upheaval in Paris, again aimed at changing the whole basis of French social organisation and culture.

The provisional government at Versailles was led by Adolophe Thiers. The provisional government had been formed to conclude a peace treaty with the victorious Prussians who were still besieging Paris. Thiers sent a unit of the army to seize some of the Paris guns so that they did not fall into the hands of the defiant Parisians. But the troops fraternised with the populace, and two army generals were seized and shot. 'The Commune' had begun.

The gulf between the repressive police of the Napoleon III's Second Empire and the Parisian working class was demonstrated by the fact that, the revolutionaries having taken over the government of Paris, the police were at once turned into what Marx called 'the responsible and at all times revocable agent of the Commune'. They were stripped of their *political attributes*' as instruments of the central government. Having dealt with the police—in Marxist theory and in Marx's words, together with the army, 'the physical force element' of internal control—the Commune broke the spiritual force of working-class repression. It disestablished and disendowed all churches. 'The priests were sent back ... to feed upon the alms of the faithful, in imitation of their predecessors, the Apostles.'[26]

There was to be no separate armed force. All citizens capable of bearing arms were enrolled in the National Guard. By restoring responsibility to the local community, Marx wrote, capitalist bohemianism and the sexual orgies of the Empire were brought to an end, and both morality and law and order were restored to their proper place:

> Wonderful, indeed, was the change the Commune had wrought in Paris! No longer any trace of the meretricious Paris of the Second Empire. ... No nocturnal burglaries, scarcely any robberies; in fact, for the first time since the days of February 1848, the streets of Paris were safe, and that without police of any kind. 'We', said a member of the Commune, 'hear not longer of murder, theft and personal assault.' The loose women had left with their protectors ... In their stead, the real women of Paris showed again on the surface—heroic, noble, and devoted, like the women of antiquity.[27]

The Commune, a revolutionary episode that looms so large in communist versions of history and contemporary society, lasted only a few weeks. The Paris Commune was elected on 26 March 1871 and began its work on 28 March. After its first actions to abolish Paris's 'morality police' and replace it with the National Guard, it remitted all payments of rent for dwelling houses due over the previous six months and stopped the sale of articles pledged at the municipal pawn shops. On 1 April it abolished state payments for religious purposes, and confiscated all church property. On 6 April the guillotine was publicly burnt. On 16 April it ordered plans for cooperative production controlled by the workers to be made for all factories. On 20 April it abolished night work for bakers, and the employment offices, that had been run 'as a monopoly by creatures appointed by the police', as Engels wrote, were transferred to the mayoralities of the arrondissements.[28]

A provisional French government had been set up after the fall of Napoleon III to negotiate peace with the victorious Prussians. On 21 May the government troops from Versailles entered Paris. For most of the rank and file, the Commune was either a protest against their social conditions, or a patriotic revolt against the peace terms. For the leaders, it was their chance to remake the whole social system. For Thiers, the provisional government's chief executive, the communards were simply a dangerous mob to be put down with a strong hand. He had been a prominent revolutionary both in 1830 and in March 1848, but had marked the lessons of the revolution of June 1848, which he opposed. In particular, he had admired the way in which the Austrian general Prince Alfred zu Windisch-Grätz had ruthlessly subdued the 1848 revolutionaries in Vienna.

Fifty-six hostages held by the communards were shot, including the Archbishop of Paris. The Tuilleries, the Palais de Justice and the Hôtel de Ville were set in flames. Guy Chapman writes of 'the ghastly ferocity' of the troops in those last days after 21 May, the travesty of justice in the courts-martial, and the executions on the Satory plateau after the savage pacification.[29] Passers-by saw the blood flowing beneath the barracks where the government troops were holding drumhead courts-martial. French soldiers smashed the heads of French civilians. The slaughter was worse than the Germans had inflicted in any battle of the Franco-Prussian War, and far worse than the Terror of 1793-94. The Terror had cost the lives of 2,596 people in Paris during 15 months. Twenty thousand communards and suspects were killed in Paris in that Bloody Week of 21-28 May 1871 (la semaine sanglant).[30] 'The exact number who perished will never be known, but it cannot have been less than 20,000.'[31]

In peaceable and orderly England, The Times expostulated incredulously:

The laws of war! They are mild compared with the inhuman laws of revenge under which the Versaillais troops have been shooting, bayoneting, ripping up prisoners, women, and children during the last six days ... the triumph, the glee, the ribaldry of the 'Party of Order' sickens the soul. There has been nothing like it in history.[32]

The suppression of the Commune led Engels to write that the bloodbath of 1848 'was only child's play compared with the frenzy of the bourgeoisie in 1871'.[33]

It was only after eight days' fighting that the last defenders of the Commune succumbed on the heights of Belleville and Menilmontant; and then the massacre of defenceless men, women and children, which had been raging all through the week on an increasing scale, reached its zenith. The 'Wall of the Federals' at the Père Lachaise cemetery, where the final mass murder was consummated, is still standing today. ... Then, when the slaughter of them all proved impossible, came the mass arrests, the shooting of victims arbitrarily selected from the prisoners' ranks, and the removal of the rest to great camps where they awaited trial by courts-martial.[34]

The Wall of the Federals, which Engels said still stood in 1891, still stood in the twenty-first century, with the bullet holes pocking the brickwork of what was by then usually called the Wall of the Communards, as a memorial of the brutality of the forces of respectable law and order. Next to it by then, too, were the memorials to the victims of the concentration camps and extermination camps of the Nazi tyranny, and of the deportations carried out with the assistance of the Vichy régime.

Some members of Marx's organisation, the International Working Men's Association, few in France, took part in the Commune. According to Engels, even they were mainly Proudhon anarchists rather then 'collectivists' (as Marxists were called in Belgium and France). The majority of the leaders of the Commune were Blanquists, who were predominant also on the Central Committee of the Paris National Guard. The Blanquists preached local autonomy, not Marxist communism. Engels said that they were socialists only by 'proletarian instinct'.[35]

The Commune was nevertheless appropriated by Marxists and socialists as a communist event, and as decisive proof of the irreconcilable and bloody antagonism everywhere between the class interests of the capitalists and those of the workers. Until the dictatorship of the proletariat replaced the dictatorship, however well disguised, of the owners of the means of production, the existing system of law and order, and the police who maintained it, were the sworn enemies of the working class.

For a century in England this theory had hardly any resonance. But Marxism in one form or another was then taken up by the radical student movements of the 1960s, without too much pettifogging attention to either Marx's writings or his times. Marx's account, vaguely known, was taken to be a description of law and order not in Paris in 1871, but in Paris,

London, Berlin and New York in 1971, and used to justify the anti-police sentiments and provocations of student demonstrators and striking workers. 'Monstrous and absurd, the Commune forms a page in socialist mythology.'[36]

In 1889 it looked as if France was on the verge of another military coup d'état. An ex-War Minister, General Boulanger, had become leader of the many sections of French society that were opposed to the whole way of life represented by the Third Republic. Boulangism won an overwhelming majority of the votes in the 1889 election, but the movement collapsed when Boulanger fled to Belgium of learning that he was about to be arraigned for treason.

At the end of October 1894 an officer was arrested because he was suspected of 'having handed the enemy confidential documents of little importance'. This was the inconspicuous overture to the Dreyfus Affair that for a dozen years tore French society, or rather was the focus of the tears in French society that already existed. Dreyfus was found guilty and condemned to deportation for life. He was imprisoned on Devil's Island. Norman Kleeblatt, in trying to understand why 'a banal spy story' should cause such deep and widespread enmity for so long, concluded that for a hundred years France had known no generation without a profound revolution or a transforming coup d'état, and *still teetered on the brink of both*.[37]

From 1933 French society was far more seriously torn than either totalitarian Germany, parliamentary England or the presidential United States. During the night of 6-7 February 1934, for example, the Communists and Royalists, with otherwise diametrically opposed notions of the way of life that should replace an overthrown French republic, came together to riot and to attack the Parisian police. When rioting broke out, the Prime Minister Deladier, who had just survived two votes of confidence for his new government, denounced the outbreak as an attack on the Republican régime, and an armed attempt against the state.

Again, *The Times* recorded this split for a public that had no experience of disorder on such a scale in England—even Peterloo, more than a century earlier, had been peaceful on the demonstrators side, the massacre being the result of the indiscipline of the volunteers of the Manchester Yoemanry.

> The first sign of anything amiss was the glare of flames in the Place de la Concorde, where two omnibuses were burning furiously. Ahead lay a dense shouting crowd. Behind it was the dull glint of steel helmets, which revealed row on row of Gardes Civiles. Up to this point it was no more than a stupid if exciting spectacle. Suddenly it turned to tragedy. To a noise that sounded like nothing more dangerous than Chinese crackers the full realisation burst upon us. The front ranks turned and ran. In a kind of mass panic we ran blindly away while the distant pop and the urgent hissing went on in our ears. Your staff photographer had a bullet clean through his hat and your correspondent himself had too narrow an escape to be pleasant.

With the Place de la Concorde cleared, the Madeleine became the storm centre. Suddenly there was a crimson glare from the far end of the Rue Royale. Some rioters had forced their way into the Ministry of Marine and set fire to it. The firemen arrived a little later, running the gauntlet of stones, bricks and pieces of iron.

The Gardes Républicaines had to give way to let them through and in a moment the crowd were upon them. Three of them were unhorsed and their wretched animals ripped to pieces with knives.

The Communists, coming down in force from Bellville and the eastern fringes of the city, joined in the rioting and alternately attacked the police and engaged in pitched battles with the Camelots du Roy. Several times they swept up the cordons in the Place de la Concorde, wrecking whatever came in their path. Both Royalist and Communist elements were present at the Hôtel de Ville, the Royalists shouting 'Vive Chiappe!' and the Communists singing 'The Red Flag'.

By 2 a.m., when the correspondent of the *The Times* sent his eye witness report to London, 12 people were thought to have been killed and about 300 injured.[38]

In the elections of 1951 the number of votes cast for parties opposed to the régime, and not just the policies of a particular government, was 46 per cent—the combined votes of the Communists and Gaullists (*Rassemblement du peuple français*). If the 1946 method of voting had been applied in 1951, the anti-constitution parties would have been in a majority. Still in 1956, Aron wrote, 'the percentage of votes I shall call technically revolutionary, meaning simply votes against the *system*, was about 40 per cent'. A social order that has at every election between 40 and 45 per cent of the votes cast against it, offers one of the characteristic features, Aron says, of societal 'decadence', namely, the breaking of the link of solidarity within the people, and between the people and those who govern.[39]

After the trauma of a society split over Algeria, de Gaulle's prestigious paternalism secured a degree of consensus up to 1968. Then, France shared and played a part in the cultural revolution of Western societies, largely student-led, the most important of all types of revolution, as Burke said, 'a revolution in sentiments, manners and moral opinions'.[40] As in Germany, the enemy was 'respectability'. In scorning and rejecting respectability, exponents of the counter-culture were the latest in a long historical line. Those who despised respectability were not just of the political or social left. To the delight of his aristocratic audiences at the court of Louis XIV, Molière mocked the pretensions of M. Jourdain who, becoming rich, had the audacity to aim at self-improvement. He had the comical audacity to take lessons in philosophy, fencing, dancing and music. In the nineteenth century, Flaubert attacked the inventors and enforcers of codes of sexual, religious and economic conduct that hampered the bohemian life. Shock the respectable middle class (*épater les bourgeois*) was the motto of the artist. The Communist, for whom the class struggle was an article of faith, found gratification in the literature and art that told him his enemy, who was economically so formidable, was morally despicable. With its insistence on obedience to the arbitrary rules of repressed good behaviour and respect for male authority, hypocritically violated as a matter of course by the family father, respectability was one of the principal means through which economic exploitation was made acceptable to those who suffered from it. In 1952 Jean Paul Sartre sanctified criminality and sexual licence as a way of life in his biography of Genet.[41]

The cultural revolution brought to the fore the problems of crime and policing connected, not with the clash of strongly held and opposed conceptions of the just society, but with the successful demands for more or less unbridled individualism. The aim and effect of the revolution was to *diminish* drastically the role that culture—shared values—played in social relationships. People were no longer to be controlled by the law, custom or public opinion in their sexual conduct, the arrangements the made if they wanted children or abortions, their consumption of psychotropic substances, their relations with their neighbours, or other 'lifestyle choices'. It was an *anti-culture* cultural revolution. France experienced the problems, with other Western societies, of what the French sociologist Emile Durkheim called *anomie*, problems not of the clash of social standards, but of their absence everywhere. All Western societies tended to become, outside the disciplines of the workplace, a multitude of people who pleased themselves in what they did.

This anti-culture cultural revolution was accompanied everywhere with a rapid rise in crime, associated simultaneously at any previously given level of police incompetence, corruption, brutality and so forth, with the strengthening of *generalised* anti-police sentiment under the impulse of anti-police agitation and anti-police provocative actions.

In the early days of the cultural revolution, in 1963, there were 0.6 million crimes in a French population of 48 million. In 1973 there were 1.8 million crimes in a population of 52 million. The crime rate per 100,000 population had risen from 14 to 34. Robberies rose by 503 per cent. 'Hold-ups' in which firearms were used rose by 2,808 per cent.[42]

By 1973 the French equivalent to *Criminal Statistics England and Wales* expressed alarm at the accelerated tendency towards 'more and more criminal violence—murders, robberies and attacks on women in the street'.[43] Hedonism and individualism, with their 'Dionysian' receptivity to drug- and crowd-induced intoxication (as Nietzsche called it) were a central feature of the cultural revolution. These were (so to speak) 'contain-able' for their own benefit by well-educated and well-to-do adults. But when the mass media of entertainment and pseudo-news propagated or connived in these values in their crudest sex-and-violence form to the young and the poor, the result was Robert K. Merton's criminal 'innovation'—their seizing by illegal or anti-social means the glamour, wealth, prestige, excitement or power that they had been persuaded was theirs by right.[44]

Already the problem of a new location of social disorder appeared around Paris. By 1972 the large housing estates implanted in many communes in rapidly growing departments on the periphery of the city of Paris were emerging as 'hotbeds for the growth of juvenile delinquency'.[45]

Parts of the inner peripheral areas (la petite couronne—Hauts-de-Seine, Seine-Saint-Denis and Val-de-Marne) were the location of the problem 'Paris' housing estates.

Figure 11.2
Population of Paris and the Paris region, 1881 to 1981

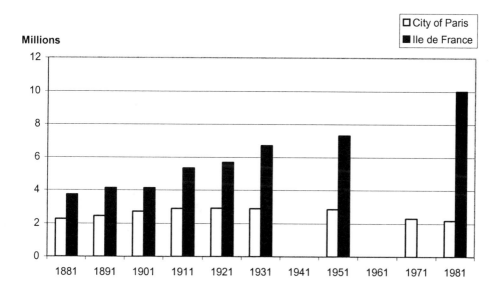

Source: Données sociales Ile-de-France

In 1981, after technocrats of the centre right had been in power for 22 years—Giscard d'Estaing was typical of them—the politician who had founded the French Socialist Party in 1971, François Mitterrand, was elected on the promise of 'a sharp break with capitalism'. With the student generation of 1968 beginning to occupy positions of influence in the media, politics, education and the churches, Mitterrand's sharp break with capitalism included drastic 'left-wing' reform of the police. In the still strongly Marxist world-view, among the settlement of other grievances against the regular and riot police, these reforms were revenge for 1871. Parallel with what was happening in Britain under the influence of the cultural revolution, the rights of suspects at the expense of the rights of victims were strengthened. Giscard's recent law that gave the police added powers was repealed. The Paris police, along with other forces, was reorganised, with 'less emphasis on bullying interrogations' and attempts to eliminate some of the more repressive aspects of policing, 'where France has frequently been criticised in the past, and with reason'.[46]

In the course of five years, 1979 to 1983, when the population of the city of Paris rose by only three per cent, crime rose by 55 per cent. Crime rose by 27 per cent in the year 1982 alone.[47] Robberies (*vols avec violence*) rose by 33 per cent from 1979 to 1983, from 9,600 to 12,800. In the single year 1984 there was a 17 per cent increase in armed robberies. All crimes increased before some categories were brought under control. But crimes in public places, controllable only by the internalisation of standards of good behaviour, informal community control or a police presence, and not by bolts, bars, alarms and vehicle immobilisers, increased swiftly and continued to increase when other categories fell.

Police strength was not falling in absolute numbers, but the ratio of police officers to crimes was falling, and the hours of work of police officers had been reduced.

Table 11.1
Police strength each year in Paris

Year	Officers
1981	13,200
1982	13,100
1983	13,200
1984	13,500
1985	13,200

Between June 1981 and April 1982, 852 Parisian police officers left Paris on transfer postings and only 102 asked to be posted to Paris from elsewhere. In the eight months February to October 1984 nearly 1,000 police officers secured a posting out and only 129 secured a posting in. Low morale owing to the growing disparity between police numbers and the crimes they somehow had to deal with meant, 'Paris seems to becoming a stopping place for police officers who want to be on their way as quickly as possible to a posting in the provinces'.[48]

Between 1972 and 1982 the average working week for police officers fell from 44 to 39 hours, and during that period they won a fifth week's annual holiday. The Inspector General of Police calculated that by 1984 the average police officer in the city of Paris worked fewer than 1,509 hours a year. (In County Durham, in England, still in the 1960s, the average police constable worked 8,736 hours a year—he was always on duty.)

Until 1970, there were never more than 100 attacks (*agressions*) on passengers a year on the whole of the Paris public transport network. The rise was then 'spectacular'.[49]

In 1984 there were 141 attacks on passengers at Strasbourg Saint-Denis station alone. There was a 358 per cent increase in 1984 compared with 1981 in attacks on passengers in which firearms were used. In 1983 there were 70 attacks on the officers of the Metro Protection and Security Service (SPSM), nearly as many as there had been attacks of all descriptions ten years before.

At rush hours, 200 pickpockets were operating on the public transport system. More than half were Yugoslav children or adolescents, working in groups of four or five for the adults who controlled them. The criminal law was inoperative, because of the age of the offenders and the difficulty of identifying them because of their lack of either a fixed address or connection with a known adult.[50]

Table 11.2
Attacks on passengers
Paris public transport network 1979 to 1982

Year	Attacks
1979	744
1980	803
1981	1,110
1982	1,585
1983	3,461
1984	4,101

More public than a dwelling or shop, but less public than the street, the public transport authorities were able to install technical means of improving security—gate controls, *monitored* CCTV cameras and alarms usable by the public.

At first, while the number of attacks was rapidly increasing, there was little augmentation of police activity—because there was little change in police numbers to meet the mounting problem. There were actually fewer interrogations by the *police judiciaire* in 1984 than in either 1982 or 1983.[51]

A vicious circle emerged of less self-regulation, more crime, less community control, more crime, more demands thrown on an unsupported police force, more crime, less self-regulation ... A survey in 1984 by the polling organisation Louis Harris asked a sample of 1,000 Parisians if they had been the victim of a crime that they had not reported to the police. Fourteen per cent answered yes. Fifty-five per cent of those answering yes gave as their reason that 'there would have been no point in doing so'. The White Paper on Parisian civic safety and crime noted that 'the refusal to come forward as a witness, and sometimes the unwillingness to come to the assistance of someone in danger (as in some recent instances) shows that it is necessary to combat the decline of public spirit, and to encourage behaviour that expresses an elementary sense of community'.[52]

Table 11.3
Police Interrogations
Paris Public Transport System 1981 to 1984

Year	Interrogation
1981	10,700
1982	11,400
1983	11,000
1984	10,800

But Paris itself—even more important as a centre of influence in France than London is in England—provided an important counterweight to the 1960s' ideology of Mitterrand and his active supporters. The tradition of 'toughness' of the French police meant that the problem of rising crime and social disorder was, in comparison with the response in England to the deteriorating situation, *quickly* confronted. At the end of 1983, in a response for which England had to wait for nearly another 20 years, Committees on Civil Safety and Crime Prevention were set up in every arrondissement by the then Mayor of Paris, Jacques Chirac. The first aim was to produce assessments of crime in their areas. In July 1984 he set up the city-wide Council on Civil Safety and Crime Prevention in Paris.[53] Six working parties of the Council dealt with drugs, crime on public transport system, street crime, vulnerable groups, vulnerable businesses and illegal immigrants. Reports were prepared by each of the arrondissement committees. Making use of them, the Crime Prevention Council prepared a White Paper covering the city as a whole.

Paris insisted that the role of the police was decisive. While in small municipalities in France the police force was responsible to the mayor, in Paris the mayor had no control over the police whatsoever, 'a fact to which attention has been repeatedly drawn'. The entire control lay with the central government through the Prefect of the Paris police.[54]

In order to raise the police force in Paris to a fully operational level, Mayor Chirac wanted 3,000 additional officers. Numbers themselves, however, could be a snare and a delusion. Raising the efficiency of the force, he insisted, was no less crucial. In particular, Paris demanded the use of the police on foot patrol, *'on the model of Britain'* (where, perhaps unbeknown to the Parisians, it was rapidly disappearing). Beat policing was 'essential' in ensuring safety on the streets. The principle of beat policing on the British model, the mayor's White Paper said, could be summarised in just six words: 'one officer, one district, one mission'. The beat police officer (*l'îlotier*—*un îlot* is an extremely small island) was someone who, together with the same small number of officers, was responsible for the safety of the streets in his or her small area. There is a *continuous* presence of the *same* people.

The continuous presence of the same officers and the relations that they form with people in the area both reduced the fear of crime among the law-abiding, and acted as an important factor in deterring delinquent behaviour. 'That is why the Working Party places particular emphasis on it.'[55]

The main principle of *British* beat policing, the report said, the permanent presence of a personally known police officer in a given small area, was not realised 'by a police car rolling by'. It was not realised 'when officers constantly changed the areas they patrolled'.

In Paris, the report said, the term 'beat policing' was often used for police practices that were not beat policing all, and beat policing in the proper sense of the term scarcely existed in the city. The work of the mobile police units (*unité mobile de police*) was sometimes wrongly described as beat policing. But in February 1985 the mobile police units had a workforce of only 1,082, including the car mechanics. When the car mechanics and so on were deducted from the total that left about 700 police officers. On any given day, only 450 of this 700 were actually on duty because, in practice, the reforms of working hours introduced in 1980 limited the level of real availability to only 60 per cent of the theoretical availability. On the basis of these figures, the police could patrol only 60 or 65 beats in the whole of the city of Paris, when it needed at least 175.

> In other words, officers in police cars, without any particular attachment to a given area, might be called 'beat officers'. But such officers are beat officers only marginally. In practice, the aims of beat policing are pushed to one side by the necessities of the moment. The reality of 'beat policing' in the city of Paris is thus very far removed from the ideal of one officer, one territory, one objective.[56]

> The advantages of beat policing of the kind we have described are recognised by others, and mainly by police officers themselves. When 100,000 police officers were asked by the

police training authority, 'Would you say that beat policing is a good a good way of deterring criminals and improving relations with the public?', 81.5 per cent said yes.[57]

The idea of auxiliary 'community beat officers', not canvassed for another 15 years in complacent Britain, was dealt with in detail by Paris in the mid-1980s. A 'vigilante' is a term with strong negative connotations in English. In French it has none—a 'vigilante' in French means 'a member of a legitimate defence group' (*un membre d'un groupe de légitime défense*).

From the mid-1980s Paris responded with control ('repressive') measures to the passenger-safety problem on the public transport system. But the response was then tough. In 1985 the Metro police were supplemented by two squads of *gendarmes mobiles*, about 150 strong. The riot police (*Compagnie Républicaine de Sécurité*) were brought in. Merely by their presence within and around the system, the riot police, though they were fewer in number than the *gendarmes mobiles*, had an immediate effective in reducing crime. The *police secours* entered the Metro system when required. In July 1985 a special police post was opened in the Halles district, responsible for the underground as well as the streets. There were 6,000 Metro and bus employees of the Paris public regional transport system in 1985. They were instructed to provide an increased measure of surveillance and security.[58]

Whereas in England people with some kind of official status, whose mere presence kept vandalism at bay, were being constantly reduced in number, Paris began to employ park security patrols from 1980 (*Inspecteurs de Sécurité des parcs, jardins et espaces verts*). They were not police officers. They had only the power that every other French citizen had under article 73 of the penal code, to intervene to prevent the commission of a flagrant crime. There were 124 parks inspectors in 1985, and double that number in 1986.[59]

'Simply having someone constantly present and responsible is one of the main factors in deterring acts of criminality or disorder in residential blocks.' But since 1979, caretakers could no longer be employed on the basis of their permanent availability, being entitled to sleep in their own homes and enjoy annual holidays. Caretakers were no longer physically present for most of the weekend, during the evenings and night, and for part of the year. That was a desirable fact of modern life. The working party therefore recommended that physical security measures, such as reinforced doors, coded locks, entry phones and so forth should be subsidised by a 30 per cent grant from the city, and a 30 per cent grant from the government.[60]

As a police matter, preventing people without fixed abode constituting a problem of safety on the streets was the responsibility of the Paris Homelessness Squad, 'the blues' (*Brigade d'aide aux personnes sans abri*—the BAPSA). The blues criss-crossed Paris to find homeless people and take them to the hostel at la Maison de Nanterre. The Mayor also recommended the existing laws on travellers (*nomades, gens du voyage*), dating from the time when France was largely rural, should be reformed so that the problems suffered and caused by the rapidly increasing number of travellers could be dealt with. Paris had five official sites for travellers, providing a total of 90 parking spaces. But it was estimated that there were 6,700 holders of travellers' licences in Paris. At the end of 1981 roughly 300 caravans were parked in the streets, mainly in the areas of the Bois de Vincennes and the Bois de Boulogne.[61]

The Mayor's report says that 'one of the generators of street crime is the presence of prostitutes'. The city had about 10,000 prostitutes in the 1980s, half of the national total of 20,000. There were three main areas where street prostitutes were to be found at any time of the day or night, rue St Denis (where 1,600 prostitutes work), rue de Budapest, and rue Joubert. A fourth area stretched from the Goutte d'Or to Belleville. The Bois de Boulogne and Pigalle were areas of transvestite prostitution.

A surge in street prostitution and the street crime associated with it had been created by the legalisation of prostitution, and the concentration of the law on the suppliers and controllers of prostitutes. As a party to the Geneva Convention of 1949, ratified in 1960, French legislation followed the principle that those who wished to be prostitutes or use (*se livrer à*) prostitutes had to be free to do so. The law should fall in all its rigour only on the pimps and madams (*les proxénètes*). The result of the police cracking down on the obvious haunts of the *proxénètes*, the hotels and brothels, was to disperse under-cover prostitution from a few definite areas, and locate it in more areas, with soliciting in the streets and 'studios' in residential dwellings.

Meanwhile, the owners of the small hotels who had formerly lived off immoral earnings had moved their businesses into legally grey areas, and now let their rooms to an indefinite assortment of petty criminals.

In 1975 French prostitutes were brought into the tax system. Because Great Britain—still socially conservative in 1960, with the cultural revolutionaries just beginning to flex their muscles—was among the countries that did not ratify the Convention that led to the legalisation of prostitution, with these unforeseen inconveniences for the prostitutes and their protectors, French prostitutes left to work in the newly permissive England of the 1970s where they were unhampered by state control. They were replaced in Paris in large part by immigrant prostitutes.[62]

'For the people in the streets affected, all these developments have brought numerous and constant nuisances in their train. Prostitution in its current form, with all the derivative pornographic nuisances, such as sex shops and peep shows, blights their lives with visual and oral, if not physical aggression.' Areas of prostitution were areas of 'incessant crime and misbehaviour'—from attacks in the blocks of flats or on the streets to late-night rowdiness (*tapage nocturne*).[63]

While both England and the United States were increasingly liberal in these matters, with the authorities and active and effective public opinion generally siding with the prostitutes rather than with the residents in the areas affected and, in particular, denying that prostitution was a crime or rowdiness problem, Paris recommended that the anti-social behaviour accompanying prostitution should be dealt with 'firmly' by the police. Extra police should patrol the area to keep such contingent disorder to a minimum. Penalties for (the possibility of such 'offences' is difficult for a post-modernist generation to grasp) 'outrages against good morals' (*outrages aux bonnes mœurs*) should be strengthened. Fines for street soliciting should be raised, so that they would act as an effective deterrent. Tax collection from prostitutes and those who lived off them should be stricter.[64]

In his introduction to his report, Mayor Chirac wrote that the findings and conclusions were nearly always fully consensual. Where they were not, they were approved by large majorities. He emphasised three things: crime had grown greatly in Paris in recent years; Paris had attacked the problem with its considerable resources; but it needed still more resources and these only the central government had the authority to provide.

> The monopoly of force and justice is the government's. Official statistics have shown violence spiralling out of control. The national authorities have evaded their responsibilities. Instead they have unleashed loud publicity about the role of local authorities and voluntary associations in the prevention of crime. It is true that even if it is the crew's fault that the ship is sinking, it is nevertheless quite understandable for them to ask the passengers to help with the bailing out—and it is sensible for the passengers to do so. But the establishment of a policy on the police, criminal justice and the penal system is the responsibility of the national government. Paris has no powers in this area. It has no juridical competence. In any case, its problems cannot be dealt with within its own boundaries. They are the problems of a vast open metropolis. Nevertheless, Paris does have at its disposal considerable means for fighting crime. I did not hesitate to use them when it became evident that the actions of the national government were insufficient or irresolute. The utilisation of the complementary means at the disposal of the national and local authorities in therefore necessary. The means that are the prerogative of the national government must be exercised firmly.[65]

Chirac said that Paris had to abandon the left's dogmatic Rousseauian approach to crime (*les a-prioris d'une idéologie rousseauiste*) that emphasised it roots in injustices that had to be removed, and prevented immediate deterrent measures being taken against criminals. For the sake of the people whose rights the criminal would violate or was violating, the authorities had to prevent him committing a crime. If prevention failed, then he and others must be deterred from committing crimes. Removing the causes of crime was a separate and long-term matter.

If someone's history or present condition predisposed him to commit a criminal act, he had to know that, if he did commit it, the offence would be known to be his. He had to know that he would be subjected to some form of action not of his own choosing, not necessarily punishment, but including the possibility of punishment. He had to know that in this process, benign to him or painful to him, the interests of the law-abiding public would be paramount, and not his interests as he or his advocates perceived them to be.

> It is not my intention to ignore the importance of prevention, support, and education in dealing with the crime problem. But the archaic ideas about civic safety that are still ideologically defended by leading intellectuals must be swept away and replaced by a modern, scientific analysis of crime. If the experiences of our inner cities and certain suburban areas are anything to go by, the question of the failure of the ideas currently dominant in France is worth pondering.[66]

The marked increase in the recreational use of drugs other than alcohol and nicotine was an aspect of the cultural revolution that surged in France in the early 1980s. Young people were now the constant recipients of aggressive messages from the entertainment industry and ambiguous ones from the intelligentsia about the harmless pleasure that illicit drugs, like legally available drugs, produced. Unlike commentators in England at this time and for long after, Mayor Chirac's commissioners did not conceptualise this as a lifestyle choice in which other people had no significant stake, and no right to any significant say. The growth in the number of drug addicts was condemned immediately and outrightly as a social scourge (*un fleau social*). It affected not merely the lives of the drug users, but was the driving force in the increase in 'murders, rapes, thefts, burglaries, armed robberies, and other aggressive acts by criminals on law-abiding citizens'. The mayor's commission on narcotics reported that, in spite of the failure of police resources to keep pace with the demands placed on them, nationwide the number illicit drug users interrogated by the police rose from under 10,000 in 1979 to nearly 24,000 in 1983.[67] The commission estimated that there were 100,000 heroin addicts aged 18 to 30 in France, and that the market for cocaine was experiencing an unprecedented rate of growth. Eighty kilos had been seized in 1982. In 1983 the figure was almost 230 kilos.[68]

The Paris region was the worst affected. There, the number interrogated rose by 29 per cent in the single year 1982-83. Almost all were young people. In 1983, 95 per cent of users of illicit drugs interrogated by the police were in the age-range 16 to 30. One third were under 20. 'More serious still: for the first time in 1983 the official figures report drug use among children under 13 in the Paris region.'

The commission dealt directly with the 'dangerous distinction' made between 'hard' drugs and 'soft'. Associated with the distinction were the two arguments of those who wished to have at least cannabis-use legalised: first, that it was wrong to suppose that there was a *chemically induced* progression from cannabis to heroin or cocaine; secondly, it was wrong to suppose that everyone progressed from one to the other. The commission dismissed both these arguments as classic examples of the logical error termed *ignoratio elenchi*—refuting an argument that an opponent has not put. The commissioners pointed out that the progression took place, for whatever reason. As in any other area of behaviour, nobody goes to hell all at once. What was unacceptable becomes acceptable, as personal standards slacken and reference groups gradually shift. Empirically, the commission asserted, when 100,000 more young people were attracted to smoke the occasional 'joint', 10,000 more young people a year would become drug addicts.[69] The commissioners proposed, among other measures, a university hospital centre for the treatment of drug users and for drug research and education, possibly at l'Hôpital Sainte Anne at the René Descartes University.

Figure 11.3
Drug users being treated in drug clinics, hospitals
and non-specialist drug centres
Metropolitan France, November 1987 to November 1999

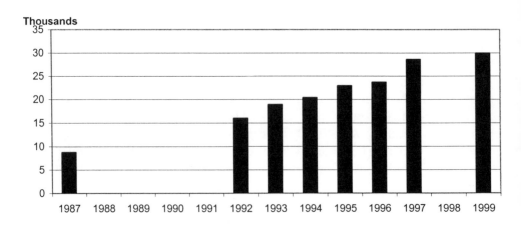

Source: Direction de la recherche des études de l'évaluation et des statistiques

The absolute figures on drug addiction, like the figures on crime, are unreliable at any one point in time for all sorts of definitional, reporting and recording reasons. But, as with the crime figures, *trends* are indicated with more certainty by the annual changes in the sets of figures showing year by year stable patterns of under-reporting and over-reporting, or experiencing changes in definition and so forth in one year compared with another.
In November 1987 there were 8,800 drug addicts (*toxicomanes*) attending for treatment in social centre clinics, health centre clinics and specialised drug clinics in Metropolitan France. By November 1995 the number was 22,900.[70] Part of the rise was due to substitution treatment being introduced in 1993, which resulted in a number of centres being opened to dispense methadone. But they had been opened because of the scale of the growing problem outside the clinics.

The figure of those attending for the first time in any year increased sharply. Drug users attending specialised drug clinics for the first time in 1987 numbered 11,100. By 1995 that figure had risen to 26,800.

Figure 11.4
Drug users attending for treatment for first time
Metropolitan France, 1987 to 1995

Thousands

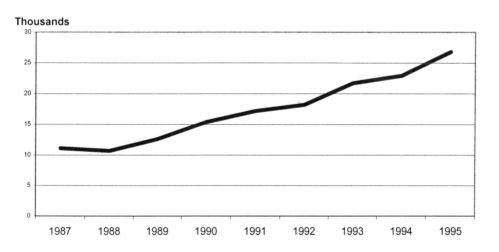

Source: Annuaire des statistiques sanitaires et sociales

'Though for a long period drug addiction affected only a small number of people in France, today the scale of the problem is disquieting. Drug taking is becoming "popularised".'[71] The *Observatoire français des drogues et toxicomanie* (OFDT), estimated that during the second half of the 1990s the number of problem users of opiates stood at somewhere between 146,000 and 172,000, a 'problem user' being defined as someone who had either sought medical help, or brought himself or herself to the attention of the police. In November 1999 there were 12,900 patients in specialised drugs clinics and in drug-treatment centres in hospitals being treated for heroin addiction.

The growth in the numbers of those consuming drugs was closely associated not only with the growth in crime. It was also associated with the growth in the number of addicts and other 'serious problem' users, and with the growth in the numbers of people suffering from AIDS and hepatitis C. A quantitative and qualitative study of drug addiction is undertaken every November by the *Direction de la recherche des études de l'évaluation et des statisitiques* (DREES). According to DREES, in 1999 a quarter of all AIDS victims were addicts, and between 12 per cent and 16 per cent of patients attending drugs clinics and hospitals tested seropositive for HIV. More than half were seropositive when tested for the hepatitis C virus. In the case of injecting drug users in hospitals, 35 per cent were seropositive for HIV, and 64 per cent for hepatitis C.[72]

In Paris, as in London, Berlin and New York, the trend in robbery was a particularly revealing index of what was happening to civic culture and police effectiveness. As in those other cities, robbery remained one of the most reliable indicators of changes in the crime rate over time.

Some other categories of crime were altered in France in 1995, thus breaking the time series of the statistics. But the definition of a 'robbery' was unchanged.[73]

The number of thefts of and from motor vehicles greatly diminished in the later 1990s as manufactures improved the security devices on their cars, but robberies grew strongly in the period. There were 60,000 recorded robberies in France in 1990. This figure had increased by 82 per cent by the year 2000, to 109,800. Robberies from women, of which there were 24,900 in 1990, rose by 48 per cent to 37,000.[74]

In the 1990s French academics argued that differences in national cultures made it more difficult for France than either Britain or the United States to adopt certain non-police, private measures of protection against burgeoning criminality and petty disorder. French solutions had to be public.

One 'Anglo-Saxon' solution had been for people of wealth and influence to remove themselves from the problem (and prolong the period during which they could belittle its importance to other people as their 'irrational and exaggerated fear of crime'). Calan called the Anglo-Saxon solution 'situational prevention' for the well-to-do (who are also the most influential in determining the priorities of public policy).[75] What the Institute for Advanced Studies in Civic Security, for example, took as its starting point was the datum that Paris had experienced since the 1960s 'new forms of urban violence and incivility', especially in the poorer areas of social housing.[76] The 'Anglo-Saxon solution' had been to flee the problem, at the extreme (particularly in the United States) by privatising public spaces and making them hostile territory to any but the inhabitants, access being limited to the residents and those authorised by them.[77] 'But what seems to be a solution to the problem in America and Britain exacerbates it in France, by creating resentment the creation of "privatised public spaces" (*espaces publics fermés*).'[78]

In the form of increased surveillance of private life in public places, France participated in the opposite tendency in the attempt to combat criminals and anti-social elements. Frédéric Ocqueteau provides the figure that from 1998 to 1999 2,512 CCTV cameras were installed in the city of Paris under the video-surveillance law of October 1996, and another 2,415 in the problem suburbs of Hauts-de-Seine, Val-de-Marne and Seine-Saint-Denis.[79] In order to deprive the criminal of his anonymity, the law abiding citizen also lost his privacy in public places. This was just one more cost the criminal imposed on his fellow-citizens.

At the beginning of the twenty-first century, with a population of 59 million, France had 233,000 police officers. There were two broad categories of police, the *gendarmerie nationale* and the *police nationale*. Approximately 98,000 gendarmes, in charge of civil safety in rural and outlying urban areas (*zones rurales et périurbaines*), operated in parts of France accounting for 29 million people. Approximately 135,000 *police nationale* covered urban areas containing 30 million people.[80] In 2002, for the first time, both the national gendarmerie and national police came under the authority of the Minister of the Interior, Security and Local Liberties. In June 2002 the crime figures began to be published monthly. Crime recorded by the gendarmerie and police had risen by 40 per cent in the previous 20 years, and the number had exceeded four million for the first time in 2001. In July 2002 the National Assembly approved an anti-crime and disorder five-year plan, allocating a supplementary budget of 5.6 billion euros for the purpose. The stated intention of the Minister of the Interior, Nicolas Sarkozy, was to renovate the culture of French policing, and in particular to ensure that the culture was one in which success in diminishing crime and disorder were paramount. He instituted a monthly meeting of all regional police chiefs so that their comparative performances in cutting crime and disorder would be made known to all of them.[81]

The costs imposed by crime and disorder are two-fold. First there are the costs of controlling crime. Secondly, there are the profits of criminals at the expense of the public, and the costs of the damage criminals and vandals inflict. Crimes hidden from members of the public, and impacting diffusely in terms of higher prices of services that rise for all sorts of other reasons as well, cost them much more in cash terms than crimes that affect directly and personally the particular victims of, say, car theft or robbery. The *Centre de recherches sociologiques sur le droit et les institutions pénales* (CESDIP) studied these two sets of costs for France from the early 1970s.[82] Considering only the second of the costs of crime, Christophe Palle and Thierry Godefroy gave the lowest estimate of the amount of tax fraud in 1996 at 50,000 million francs. The investigated figure for the proceeds of armed robberies was 246 million francs.[83]

Figure 11.5
Robberies
City of Paris, 1973 to 2000

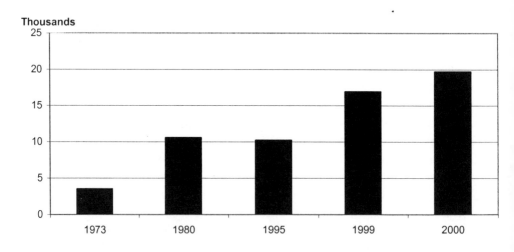

Source: Aspects de la criminalité

Robberies in the city of Paris rose in the 1970s from 3,500 in 1973 to 10,800 in 1980. Jacques Chirac was elected mayor in 1977, and remained in office until 1995. Under the mayorality of Chirac, robbery did not, indeed, fall as it did in New York under Mayor Guilliani, but in the 1980s and the beginning of the 1990s it was stabilised. In the second half of the 1990s the number of robberies again surged, to 16,900 in 1999, and to 19,700 in 2000. The *increase* in the single year 1999/2000 was therefore more than the *total number* of robberies in 1973 when the cultural revolution was beginning to make its criminogenic effects felt. Most unarmed robberies took place in public places. In the year 2000, 15,642 out of the total of 15,812 unarmed robberies (8,441 of them being robberies of women) took place in the street or other public place. Armed robberies rose from 286 in 1973 to 1,167 in the year 2000, the vast majority being robberies from premises or security vans.[84]

In Seine-Saint-Denis, with a population of about 1.4. million throughout the period, robberies rose steeply from 797 in 1971 to 2,100 in 1980, to 4,000 in 1995, to 7,000 in 1999, and to 8,300 in the year 2000.

There was the same uninterrupted growth in Hautes-de-Seine, the population of which remained stable at about 1.5 million. In 1973 there had been 766 robberies, in 1980 there were 1,400, in 1995 2,700, in 1999 4,300, and in the year 2000 5,300. In Val-de-Marne, with a stable population of about 1.2 million, the figures were 497, 1,500, 2,600, 4,200 and 5,800. In all cases the *increase* in 1999/2000 was far in excess of the *total* for the year 1973.

Figure 11.6
Robberies in the Paris banlieus
Seine-Saint-Denis, 1973 to 2000

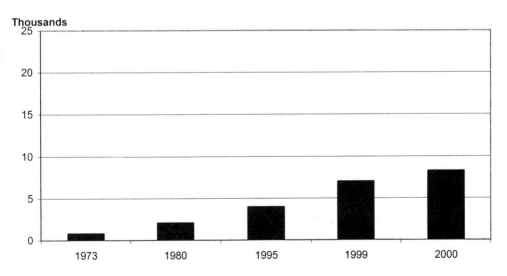

Source: Aspects de la criminalité

In 2002 ex-Mayor Chirac, now President Chirac, found that the electorate strongly endorsed his law-and-order views and programme. The crushing defeat of his Prime Minister, Lionel Jospin, was at least partly a rejection of the French left's (which had not been until the 1960s English Labour's) tenderness towards the criminal as rebel. This freed ex-Mayor Chirac from the constraints imposed by *cohabitation* with the socialists. A Labour Party Home Secretary in England, David Blunkett, and a *Union pour un Mouvement Populaire* (UMP) Interior Minister in France, Nicolas Sarkozy, had now adopted much the same standpoint, namely, that where, and to the extent that, internalised personal motivation or informal community constraints for the time being were failing, it was necessary to impose police control on people who were criminals or social nuisances. On the premise that whatever was done must be within the terms of the dominant culture of permissiveness, and the assumption that the past ('the forces of conservatism') had nothing to offer, the moulding or remoulding of their personalities by a change for the better in their education, experience of discrimination, incomes, housing, leisure facilities and so forth, was a longer-term and uncertain project. So was building, with the intellectual and moral presuppositions of the alternative culture, community control and a spirit of civic responsibility in the general population. But fundamental improvements in the future could not be accepted as a reason for hindering effective prohibition and deterrence in the here and now.

On 13 November 2002 the French Senate held the first reading of Sarkozy's proposed law on internal security. Although there was little in its 57 sections that was not already covered by existing law somewhere; and although the draft had 'stamped heavily all over the flower-beds' of its predecessor (as *Le Canard enchaîné*, France's *Private Eye*, mocked),[85] in the law there was at least this simple symbolism: the French government, with the support of the law-abiding population of whatever class, creed or party, now indeed did 'mean business'.

Part IV

The United States

12

Dealing with Diversity:
Extermination, Segregation, Assimilation

The domestic history of the United States has been in one sense that of a torn society, and it has been at least as bloody as the internal history of France.[1] The War of Independence was a quasi-civil war, in that many of the rebels shared the same cultural heritage as the English authorities. The American Civil War of the nineteenth century, unlike the English Civil War of the seventeenth, was fought with modern munitions, and the result was mass slaughter in its battles. But until the cultural revolution of the 1960s, there was rarely any doubt about the content, power or overwhelming confidence in the 'manifest destiny' of the dominant culture. American minorities were either exterminated, civilised, dispossessed, enslaved, segregated or voluntarily assimilated.

The fate of the Amerindians was forecast in the early days of the USA by Tecumseh, chief of the Shawnee in what is now Indiana and Ohio. 'We gave them forest-clad mountains and valleys full of game, and in return what did they give our warriors and our women? Rum, trinkets and a grave.' The white invaders 'grew from the scum of the great water, when it was troubled by an evil spirit'. General Sherman had no compunction about putting himself on record with such opinions as this: 'We must act with vindictive earnestness against the Sioux, even to their extermination, men, women and children'. 'Extermination', according to Angie Debo, author of a standard history of the Amerindians, was Sherman's 'favourite word'.[2] By 1892, the Indian Wars were over. The apocalyptic religions had been killed off. The despoliation of Indian lands then moved silently towards its end. Indian tribal funds were diverted to meet the cost of the Indian Bureau. Indian-owned timber was commercially harvested. In 1917, the Assistant Indian Commissioner explained to the Indian Committee of the House of Representatives that since Indians were being 'liquidated', it was policy to liquidate their forests at the same time.[3]

Diversity among white Americans was handled in one prominent case by members of the Church of the Latter Day Saints who, driven from their communities because of their un-American beliefs and practices, proved large enough in numbers, and strong enough in their alternative culture and leadership, to establish their own durable and economically highly successful cities and theocratic state in the wilderness of Utah.

The Civil War destroyed slavery, but created *legally enforced* segregation in the South, that is, institutional racism in the proper sense of the term. [4] As Walt Whitman wrote in 1873, 'the problem of the future of America is as dark as it is vast. ... Unwieldly and immense, who shall hold in behemoth? who bridle leviathan?'[5] The practical answer to the indigenous population of African-Americans was their subjugation, in part by the Ku Klux Klan.

The first practical answer to immigrants was their unapologetic and relentless 'Americanisation', in part by Nativism and anti-Catholic violence.[6] Domestic science night classes before the Great War taught immigrants that it was unseemly to mix food in one dish, with unwholesomeness heavily disguised by spices as peasant poverty dictated—pizzas, goulashes and so forth. Each portion of perfect American food had to be placed separately on the plate, good meat, good vegetables, good potatoes. In an annual ceremony at Soldier Field, Chicago, immigrants in the traditional clothing of their native land stepped into a giant melting pot, to re-emerge dressed as 'proper Americans', the men complete with their Eversharp propelling pencil in their top jacket pocket. Total immigration from 1820 to 1930 was 37.8 million. In the single generation from 1880 to 1910 almost 18 million immigrants entered the United States; most of the men were farmers or unskilled labourers from the countries of southern and eastern Europe.[7]

When immigrants became less willing to assimilate, the second answer was violence. In 1943 Mexicans dressed in an un-American fashion suffered a week of attacks in Los Angeles in the so-called Zoot-Suit Race Riots. The Los Angeles riots had started with fights between zoot-suited Mexicans and US navy personnel. They were exacerbated by race attacks on youths of any race who were wearing un-American zoot-suits, and spread to San Diego, Philadelphia, Chicago and Evansville, Indiana.[8]

Before the 1960s, race riots were almost exclusively riots by whites against members of other races. The police were part of this process, enforcing Americanisation where they did not enforce segregation. In pre-1960s American communities, committed as they were to Americanisation, the police assisted in the assertion of American normality, acting on behalf of the Americanised or willingly assimilating law-abiding adults in their neighbourhood. In some places they acted well beyond their authority—but with the approval of the majority in the local community. Young white toughs were roughed up. People were arrested on catch-all charges —'on suspicion' or for 'vagrancy'. 'Rights' were for the protection of decent Americans and would-be Americans.

From the earliest days, therefore, where the problem was not segregation, the police function in normal times was seen primarily as maintaining order against 'disreputable behaviour', with the support of the assimilated and assimilating population.

In the year ending 1885, for example, Chicago was still a city in a phase of rapid growth, with all the problems of social order posed by that state of affairs. Its population had been only 29,963 in 1850. In 1880 its population was 503,000. It was more than twice that number in 1890, 1.1 million.[9] In the middle of this decade of population expansion, the city expended $1,079,344 on the police. The total number of men constituting the police force was 926, of whom 568 were assigned to patrol duty. There were 84 'plain dress' officers. They made slightly fewer than 41,000 arrests in the year—63 arrests for each patrol officer and plain-clothes detective.

But by far the largest number of arrests were not for crimes. They were for offences against public decorum. Over half were for 'being disorderly' (23,000). There were 1,554 arrests for 'being an inmate of a house of ill-fame' and another 108 for 'being an inmate of a disorderly house'. There were 146 for 'lounging on street corners'. There were 673 arrests for violations of the dog ordinance and 192 for violations of the saloon ordinance. Rioting in July 1885 resulted in 175 arrests. There were four arrests for 'a crime against nature'.

By contrast, in this city that was growing from half a million to a million in ten years, there were only a small (by modern standards) number of arrests for robbery: 355. There were 2,000 arrests for larceny, 814 for burglary, and 93 for 'shooting within the city limits'.

To dismiss this account as an unreliable description of the *amount of crime* in Chicago is to miss the point. It is a description of the *work the police undertook* in Chicago at that time.

The role of maintaining petty public order, rather than pursuing criminals, is seen even more clearly in the account given in the 1875 annual report of the police department of the work of the officers at Desplaines Street Station. They 'suppressed 200 disturbances without arrest'. They took 95 sick and injured people to hospital and 80 to their homes. Forty-five sick and injured persons were taken to back to the police station 'and cared for'. The Desplaines Street officers 'cared for' 42 insane persons and 20 destitute persons. Twenty-seven lost children were taken to their parents. Thirty-five dead bodies were taken to the morgue, and three to their homes. Thirteen destitute children were taken to St Vincent's Orphan Asylum and ten abandoned children to the Foundlings' Home. Twenty 'inebriates' were taken to the Washingtonian Home. Eight 'wayward girls' were taken to the House of the Good Shepherd. Two mad or crippled animals were killed and one runaway horse was stopped.[10]

The police were assisted in all this work of keeping good 'American' order, or pushed into doing this, by citizen Reform movements whose objective it was to bring law, order and 'decency' into, or back into, their own neighbourhoods or cities.

Samuel Wilson gives an account of neighbourhood vigilantism against prostitution in a residential district of Chicago before the Great War.[11] The most remarkable thing is not what he says directly about the red-light district of Chicago, but the latent assumption that as an 'investigator' for the Douglas Neighborhood Club he could and did make arrests without interference even from suspect's own immediate circle in the brothel or saloon. Much less did he expect interference from a hostile crowd from any 'ethnic'—cultural—community with different standards that, unable or unwilling to control its own criminal and vicious elements, hindered the work of the others in doing so. Wilson, and the suspects he apprehended, must have taken it very largely for granted that 'right' was on Wilson's side.

Wilson's job was to investigate 'vice' and, basically, clear it out of the Douglas neighbourhood. He reports on some of his work for the vigilante club in the previous six months. He gives details of 26 cases, of which the following are examples.

> Arrested and convicted Mrs—, house of ill-fame and harboring girls under age, in the Silverman building.
>
> Reported Miss— and three inmates to Lieut S—, who removed them at once. Arrest and conviction of Miss—, house of prostitution. Took minimum fine and agreed to leave the city.
>
> The arrest and conviction of Mr—, corner of 32nd and Indiana Avenue, keeper of saloon and house of assignment.
>
> Arrested Mr—, owner of saloon and assignment house, corner of 35th and South Park Avenue. He was compelled to leave the district.
>
> We have closed up and put For Rent signs at about sixty-five houses of assignation. These are places where men take young girls and women for immoral purposes.
>
> Closed up twenty houses of ill-fame where women are kept for immoral purposes.
>
> We arrested the notorious Madame—, 3000 Indiana Avenue, for keeping a house of ill-fame and hooche-cooche (sic) dance. Forced occupants to move from 192 East 32nd Street without arrest.
>
> Reported to police and had tenants move from house on Michigan Avenue. Arrest and conviction of Mrs—, 3447 Prairie Avenue, assignation house for married women.
>
> One of the most aggravated cases we had to contend with was that of Mrs—, whom we arrested on a charge of pandering. She very willingly sold a girl to us for $50, but as the investigators did not purchase the girl for the purpose of taking her to a house of prostitution, we had no particular standing in court, as the law reads that the person purchased or sold must be used for that purpose.

The 'legitimacy' of the Douglas Neighborhood Club's actions was acknowledged by the perpetrators themselves. In some sense they were still part of the same 'moral community' as their critics, and personal shame and loss of community reputation for sexual misconduct were still disincentives to bad behaviour. It needed much intellectual work and a great deal of propaganda before that state of affairs could be changed, and the notion of sexual misconduct could be dismantled. 'We find that publicity is one of the greatest weapons we have in fighting the disreputables in our district. Invariably the women ask whether it will get into the papers, and have more dread of publicity than they do of the police courts.'[12]

In his *obiter dicta* we also hear about the role of the Chicago police at that time. Wilson's view was that the police officers were not proactive enough. 'The dishonest policemen are few. ... We do know, however, that they seem to be shackled, and seldom, if ever, go after the evildoer until driven to it by the Reform movement. ... The dark shame of all this is, that the public ... do not rise up as a man and break the chain that has held decent citizens captive for past generations.'[13] To the Reform movement in Chicago and other cities, criminality, vice and disreputable behaviour were the work, to use Virgil Peterson's phrase, of the 'barbarians within our midst' who had to be civilised, that is to say, Americanised.[14]

The American tradition of powerful groups of citizens coming together to 'clean up the city', including groups demanding a more effective police service, is illustrated the work of the Citizen's Police Committee of 1931. Chicago Police Commissioner William F. Russell had written to the Chicago Crime Commission, Chicago's Northwestern University, the University of Chicago and the American Institute of Criminal Law and Criminology, asking them to undertake a study the work of his Department. The Supervisory Committee included the President of Northwestern University and the Vice-President of the University of Chicago. The invitation was at once accepted by the presidents of the four institutions. 'It is my hope', Russell wrote, 'that when its full needs are studied ... by a disinterested expert committee, the people of Chicago will promptly and amply support and demand all measures ... for enabling the department to reach its highest ideals of efficiency.' He said he was 'keenly aware of the great responsibility' of protecting the 'lives, liberty and property of three million citizens in their homes and livelihoods'.[15]

The Operating Committee included Ernest W. Burgess, Professor of Sociology at the University of Chicago. He showed from the 1926 Chicago crime statistics that the police concealed the evidence of most of the city's crime. 'An amazing percentage of the records of offenses known to have been committed, and also known to have been reported to the police, have been suppressed, and only reported to the criminal records bureau when the offender has been apprehended.' The district captains reported as known crimes only those where arrests had been made.[16] (The 1926 'crime' figures are therefore really comparable only with the 'arrest' figures of earlier years.) Comparing the number of crimes on the station files with the numbers that eventually found their way Chicago's criminal records bureau, the Crime Committee showed that in 1926, of 14,110 burglaries on station files, only 896 were passed to the bureau; of 12,924 larcenies on station files, only 334 were passed to the bureau; of 7,191 robberies on station files, only 1,311 were passed to the records bureau; of 941 assaults with a deadly weapon and assault to kill on station files, only 46 were passed to the bureau; of 2,831 cases of malicious mischief on station files, including bombings, only nine were passed to the bureau. In 1926, only 6.33 per cent of the crimes reported and recorded at station level actually appeared in the Chicago crime statistics.[17]

The Crime Committee developed two manuals of crime records, and Chicago then adopted a much more reliable system based on the Crime Committee's 'Uniform Classification of Offenses', which included the, to us, strange but striking crime of 'assault where the circumstances show an abandoned and malignant heart'.[18]

The American police officer's traditional role up to the 1960s had been to maintain the white, and to a large extent 'Anglo-Saxon' American order. The Peelite principle of the police officer as citizen and the citizen as police officer could be applied to both immigrants and those African-Americans who sought assimilation. All this was drastically changed in America by the cultural revolution of the 1960s.

13

Dealing with Diversity:
Libertarianism and Multiculturalism

No social movement can be allocated a precise starting date. In 1951 the Kefauver Commission had reported on crime in America—a sensational document in its day, now the faint echo of a tranquil age.[1] But the forces of the American counter-culture certainly gathered momentum from the late 1950s. Jack Kerouac's accounts of his the drug-fuelled journeys in *On the Road* and Norman Mailer's 'The White Negro' can stand as markers of some sort.[2] In the 1960s immense impetus was given to the counter-culture by opposition to the Vietnam war, by a greatly intensified demand for equality for African-Americans and, later, by militant feminism in a new form, all empowered by the hospitality of the new electronic media to any breaker of taboos.

The counter-culture was strongly libertarian, and expressed its libertarianism in the increase in sexual permissiveness (with the help of the Sanger/Pincus contraceptive pill) and in the addition of illicit drugs to alcohol and nicotine as recreational substances. By 1970 a survey of the consumer market for selected organised crime services in the Chicago area gave a maximum likelihood estimate that four per cent of the adults had used heroin.[3]

Libertarianism is also synonymous with moral dissensus, or what the Illinois Institute of Technology and the Chicago Crime Commission, in its study of organised crime, called 'idiosyncratic morality'. Not only the idealists of the 1960s sought to create a society rich in idiosyncratic morality. Organised crime, in its most sophisticated form, joined them in working to achieve this goal. But it did so in a manner that created the minimum amount of visible moral conflict, that is say, it quietly supported every movement that *normalised* drugs, prostitution and pornography.[4] 'Organised crime prospers when the public is willing to tolerate a high degree of attack on the general social morality by idiosyncratic morality.'[5]

University students and staff played a large role in all the movements aimed at changes in American lifestyles.[6] Carl Rogers was influential in bringing the idea of 'non-directive' upbringing into even the primary school. The one guarantee of my values being my own is that they are not those of my parents or other would-be mentors.[7] *J'agace donc je suis.* Even

though Rogers repudiated his own doctrine when he saw what catastrophic effects it had in a society with the highly self-centred values of late-
1960s California, as distinct from the communitarian values of his 1950s
mid-west students in his Chicago days, this made little difference to the
spread of his ideas through the schools in the 1970s and 1980s.

By definition, libertarianism is anti-authoritarian. It rejects the constraints
either of an internal commitment to customary behaviour, or of community
control, or of the police.

Assimilation to American standards of respectability was what was
repulsive *par excellence* to the exponents of the American counter-culture,
where the anti-political libertarian strand was stronger than the political
revolutionary strand of the German, French and imitative English students.
In a society of diverse cultural origins, the role of the police officer in
maintaining 'all-American' order came under particularly severe challenge.
The aspirational myth of the small town hero of the 'High Noon' type
standing alone to maintain community order even when other responsible
citizens have deserted him—'I only know I must be brave'—was replaced
with the myth of 'First Blood', Rambo the heroic outsider, the lone drifter
let down by society, who wreaks complete destruction on a community
that interferes with his right to move or stay anywhere, as he pleases.

In the 1960s and 1970s the American police officer was systematically
stripped of his power to be abusive, but at the same time stripped of his
power to be effective. For university students, even from well-to-do all-
American families in the staid towns of the mid-west, the police became the
'pigs'—and there were abuses in American forces that fed any predisposi-
tion to be anti-police in general. In 1993, for example, the Chicago Police
Board fired Commander Jon Burge, finding that he had tortured a man
being questioned about the killing of a police officer.[8]

The compromise position between the complete individualism of the
libertarian and the uniformity of 'Americanism', as it was called, was
'multiculturalism', the third mode of dealing with diversity. The libertarianism originating in 1960s was a boon to college campuses and to the
beneficiaries of the new economy. Multiculturalism was a boon to ethnic
newcomers who suffered less interference and enjoyed more assistance in
maintaining their original way of life. But libertarianism and multiculturalism did not always and everywhere increase the already rich diversity in
the free life of the American city. Many neighbourhoods were plunged into
the restrictive, grey and monotonous squalor of drug addiction, teenage
gang violence and petty criminality.

In the 1960s, cities in the United States were the scene of race riots of a
frequency and ferocity never seen in England, and tasted on only one
occasion when P.C. Blakelock was hacked to death by unknown assailants

during a race riot at Broadwater Farm, Tottenham, in October 1985. 'And the end men looked for cometh not,/And a path is there where no man thought;/So hath it fallen here.'[9]

In the 1964 presidential campaign both the conservative candidate Barry Goldwater and the liberal Lyndon Johnson made an issue of the rise in crime and violent riots. In office, Johnson initiated the President's Commission on Law Enforcement and Administration of Justice in response to it.[10] Urban riots remained a major problem. In 1992 rioting in Los Angeles resulted in 52 deaths, 2,500 injuries and at least $446 million in property damage. Using international data, evidence from the race riots of the 1960s in the US, and Census data on Los Angeles, Denise DiPasquale and Edward Glaeser concluded that it and the 1960s' riots had little to do with poverty. On a community level it had much to do with the cultural diversity of a city. On an individual level it had much to do with the feeling that there was little risk of being punished.[11]

As in Great Britain, France, Germany and other Western countries, crimes that had an impact on particular victims—robberies, burglaries and so on—also began their dramatic increase in the 1960s. Chicago's population, 1.1 million in 1890, had risen threefold to 3.4 million by 1970. It was to fall to 3.0 million in 1980 and to 2.9 million by the year 2000.[12] But the workload of the police had been increasing at what the 1975 annual report of the Chicago police described as a 'staggering rate' since the 1960s. In 1965 the Chicago police had to deal with 30,000 reported burglaries; in 1975 with 47,000. In 1965 they had to deal with 15,000 robberies; in 1975 with 22,000. In 1965 they had to deal with 10,000 cases of aggravated assault; in 1975 with 13,000. In 1965 they had to deal with 1,200 cases of rape; in 1975 with 1,700. In 1965 they had to deal with 395 murders, in 1975 with 818.

Predictably, the chances of the perpetrator of a crime escaping detection improved. In 1965, 94 per cent of murders were cleared up; in 1975, 85 per cent. In 1965, 73 per cent of the aggravated assaults were cleared up; in 1975, 55 per cent. In 1965, 63 per cent of the rapes were cleared up; in 1975, 55 per cent. In 1965, 44 per cent of the robberies were cleared up; in 1975, 40 per cent.[13]

In 1975 the Chicago Police Department did try to increase its foot patrols in shopping areas, but the available resources were necessarily miniscule. The strength of the mounted police was increased from 14 to 25 officers to provide greater protection in Grant Park, Lincoln Park and outlying park areas, and officers were released for other duties by the employment of 181 civilians to attend to detention facilities, with more civilians being hired to work in the auto pounds and in the equipment and supply and animal care sections. But the increases in resources were out of scale with the increases in crime, and the possibilities of police officers being available to maintain civil peace and prevent crime by their uncommitted presence on the streets were drastically reduced.

Mechanical means to protect one's own property were increasingly advocated. A Preventive Programs Division attempted to tackle crime with more and better locks and bolts.

Public relations became more important. A community consultative programme was instituted in 1975. In 22 police districts citizens and police officers 'worked together to reduce crime'. The programme offered 'an opportunity for citizens and the police to meet regularly to discuss community problems and work out solutions'—that meant, in practice, public-relations police officers talking to a handful of community activists about how to make bricks without straw, an in practice bogus if in intention well-meaning 'participation' device copied in England 20 years later.

Since 1975 a civilian Office of Professional Standards to impose stricter control on the police had been in operation, with 33 civilian investigators under the direction of 'a black, a white and a latino', as the annual report of the police department says. It was responsible for investigating all allegations against the police of the use of excessive force, of corruption and of bribery.[14]

In 1969 James Q. Wilson gave an account of how the police role in the United States generally had already begun to change. From keeping the streets clear of minor breaches of seemliness in behaviour, the police were having to control major riots in the large African-American districts of many cities. Order maintenance became synonymous with 'community relations' aimed at damping down the risks of serious urban violence. From preventing crimes by maintaining good order, by 1969 the police were primarily responding to crimes that had been committed.

In the face of the enormous new demands placed up them, what Jane Jacobs called the 'small change' of urban life was neglected.[15] Urban life, Jane Jacobs said, was essentially the interaction of strangers, and the interactions could be productive only if there existed the *fine mesh* of mutual restraint, and respect for a multitude of unwritten rules of good behaviour—the 'built-in equipment allowing strangers to dwell in peace on ... dignified and reserved terms'.[16]

Attention shifted to gathering evidence against criminals, arresting them and processing cases into the courts. The link between order maintenance and crime prevention, so obvious to earlier generations, Wilson said, was forgotten.

Police forces focused on the FBI's 'index' crimes—murder, rape, aggravated assault, robbery, burglary, and other types of theft—and commentators focused on ways of combating them: capital punishment, gun control, more prisons, 'three strikes and you're out' and so forth. The results were that federal programmes and expenditures did not satisfy the demands of ordinary people for the control of constant daily disorder. But the supposed pay-off, the reduction in sporadic crime itself, did not materialise.[17]

A few academics began to argue that the reduction in police forces in proportion to the volume of crime and serious disorder, in the belief that technology could make up for the shortfall—that rapid response by radio control and fast vehicles were an adequate substitute for the hum-drum and trivial work of the foot patrol officer—was a strategic error.[18]

Albert Biderman and his colleagues examined the complex of cultural change, a torn society, and a relative diminution in the utilisation of police resources to deal with the 'small change' of urban life, namely neighbourhood nuisance. In a report prepared for President Johnson's 1967 Commission, they argued that nuisance behaviour in the streets and parks was a phase in a vicious spiral of crime and neighbourhood neglect. If low-level unruly conduct went unchecked, it formed the seed-bed for worse conduct. With an increase in unruly and criminal conduct, the disproportion grew still further between the number of crimes and the number of police officers. The police could not deal with the growing number of trivial and vaguely defined offences, because they had to deal as best they could with the growing number of serious and definite crimes. In the worsening situation, residents lost both the motivation and the capacity to keep in check their own anti-socially inclined neighbours. The unruly encroached then still further on the rights of the law-abiding, and petty offenders felt an ever-increasing sense of power, control and safety to graduate into the class of more serious criminals.[19]

James Q. Wilson proposed that, just as one broken window left unattended led to all the other windows in a building being broken, so trivial breaches of urban decorum, left unattended, led to an increase in bad behaviour generally, including an increase in crimes.

The citizen who fears the appearance in his neighbourhood of the drunkard, the drug taker, the prostitute, the rowdy teenager or the beggar, therefore, not merely feels and expresses distaste for particular acts of unseemly behaviour. As Hobbes said of libertarianism, many people behave well when 'everyone is governed by his own Reason'—the only trouble is, not enough of them do so.[20] The citizen's common sense—the experience of generations—tells him that his neighbourhood is on a slippery slope. 'The unchecked panhandler is, in effect, the first broken window.'[21]

In 1982 Wilson joined George Kelling in putting their ideas to *The Atlantic*, in what became an influential article. They dealt with the triad of factors that produce a community of considerate neighbours whose mutuality maximises everybody's possible degree of personal freedom, namely: the self-control based on personal commitment to behaviour that does not invade other people's rights; police surveillance and action; and community control. They suggested that bad behaviour that went unchecked and physical damage left unrepaired led to the breakdown of community controls. 'A stable neighbourhood of families who care for their homes, mind each other's children, and confidently frown on unwanted intruders can change, in ... even a few months, to an inhospitable and frightening jungle.' A window is smashed. Adults stop scolding rowdy children. The children, emboldened, become more rowdy and defiant of any checks on their conduct. Families move out, unattached adults move in. Teenagers gather in front of the corner shop. The shopkeeper asks them to move; they refuse. Fights occur. Litter accumulates. People start drinking in front of the off-licence; in time, an inebriate slumps on the pavement and is allowed to sleep it off. Passers-by are approached by beggars. At this point it is not inevitable that crime will begin to flourish. But from fear of crime, many residents will modify their behaviour. When on the streets or using public transport they will more frequently make certain that they don't get involved in what is going on around them. Confrontation with a foul-mouthed and aggressive teenager, not just a mugging, is a perfectly good reason to make a defenceless or peaceable person fearful of the streets.[22]

For centuries, Wilson and Kelling argued, the role of the policeman was that of watchman. He was judged primarily not in terms of compliance with appropriate procedures but rather in terms of attaining a desired objective. That objective was 'order'.

'Order' is a vague term. It is a condition recognised by people in a particular neighbourhood when they see it. The means employed by 'the police officer as watchman' were the same as those the members of the community would employ, if they were sufficiently determined, courageous and authoritative. Ordinarily no judge or jury sees the people caught up in a dispute over the appropriate level of neighbourhood order. This is because there are no universal standards to settle arguments over disorder, and thus a judge as such is no wiser or more effective than a police constable. Until quite recently, and even today in some places, the police made arrests on charges 'with scarcely any legal meaning'—'suspicious person', 'vagrancy', 'public drunkenness'. These charges existed not because society wanted judges to punish vagrants or drunks, but because it wanted an officer to have the legal tools to remove 'undesirable' people from the neighbourhood, when informal efforts had failed.

Since 1960, the American police had moved in their normal routine from the trivial order maintenance to prevent crime, towards responding to calls for help when a crime had already been perpetrated.

Meanwhile the informal rights conceded to the police officer to control petty breaches of order were increasingly the subject of explicit legal prohibition. Provoked by media complaints in the increasingly libertarian 1960s, controls on the police were enforced by court decisions and departmental orders. The result was that order maintenance was brought under the influence of legal restrictions appropriate to crime suspects only. The control of 'disorderly', 'undesirable' or 'disturbing' conduct was now governed by rules developed to control police relations with suspected criminals.

This development, said Wilson and Kelling, was 'entirely new'. It was now necessary to justify in legal terms why 'undesirable' behaviour should be 'criminalised'. If it could not be criminalised, then it must be permitted, without let or hindrance by anybody at all. Least of all should it be hindered by the police.

In the Wilson and Kelling view, this permissive and libertarian treatment of 'disreputable behaviour that harmed no one else' was a mistake. A single drunk damaged no other identifiable person. But failing to do something about *any one* of a score of drunks adversely affected the living conditions of everyone in an entire neighbourhood. State and charitable social-work agencies should be available. But, for as long as they did *not* attend to the needs of alcoholics and the homeless as a matter of social work, for so long residents would properly want the police to control them as a matter of public order.

The Wilson/Kelling thesis was that individual users of illicit drugs, vagrants, homeless people, drunks and prostitutes who had freely chosen their own lifestyle, and were happy with it, may or may not be individually admirable people, considered all round. Among those individuals who had not freely chosen these conditions, ill-luck or victimisation may have driven them into a life they thoroughly detested. But the prejudice against them all, indiscriminately, is based on the correct generalisation that serious street crime flourishes in areas in which such unseemly behaviour goes unchecked, whatever its origin in personal choice or personal pathology. An area where the trivial vandal and harmless beggar are on the streets every day, and where every night the streets are taken over by the blameless rough-sleeper, the single-mother prostitute working selflessly for her child and the high-spirited, noisy party-maker, is more likely, compared with an area where the residents still feel they have some control over what happens, to be one where, before long, heroin and crack cocaine would also be traded, drunks would also be robbed, 'johns' would also be 'rolled' by prostitutes' pimps, passers-by would be mugged and houses would be broken into.

Nathan Glazer argued that an area where graffiti are found is intimidating even when they are not obscene. Graffiti signalled to the passers-by or passengers that they were in a place out of control, at its worst, a place 'that anyone can invade to do whatever damage and mischief the mind suggests'.

In response to their fears, people avoid one another, weakening informal controls. In the absence of informal control, at first they turn to formal controls. They call the police. Disorder is not abated. The police explain that they are low on personnel, and they cannot afford to allocate resources to trivial incidents. The courts, their personnel or buildings from more orderly days lagging far behind the increase in the number of cases, adjust their through-put to their resources. They do not punish petty or first-time offenders.

To dismiss the 'fear of disorder' or the 'fear of crime' as something irrational, and to say that one of the jobs of the police is to talk old people in particular out of their allegedly irrational fears, is to miss the point. Logically, the implied argument is absurd, namely, that if only one in a thousand old people is verbally abused or mugged, only one in a thousand old people should fear being verbally abused or mugged. Empirically, the level of harassment or crime against old people is kept down precisely by their fear of being the victim of harassment or crime. Young men are subject to violence more than old women at night, partly because more young men are in the pubs. Old women are less likely to be the subjects of violence because they confine themselves to the comparative safety of their home more often than they once did.

As a neighbourhood loses the sense that it has the capacity to stop drug-use and drug-dealing in its residences and on its streets, prostitutes from soliciting local sons, husbands and fathers, and the clients of prostitutes from propositioning local daughters, wives and mothers, so the residents lose the sense that they have the capacity either to interfere when a mugging is taking place, or to muster the courage to testify as witnesses for fear of retaliation from the culprit or his friends. The essence of the police officer's traditional role in maintaining order was to reinforce the informal control mechanisms of the neighbourhood itself. A police force could not, without committing extraordinary resources, provide a substitute for that informal control.

As Kelling and Coles said, discrediting the role of the American police in maintaining 'the American way of life' did not affect the fact that, in all circumstances, responsibility, respect and concern in the neighbourhood did not divide rich from poor, black from white, or people pursuing different lifestyles among the infinite number that were mutually compatible. It united all the people in neighbourhoods of optimally free people against those whose behaviour disproportionately restricted the freedom of others, and who preyed on the weak and the vulnerable.[23]

In the mid-1970s, the state of New Jersey announced a programme of 'Safe and Clean Neighborhoods' for 28 cities. As part of the programme, the state provided money to help cities take police officers out of their cars and assign them to foot patrol. But many police officers disliked foot patrol. It was hard work. It kept them outside on cold, rainy nights. It reduced their chances of making a 'good pinch'. In some departments, assigning officers to foot patrol was used as a form of punishment—and was further disliked for that reason. Many police chiefs were sceptical about the scheme. Foot patrol reduced the mobility of the police in responding to calls for service from the public. It weakened the control of police officers by headquarters. In the opinion of most academics, foot patrol had little impact on crime rates, and was merely a sop to ill-informed public opinion.

But the state was paying for foot patrol, so the local authorities went along with it. Five years after the programme started, the Police Foundation (an organisation based in Washington DC) published an evaluation of the initiative, based chiefly upon the experience at Newark. Residents in the foot-patrol areas tended to feel more secure than residents in other areas. They believed that the rise in the crime rate had been halted, and crime was being reduced, even if neither of these beliefs were true. Those whose personal liberty had been most restricted by rising crime took fewer precautions against crime (staying at home with the doors locked, for example).

Residents in neighbourhoods patrolled by police on foot tended to have a more favourable opinion of the police generally than residents in other neighbourhoods. Police officers walking the beats, for their part, had a more favourable view of the residents in their neighbourhood than did officers patrolling neighbourhoods in police cars. They also had higher morale and greater job satisfaction.

The immediate impact was on trivial nuisances. This was not an inconsequential benefit to the people in the neighbourhoods who had suffered from them, however dismissive people in neighbourhoods not affected could afford to be. Residents wanted a higher standard of conduct than simply the absence of crime. People felt that criminals were depriving them of their human rights to go about their useful business unmolested and enjoy the fruits of their efforts without being illegally deprived of them. But they also felt they were being deprived of their human rights to go about their useful business unmolested when there were people about who interfered with those rights. These were the disreputable or obstreperous, unpredictable, disorderly people who had been increasing in numbers in their neighbourhoods—people who engaged in activities that easily gave rise to quarrels and fights, kept people awake, or threatened to damage or did damage residents' property. Among these were beggars, drunks, drug users, petty vandals, graffiti artists, rowdy neighbours, mentally ill people, street gamblers, prostitutes, men looking to pick up a prostitute and children who would not go away when asked, playing with a ball that could break one's window, or playing with an exuberance that kept the night-shift worker from his or her daytime rest.

Though the Newark neighbourhoods in the foot-patrol experiment were predominantly black, and in those days the patrol officers there were still mostly white men, the order-maintenance function of the police was performed to the satisfaction of both the black communities and the police force. If a stranger loitered, the foot patrol officer would ask him what his business was. Unsupervised groups of noisy children and teenagers were told to keep quiet. Drug takers could sit on the pavement where they did not obstruct it, but they were not allowed to lie down. Drunks could drink more or less out of sight in an alley, but not in full public view on the street. They could drink from a bottle, so long as it was partly hidden in a paper bag. A beggar could ask someone passing by for money, but he or she was not allowed to accost someone say at a bus stop or on a bus. (A person who is on the move has more control over the situation than one who is standing still.) In any dispute between a shopkeeper and a customer, the shopkeeper was generally assumed to be right, and the customer assumed to be 'trying it on' or mistaken, especially if the customer was a stranger.

Only sometimes did the foot patrol officer 'enforce the law'. Much of the time he was taking informal measures outside the scope of the law to help protect what most of the residents agreed was the appropriate level of public order for that neighbourhood. The residents turned to the foot patrol officer to attend to violations of their informal neighbourhood code. But because they felt they had ultimate control of the situation through their ability to call in the foot patrol officer, they also themselves ridiculed the violator, or otherwise let the violator know of their disapproval of his behaviour. In all neighbourhoods most residents assigned a high value to such 'public order', and felt relieved and reassured when the patrol officer was there to help them maintain it.

Many other studies showed that sub-criminal disorderly conduct was linked with the *eventual* level of crime. Philip Zimbardo illustrated the existence of the slippery slope from neglect, to vandalism, to intimidation and fear, to crime, and showed that this was as true of a good as it was of a bad neighbourhood. The only difference was in the pace of the process. Zimbardo left two cars without licence plates, one at the Bronx, one in Palo Alto, California, the town of the élite university Stanford. In the Bronx, within ten minutes a father, mother and son had arrived to remove the radiator and the battery. Within 24 hours everything of value had been taken. Then the vandalism began. Windows were smashed, the upholstery ripped and panels torn off. At Palo Alto, nobody touched the car for as long as it was not damaged. Then Zimbardo himself smashed part of the car with a sledgehammer. Soon, passers by were joining in, without checking on his right to destroy it—some of them therefore were 'helping a neighbour'. But within a few hours the car had been destroyed. Unattended property was fair game for fun or plunder.

By the 1980s the community control of the 1950s was a distant memory in the United States, as it was in England. A Hollywood 1950s film starring the young Marlon Brando, *The Wild Ones*, was banned in England because of what was thought at the time to be its violent content. Yet in the days when that film was made, it was not absurdly unrealistic in either country to portray, as the film did, an unaided ordinary resident fearlessly chasing the motor cyclists from his lawn—and, without a word or gesture of abuse, or any show of force, the motor cyclists leaving it.

Susan Estrich drew together a number of studies of sources of fear when using public places. In Portland, 75 per cent of all adults interviewed said that they crossed to the other side of the street when they saw a gang of teenagers in time to do so. In Baltimore, 50 per cent said they would cross the street to avoid passing even a single unknown youth. The greatest fear of the place where they lived was expressed by residents of buildings where disorderliness and incivility, not crime, were the greatest. People in a particular housing project chose as the most dangerous spot a place where young people gathered to drink and play music, despite the fact that not a single crime had been committed there.

A police officer on foot cannot separate himself or herself from people. Only his uniform and personality can help him manage the situation. In contrast, the car can be used by the police officer to protect himself from problems.

> The police car pulls up to a corner where teenagers are gathered. ... The officer says to one, 'C'mere.' The youth saunters over, conveying by his elaborately casual style that he is not intimidated by authority. 'What's your name?' 'Chuck.' 'Chuck who?' 'Chuck Jones.' 'What'ya doing, Chuck?' 'Nothin'.' 'Got a PO [parole officer]?' 'Nah.' 'Sure?' 'Yeah.' 'Stay

out of trouble, Chuckie.' Meanwhile the other boys laugh and exchange comments, probably at the policeman's expense. ... The officer has learned almost nothing, and the boys have decided that he is an alien force who can be safely disregarded, and even mocked.[24]

Wilson and Kelling present a case study of a Chicago housing estate with a population of 20,000, built in 1962. Crime rates soon soared on the estate. Only a tiny proportion of gang-related crime could be solved by arrest. Gangs need only stand around in a menacing fashion to secure control of an area. Thus, if arrest on a *criminal* charge was the only recourse for the police, the police would be helpless. The residents would feel that the police were useless. But what the police in fact did was to simply chase known gang members from the estate.

The police and the residents were allies. Since both the residents and gang members are black, the police action cannot be condemned as 'racist'. It is a collaborative effort to maintain certain standards of neighborly life. But no citizen is likely to feel the sense of personal responsibility that a police officer feels that he or she must intervene in a threatening situation.[25]

On streets and in public places, where many other people are around, the chances are reduced that any particular individual who is not a police officer will act as the agent of the community.

In residential areas, where respectable people far outnumber disreputable people, informal social control is effective. Where an area is in jeopardy from disorderly elements, citizen action without substantial police action may be sufficient to contain the situation.

Where disorderly people are present in greater numbers, volunteer watchmen—using no vigilante force to either arrest or punish people —might help the residents regain control of their streets. A private security guard may deter crime or misconduct by his presence. Being a sworn officer supplies the confidence, the sense of duty and the aura of authority needed to perform this difficult task.

But past a certain point, neighbourhoods become so demoralised and crime-ridden that community control is non-existent and it is beyond the capacity of even the foot patrol officer to make an impact. At the depths of the vicious spiral, the best the police can even hope to do is to make a symbolic response by police car to the enormous number of calls for service. Policing, Wilson and Kelling insist, consists in seeing to it that the vicious spiral is interrupted at an early enough stage.

The most important requirement is to think that to *maintain order* is a vital job. Without that, police training turns to an emphasis on the police officer's legal scope for questioning and arresting people suspected of crimes, and neglects training in what Wilson and Kelling call 'the management of street life'. But rowdism, intimidation, prostitution, drunkenness, drugs and pornography can destroy a community. Professional burglars can only damage individual householders.[26]

Wilson and Kelling's main argument is that the police had to return to their long-abandoned view that the police ought to protect *communities* as well as protect individuals. Crime statistics measured individual losses, but they did not measure communal losses.

> Just as doctors now recognise the importance of fostering health rather than just curing illness, so the police—and the rest of us—ought to recognise the importance of maintaining, intact, communities without 'broken windows'.[27]

Citizens and retailers regarded the major problems of the worst neighbourhoods in their cities—San Francisco, New Haven, Chicago, New York, Minneapolis, Milwaukee—as abandoned cars, graffiti, public drunkenness, street prostitution, youth gangs in parks and other 'disorderly behaviour'—not the rarer prospect of a crime being committed and the even rarer prospect of a riot.

People responded to these things by leaving the city or reducing their use of local shops, parks and public transport. A study of New York City by the Commonwealth Fund reported that of those who left the city to live elsewhere, 17 per cent said that if the Police Department had taken minor complaints more seriously, it would have had an impact on their decision whether to stay or to leave. Of those still living in the city, 60 per cent said that their quality of life had been worsened by dirt, graffiti, begging and homeless people. Jeremy Travis, New York City's deputy police commissioner, and later head of the National Institute of Justice under President Clinton, said that such problems were '*the central issue* for the future of New York City'.[28]

In the *Roulette* case, 1994, elderly residents of a non-profit housing association, many of them formerly homeless, together with a centre for homeless alcoholics, the Indian Center, filed 'a friend in court' brief to support 'street civility laws', including an ordinance to make it illegal to sit or lie down during certain hours in certain places in Seattle. As the streets emptied of ordinary people, they themselves felt less safe when walking to the corner shop. Setting standards for good behaviour in the area was not an assault on the homeless, but a help to them.[29]

In central London, giving the homeless the freedom of the streets turned Lincoln's Inn Fields from a pleasant oasis for anyone who wanted to visit it for any of a wide variety of purposes into the unpleasant possession of a few dozen 'bendy' squatters, so called because of their make-shift 'bendy' tents. The park was soon invested with rats, feeding on the surplus Marks and Spencer sandwiches left by well-wishers and discarded by the recipients. By the end of 2002 one of the great defenders of the homeless,

John Bird, founder of their street magazine *The Big Issue*, was pleading not on behalf of the offended general public, but of the street people themselves, for the cessation of police tolerance and gifts from the public. Money and charitable aid, Bird argued, simply maintained them in a life of disease, slow decay and death: the more money we gave them, the greater were their problems.

Bird realised he was dealing 'a cruel blow' against the progressive opinion, that people should be allowed to do what they wanted. He traced the rise in street living in England to the 1970s. The earliest and most important cause, Bird argued, was that in the 1970s central and local government, the police and others stopped enforcing the vagrancy laws. Begging became commonplace. Then, because of the trend in progressive thinking that attacked institutional care for the mentally ill, the institutions that cared for mentally ill people were closed for those who could not look after themselves. Later, benefits were withdrawn from 16- and 17-year-olds living at home. His conclusion was that the vagrancy laws should be enforced in the interest of the 'homeless' themselves, with help given being that which was really helpful to them, suitable accommodation and rehabilitation or treatment for the sick, the addicted and the mentally ill.[30]

14

Dealing with Diversity:
Destroying Crime and Disorder

City mayors and powerful politicians in the United States began to address these problems of crime and petty disorder, which had such large mulitplier effects for their cities—Jane Byrne in Chicago, George Latimer in St Paul, Minnesota, Keven White and Raymond Flynn in Boston, Stephen Goldsmith in Indianapolis, Bret Schundler in Elizabeth, N.J., Frank Gordon in San Francisco and Rudolph Giuliani in New York.

In our daily fleeting interactions with strangers in the everyday life of the city, we cannot know from a person's history or reputation how he or she is likely to behave. We have to rely on conventional cues. The cues by which people communicate their honesty, trustworthiness, reliability and readiness to co-operate (or not disrupt co-operation) are innumerable and mostly uncodified. Civilised urban conduct, to the extent that it is acquired, is imprinted in the course of a person's upbringing in family, school and neighbourhood. Most people for much of the time find a balance roughly acceptable to themselves and others between their freedom, which implies having their own way against other people's wishes, and civility, which implies self-imposed restraint and obligation. Some people do not. At the extreme are predators who murder, rape, rob and assault the innocent and weak, for a religious or political cause, or for their own gratification. Their conduct is glorified or excused by some revolutionary intellectuals and, successfully in recent years, by many existential subverters of all conventional moral assumptions.[1]

But nearly all societies more or less successfully inculcate condemnation of such conduct through family upbringing and the education of the young. They condemn it in their value systems and customs, and prohibit is in their laws. Both personal morality and compliance with custom sometimes fail. Nearly all societies therefore have, in addition to morality and custom, legal prohibitions to define it, and police officers, judges and gaolers to prevent, detect and punish it.

Less extreme are actions , some of them criminal misdemeanours, 'petty' offences, punishable by fines and community service, that themselves directly destroy or degrade property (vandalism, graffiti), or are unusually

prone to give rise to disturbances of the peace (intimidation, public
inebriation, the use of obscene language, street prostitution), and create the
conditions in which serious crime thrives when carried out by more than
a few scattered people.[2]

Public relations' approaches

Chicago initiated its Chicago Alternative Police Strategy (CAPS) in April
1993. Introduced in five police districts, the programme was then expanded
to encompass all 25 police districts of the city. Teams of what the CAPS
called 'beat' officers were given long-term assignments to each of the city's
279 police beats. They were to spend most of their time, not patrolling on
foot, but responding to calls and working on prevention projects. They
were 'problem-solvers', supported by a co-ordinated system for delivering
city services. By May 1995 virtually all officers had completed *two days* of
'problem-solving training', including instruction on how to use the service-
delivery process. Officers should not only be responding to individual calls
for service. They should be dealing with the 'causes of crime'. They should
'proactively be working to solve chronic problems'. Through pro-active
work of problem solving, officers' efforts should result in a more lasting
impact on crime.

In the winter of 1995, all patrol officers were given further training in
understanding and applying the CAPS problem-solving model. The model
consisted of five basic steps: identify and prioritise; analyse; design
strategies; implement strategies; and evaluate and acknowledge success.
This five-step model was based on the 'established format' known as SARA
(scan, analyse, respond, assess). Another aspect of the model was 'the crime
triangle', which called for officers to gather data about offenders, victims
and locations of crimes. 'For police officers this is a new way to approach
the problem; in traditional police work, officers focused on the offender
aspects of the problem only.'[3]

A CAPS Implementation Office was composed of a staff of civilian
community outreach workers who are charged with assisting beat and
district projects and sustaining participation in beat community meetings.
Over the years the office added staff members to support the court
advocacy program and assist in problem-solving in the areas of 'housing
and land-use issues'.

Civilian district advisory committees were created in all 25 districts, and
the districts all began holding beat community meetings on a regular basis
by June 1995. Each police district had the capacity to 'generate basic
analytic crime maps'. By the autumn of 1995, 'organising and problem-
solving training sessions' were being conducted for the general public by
teams across the city of civilians and police officers.

A new planning process was created in 1996. It began with the formal identification of beat problems and the resources required to attack them, and culminated in the formulation of beat, district and area plans that respond to those needs. Residents were to be involved in the development of beat plans, through regular community meetings and advisory committees.

Beginning in the same year, the city mounted a substantial civic education effort to support CAPS. Television and radio programmes, billboards, videos, brochures, mailings, festival booths and district and city-wide rallies were targeted at promoting CAPS. In 1997, civilian and police trainers were added to the staff of the police department's Education and Training Division. They were to deliver training and technical assistance to neighbourhoods, community organisations and police beats.

During 1997, 'high-level tutorials' were held for 'district managers' to help them develop better plans. An advanced crime mapping system was developed; data terminals were installed in patrol cars, and a modern database management system was been developed.

The city's Office of Emergency Communication was formed to manage police and fire calls. Interagency task forces and a bureau charged with enforcing city ordinances was formed, and the city attorney's office was 'mobilised to address' problems created by drug houses and negligent landlords.

In 1998, the CAPS Implementation Office expanded to include 'organis-ers', whose job it was 'to conduct a new community mobilisation effort'. The Implementation Office also took over the co-ordination of city services, a task earlier assigned to the Mayor's Office of Inquiry and Information.

City-wide, total participation by members of the public at meetings averaged 6,000 a month during 1998. The conclusion of these formal efforts to replace destroyed cultures of informal, continuous and dense commu-nity control left the distinct impression of a mountain labouring and bringing forth a mouse. 'The average gathering was good on the mechanics of meetings and on airing the issues, but weak in finding solutions to problems.'[4]

New York's solution[5]

The city that at last succeeded in halting the apparently inexorable growth of crime and disorder, and that succeeded in doing it dramatically, was New York. Although New York had never been famed for law-abiding-ness, its street-crime problem sharply worsened in the mid-1970s. There was a multitude of coincident causes, among them serious budgetary problems that afflicted the city from 1975 to 1983, some of them the direct result of the sharp increase in welfare costs.[6] A famous front page headline of the New York *Daily News* announced on 30 October 1975 the decision of the President of the United States not to rescue it from its financial difficulties: 'Ford to City: Drop Dead'.[7]

One of the city's solutions was to economise on its police force. Faced with growing crime and disorder since the early 1960s, the police department had been expanding. In 1968 alone it brought in an extra 3,600 recruits, raising the number of uniformed officers to 29,900. Over 1,000 more civilians were also recruited. The particular significance of these increases was noted by the police commissioner, E.R. Leary, as greatly increasing the NYPD's 'street patrol strength'.[8] By 1974 the number of uniformed officers had slowly increased further to reach 30,600.[9] Eight years of cuts followed, and the low-point of 21,800 was reached in January 1982.[10]

Quite suddenly, crime and disorder on its streets meant that New York's demise as a functioning city was routinely expected. The novelist Saul Bellow remarks somewhere that New York made him think about 'the collapse of civilisation. ... Many people already bank on it'. Jason Epstein, a leader of New York's cultural élite, and in 1970 the defender of the Chicago Seven's right to foment an intensely violent riot against (and by) the police at the Democratic National Convention in 1968, later came to write an article called 'The tragical history of New York', in which he declared that the city's engine had failed, and it was adrift on an uncharted sea.[11]

New York was frequently portrayed in the cinema as a place of violent nihilistic shoot-outs or as a city that had turned into a junk yard or even an enormous walled-in prison ruled by underclass war-lords (*The Warriors* [1979], *Escape from New York* [1981]). Tom Wolfe's *The Bonfire of the Vanities* (1987), depicting the chaos in the judicial system under the pressure of lawlessness on the city streets, was a film as well as a famous book. The *Death Wish* films appealed to audiences who felt that neither the police nor the courts were any longer capable of containing street disorder or crime.

The acute and chronic shortage of patrol officers made the NYPD into a reactive force. It did not have the resources to notice and process 'trivial' and 'victimless' crimes. But as often happens, a virtue was made out of necessity. It came to seem *good* policy to overlook petty crime and disorder, and to deal only with major crimes after they had been committed. Arrests of 'real' criminals became the criterion for success, not the old Peelite criterion of a low crime rate. And, of course, a high rate of arrests was an achievement that could go on for ever, if the crime rate was forever rising. The smaller the police force, the more repressive it became.

What happened in Times Square can be selected as a particularly vivid example of a widespread process. Before the 1970s Times Square was a safe place. Its problems began when the NYPD ignored petty disorderliness, street prostitution and 'soft' drug use. With prostitutes on the street at all hours, some of them taking drugs to keep themselves going, the drug dealers came in. According to the economic maxim 'supply creates its own demand', users followed the dealers. The prostitutes' clients, the johns, proved easy targets for robbers and car thieves. Rubbish was discarded everywhere. The walls became the target of paint-sprayers, until nothing but graffiti, unsightly to most people, praised only by those for whom dissidence is a cardinal virtue, could be seen on the walls. Fights over prostitutes and drugs led to assaults and homicides.

Places like Washington Square Park became a drugs bazaar, where Ivy League students could step out of the doors of New York University to keep themselves supplied with marijuana. Bryant Park, right next to New York City's magnificent privately funded public library, became a no-go area for ordinary workers in the daytime, and for visitors to the area in the evening. Hard-drug availability and use followed 'harmless' drug availability and use.

The police, furthermore, were intimidated by the by now normal reaction of the broadsheet press and mainstream news media to any *enforcement* of the criminal law and communal order by the police. Paradoxically, the concentration on the police of the right to enforce public order, and the high degree of public order that resulted from that, had depended upon a growing abhorrence of the use of any private violence. This abhorrence spread to the police's use of any force. The idea gained ground—a self-indulgence possible only in a society with a long history of civic safety—that if civilians doing illegal things used illegal force against the police, the justice of their grievances exonerated them, and the police were to blame if they used force to maintain or restore lawful conduct.

A clear example was the intimidation of the police in the aftermath of the Tompkins Square Park riot in August 1988, reminiscent of the intimidation of the Metropolitan Police at the Macpherson inquiry of 1998.[12] Tompkins Square Park is located in East Village, a racially, ethnically, economically and politically diverse corner of the lower east side of Manhattan. It had been known since the 1960s for its tolerance of a wide variety of lifestyles. But by 1988 the tolerance of the residents around the park was wearing thin as one of the 'lifestyles' stifled the possibility of people pursuing many other lifestyles.

Individual residents, as well as local block associations and community boards, increasingly complained to the police about disorderly groups of men and women who were playing loud music in the park and generally partying from 9 p.m. to 5 a.m. Drugs traffickers were using the park to shield their activities from police observation. Large numbers of the intentionally homeless, as well as the unintentionally homeless and mentally ill, preferred summer residence in the park to the services of the city's Human Services Administration. However carefully private or public owners of property had faced, painted or decorated the walls of their buildings to suit their own tastes within the limits of what was aesthetically acceptable to neighbours and passers-by, individual graffitists decided that every sprayable surface should bear their signature, and take on the appearance they alone dictated. Litter, used condoms, discarded needles and human waste abounded. The police accordingly moved in to enforce the park's ordinances and the 'quality of life'—the general public's quality of life—regulations of the city.

The park's closing hour was 1 a.m. Visitors were required to leave at closing time, though the police made the concession of allowing homeless people to remain in one part of the park. The curfew was strongly supported by local residents and their representative organisations, but opposed over several weeks of discussions and rallies by the park's occupiers. On the night of 6/7 August, however, demonstrators threw bricks, bottles and fireworks at the police. The local police called for the assistance of officers from other precincts, and eventually not only mounted police, but a police helicopter was involved in the incident.

The police on the scene then used their truncheons. The NYPD's own internal report on the riot emphasised that 'extensive broadcasting of film and video taken by the media and private citizens' meant that 'most residents of the city' had witnessed police officers 'striking demonstrators'—and this was 'appalling behaviour', not only in the eyes of the rioters, the news commentators and the private citizens whose video record was broadcast by the television stations citywide, but also in the eyes of senior police officers themselves.[13]

In such circumstances the police, acting on behalf of local residents, businesses and the public, lacked any incentive to attempt to retake public thoroughfares and public places for general use. The public that was not immediately affected by the restrictions on their lives imposed by violence, drug use and the myriad associated public nuisances had been persuaded that drug use was harmless, violence a justified reaction to economic deprivation or racial discrimination, and homelessness always the consequence of society's harshness or indifference.

In Britain as well as the United States influential academic commentators and broadsheet journalists were astonishingly successful in propagating the view—it can still be heard, even today—that crime, violence and public nuisance had not increased at all. These things had been as prevalent or worse in the past, and the ignorant, hysterical and contemptible general public was simply in the grip of one of its periodic bouts of 'moral panic'.[14] As we have argued above, the implication of the moral panic view of crime and disorder was that, as there was no new problem, then obviously nothing new needed to be done to solve it, least of all by the police.

People who could do so abandoned the invaded areas of the city in droves. In mid-town Manhattan, the great shops and theatres languished. Tourists gave the city a wide berth. Potential investors were deterred from considering New York as a destination for their developments. Whole 'projects' (municipal and federal housing estates) were abandoned to drugs and violence.

In the early to mid-1980s apocalyptic projections of existing trends continued to draw a picture of drug-fuelled anarchy on the streets, with young criminals running amok with machine guns, in a city being bled dry by the expense of caring for AIDS victims and babies addicted to crack cocaine.[15]

The peaceable control of the real situation on which these projections were based, on behalf of the people whose 'lifestyles' did not prevent the pursuit of other lifestyles, would have to wait until the culture of 'the victim of society' and 'the rights of the deviant' had shifted in favour of the rights of the law-abiding and the victim of the criminal; and until the NYPD had the sheer numbers to concentrate an overwhelming weight of police officers' bodies in opposition to an unco-operative crowd.

In 1975 there had been 83,000 robberies in New York City. This was already a vast rise on, say, 1955, when the New York robbery figure had been 7,400. By 1981 there were 107,000 robberies. From 1982, police numbers slowly built up again. But the police culture of rushing in powerful cars to the scene of major crime did not weaken. Robberies were cut to some extent, just as they have been cut with the extraordinary and temporary resources of Britain's street crime initiative and London's Operation Safer Streets. But they still numbered 100,000 in 1990, and 86,000 in 1993.[16]

In 1994 Rudolph Giuliani was elected mayor of New York City on the promise that he would deal with crime. Many politicians before him had promised to be tough on crime and the causes of crime, and gained the kudos of being tough (or sustaining the image of being tough), whatever happened to the crime figures themselves. Before 1994, too, there had been much talk of 'citizen-police partnership', 'community policing', 'police problem solving' and so forth.[17] Mayor Giuliani publicly undertook to *reduce* crime by *applying* these strategies, a very different sort of promise. He appointed as his first police commissioner William Bratton, who was fresh from his triumphs in restoring security to the subway as chief of New York's transport police.

Giuliani greatly expanded the size of New York's police force. The 'uniformed headcount' was 28,700 in 1993. By the end of 1994 it was 30,500, and by the year 2000 it was 40,300.[18]

Several functions that in England are performed by the Metropolitan Police, are performed in the United States not by New York's police department, but by the FBI, the CIA or other special agencies. In so far as the sheer number of police officers present on the streets is an element in controlling street crime, this fact simply strengthens the case for more police officers to carry out low-level policing (so long as that is what they are actually used for).

With the larger number of officers at their disposal, Giuliani and Bratton bore down heavily on 'harmless' quality-of-life social nuisances and 'victimless' crimes that had gradually become too trivial for the old beleaguered police to bother about, especially when progressive public opinion insisted that it was quite wrong to bother about them anyway.

The enforcement of the law against minor crimes, non-criminal breaches of the peace and 'quality of life' offences, was achieved by the increased visibility and accessibility of many more officers on foot patrol. 'Enforcement' did not mean rigidity of response. According to the circumstances of the infringement, the police officer's response in policy terms properly ranged from citations and arrests at one extreme to admonitions and reminders at the other.

Getting prostitutes off the streets (much the easiest police job compared with removing drug dealers and users and the homeless, whether mentally ill or not) was the start of the virtuous circle, just as allowing the prostitutes to occupy the streets had been the start of the vicious circle. With the disorderly street-life engendered by street prostitution gone, the drug dealers left. With the prostitutes' clients gone, people who were easy to rob and the cars that were easy to steal left too, and so the robbers left. The streets were once again occupied by people whose interest was in safety and the freedom to go about their own business. Public places were once again occupied by the endless variety of the well behaved, instead of the bleak and threatening monotony of a city's low-life.

Bryant Park was closed for two years. It was reopened as a place that could be enjoyed by thousands of workers and visitors a day, instead of a place where a few tens or hundreds of drug users, drug dealers and homeless people permanently occupied as their own.

The Regents of NYU appealed to the police to free Washington Square Park from gangs, prostitutes and drugs dealers and users. A permanent NYPD command centre was placed in the park, and without its crack and its guns it became available once more for general use by large numbers of students, residents, workers and visitors.

The NYPD's policy from 1994 was a major attempt to take back from criminals, and sub-criminal perpetrators of petty and (in the short run) 'victimless' offences the control of public spaces (and definitions of what is acceptable behaviour in public) and return it to the people who are respectful of the rights of others to a socially peaceable and physically salubrious environment.

The agent of change was the officer on foot patrol, as the member of the community who was clearly authorised and readily available to *take responsibility* for responding decisively to sub-criminal neighbourhood disorder. In some major city-centre locations in New York the police officer had been supplemented by privately uniformed 'public safety officers', even prior to the institution of the Giuliani/Bratton policing régime. With no more authority than any other citizen, they acted solely by being present on the streets as people who would take responsibility for dealing with any crime or other banned activity, in their case by calling in the NYPD foot patrol officers or further police backup.[19]

Away from the glamour of 42nd Street and Broadway, in Harlem's five police precincts there were 6,500 robberies in 1981. This had been reduced to 4,800 by 1990—a reduction of 26 per cent. But the cuts in the numbers of robberies were much greater in the 1990s under the *steady and consistent pressure* of police commissioner Bratton's policies.[20] Robberies dropped from the 4,800 of 1990 to 1,700 in the year 2000 (a cut of 65 per cent). In the most notorious of New York's precincts, Precinct 67 in South Brooklyn, the numbers were cut in the 1990s by almost exactly the same extent—from 2,200 robberies in 1990 to 743 in the year 2000. In the 28 days to 19 October 2002 there were 61 robberies in Precinct 67. In the 28 days to 19 October 2002 there were 33 robberies. In 1990 there were 2,300 cases of murder and manslaughter in New York. In 2001 there were 642.[21]

Figure 14.1 shows the fall in the number of robberies in all of New York's boroughs in the 1990s and into the twenty-first century.

For 30 years the police (not only in New York and the United States) had been increasingly defined—and had thus increasingly come to define themselves—as oppressors of working-class communities. But statistical data have increasingly made evident what common sense had always indicated, that the most victimised part of the community looks most anxiously to the police for protection. The US Criminal Victimisation Survey for 1995 indicated that while 54 per cent of white victims of robbery reported the crime to the police, 60 per cent of black victims did so.[22]

Giuliani and Bratton imposed a system that made it incumbent upon precinct commanders to justify their leadership at police headquarters by

showing results in one thing only—crime reduction. This involved much
more than trivial crime. The sinews of the system were the data collected
for and analysed and presented by computer hardware and software
systems known as Comstat. Police headquarters knew quickly what was
happening in the precincts. Each precinct commander had to be ready to
come to police headquarters at short notice to describe and assess his or her
tactics, and the results that were being obtained in the precinct. Many old
guard precinct commanders were demoted, and many resigned. Many
young officers brought their merits immediately to the attention of the
commissioner in face-to-face meetings, and secured rapid promotion. On
a daily basis precinct commanders were expected by their superior officers
to identify particular outbreaks of robbery or other crimes, and quickly
devise tactics to combat them. Woe betide the commander who did not
spot a problem in his precinct before his superiors at police headquarters
saw it! Woe betide the precinct commander who did not produce effective
strategies for dealing with a crime problem in his precinct! Woe betide the
precinct commander who did not deliver the one thing that now counted,
crime reduction.

Figure 14.1
Police action results in steep reductions in street crime
Robberies, New York boroughs, 1993, 1997 and 2002

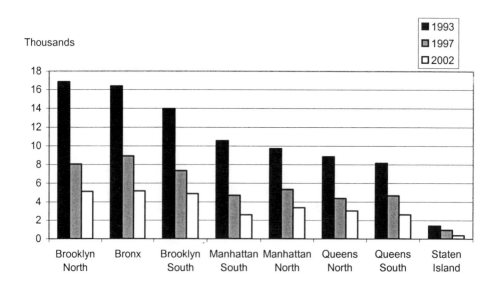

Source: NYPD *CompStat* 10, 42

A third change was in 'multi-agency' work. The political and administrative set-up in New York facilitated the *effective* use of multi-agency approaches to the solution of street-crime problems. Multi-agency work did not mean setting up a talking shop on the Chicago or English model. It meant that if a dark and derelict part of a neighbourhood was being used for drug dealing and drug use, the sanitation department would be instructed to clear the site of abandoned cars and other rubbish. The transportation department would be instructed to fence the site. The site would be strongly lit with vandal-proof lamps. The drug dealers' and drug users' territory would be permanently taken away from them and permanently reoccupied by the city as a salubrious part of the neighbourhood.

The Times Square district, Washington Square Park and Bryant Park provide striking and particularly clear examples of this policy of the permanent reoccupation of neighbourhood territory for pleasant use of the general public, and not just for the use of criminal, intimidating, or other nuisance-creating elements in the city's parks and streets.

The task was prolonged by the success of propaganda that assimilated criminals and public nuisances in public places to the *unintentionally* homeless, and homelessness to a constitutionally protected right to free expression.

In some cases—the heavy-handed aspect of the Giuliani/Bratton policy—to deny criminals a territory from which to operate, the NYPD would close off, to any but the residents and other people authorised by the NYPD, whole blocks of properties identified as being among the most badly affected by intimidatory gangs, by drug dealing and by drug use. The old police tactics had been to arrest dealers—who were immediately replaced by others in the same locality. But intimidatory gangs and drug dealers permanently deprived of their territory did not find it easy to find another place from which to operate, if for no other reason than that it was difficult to encroach on areas already occupied by rivals. Arrests as the criterion of success were now seen to have been as misleading as body counts of Vietcong. No real advantage was gained where either aim was accomplished. What had been essential then in the case of war, was essential now in the case of crime and disorder: to take and hold permanently the enemy's territory.

Whether Mayor Giuliani and Police Commissioner Bratton were right or wrong in what they did, they were not cynically picking easy targets. They were acting on 'broken windows' theory, the common-sense view that 'one thing leads to another'.[23] George Kelling played a prominent role in the formulation and implementation of the Giuliani/Bratton innovations. The catalytic role of unchecked 'trivial' and 'victimless' crimes was emphasised in NYPD's policing after 1993.[24]

George Kelling and W.H. Sousa tested the four most frequently adduced arguments for the decline in crime by the statistical analysis of trends in crime and social conditions in different New York police precincts. The results showed that neither the improvement in the economy (the decline in the rate of unemployment), nor the decline in the use of crack cocaine nor the reduction in the number of young males was significantly associated with the decline in the crime rate in the different precincts. The change significantly associated with crime reduction statistically was the changed activity of the reformed New York police.[25]

The NYPD, helped by the Business Improvement District (BID) 'public safety police', again keeps the peace in Times Square.[26] The Port Authority Bus Terminal is busy, clean and pleasant. Late in the evening, if you ask the way in some formerly notorious neighbourhoods, you will be given the walking directions for several blocks, without any warning or premonition of danger. The new-found safety of New York's streets was an element in its being selected as the American city that should bid to host the Olympic Games.

In the year 2004, New Yorkers talked of the time when Bryant Park and other public spaces were unusable by ordinary people because they were occupied by muggers and dealers in and users of illicit drugs; when a wide area on Eighth Avenue at the Port Authority terminal was avoided for the same reason; and how the threat of being robbed was pervasive, as old, forgotten, far-off things and battles long ago. In such locations only the occasional beggar was to be seen, like the man in Times Square whose placard cheerfully asked for money for drink and drugs, accompanied by the claim that he deserved to be rewarded for his honesty.

The attack on the World Trade Centre (very close to City Hall and police headquarters) had the effect of placing Metropolitan Police-type burdens on the NYPD—guarding bridges, embassies, railway stations and key tourist areas against terrorists. Renewed financial stringency generally —the police can go on short commons—pointed to cuts in the police budget. On the national level, President Clinton's administration had backed 'broken windows' policing by inaugurating an $8 billion prog-ramme to recruit 100,000 locality police officers, the so-called Community Oriented Policing Service (COPS)—a policy that coincided with annual reductions in the crime rate. Surprisingly, the Bush administration cut the programme, halting the decline nationally.[27]

The great increase in the numbers of police officers, the campaigns of low-level policing by foot patrols, Comstat-driven control of precinct commanders and multi-agency problem-solving partnerships (not multi-agency talking shops) resulted in the the robust reoccupation of the streets and residential areas by the forces of law and order. In his second term, therefore, Guiliani was faced with the revival of the élite criticism that had been hegemonic from the mid-1960s to the late 1980s. There was a revival in books and in discussions of the libertarian complaint that disorderly or nuisance elements in New York were being denied by the narrow-minded and uncompassionate respectable majority the scope for self-expression to which they were entitled.[28] Short memories or ignorance of crime and petty disorder in New York from the end of the 1960 to the end of the 1980s meant that zero tolerance seemed burdensome to people who benefited from it. In the 28 days to 19 October 2002 there were 23 robberies in Precinct 25. This had increased to 29 robberies in the 28 days to 19 October 2003. In Harlem's Precinct 26 the increase was 20 to 23. In Harlem's Precinct 28 the increase was from 16 to 23. In Precinct 34 the increase was 19 to 23. Only one of Harlem's precincts showed a continuation of the long reduction in the number of robberies, Precinct 32, where the fall was from 26 to 17.[29]

Figure 14.2
Crimes peak in 1991 and return to level of early 1980s
All Index Crimes, USA, 1983 to 2002

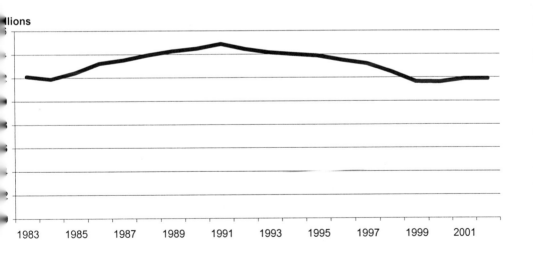

Source: Uniform Crime Reports

Figure 14.3
Robberies peak in 1991 and fall below level of early 1980s
Robberies, USA, 1983 to 2002

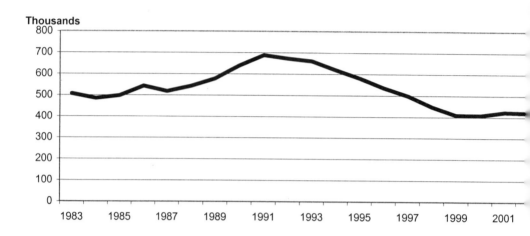

Source: Uniform Crime Reports

John Timoney, from his experience as deputy commissioner in the NYPD, took 'broken-windows' policing, Comstat and the frequent meetings with precinct commanders, and the other features of the Giuliani régime to Philadelphia, and enjoyed the same sort of success in bringing down the crime figures.

One of his main targets was Kensington, a crime-ridden black neighbourhood of Philadelphia. He attacked the 'petty' as well as the 'serious' drug users and dealers who had been increasingly ignored by a demoralised police force that, with the approval of main-stream media, had come to rationalise its self-defined impotence as toleration of what was ethnically 'cultural'.

Police Commissioner Timoney's chief of staff was formerly a Home Office official. In Britain, he said, most police officers still did not think they could do anything about stopping crime going up, much less do anything about bringing crime down. 'No one is blamed when crime goes up, unemployment and race are blamed instead.'[30]

More or less properly understood, and more or less actually applied, all or some aspects of the New York model of 'broken windows' policing appeared in many other places in the United States. In May 2000 Edward

T. Norris, who rose in the NYPD to become director of Compstat and the NYPD'S youngest Deputy Commissioner, was appointed chief of the Baltimore police force. Prior to his appointment, Baltimore was the worst of the 30 largest cities in the United States for murder, violent crime and property crime. In the six months before his arrival, the murder rate was 34 per higher than during the same period a year previously. By applying the full range of the Wilson/Kelling/Bratton/Guiliani policing methods, in the next two years Baltimore achieved the largest percentage falls in these crimes in the United States.

Conclusion

15

Making Up Lost Ground

Crime and disorder lie in the loss column of the profit-and-loss account of the material and cultural changes experienced by the rich and free societies of the West. Crime and disorder are not accidental and disposable aspects of post-1960s society. They are part of the price that has been paid for its advantages. The values of the now hegemonic cultural revolution deplore as a major evil the inculcation of uniform minimum standards of good conduct through parents and other kin, teachers, neighbours, journalists, entertainers and so forth. The notion of the citizen's responsibility to uphold the social order of the small community of his neighbourhood or membership organisation, and the large community of his nation, has been largely transposed from virtue to vice. A good citizen is now much more frequently one who helps ameliorate the consequences that people suffer as a result of the pursuit their own permissive lifestyles. The human right of perpetrators to respect for their private lives has been claimed as grounds for shielding them from public disapprobation.[1]

Post-1960s democratic Germany shared this situation of a decline in self-control deep-seated in the conscience, and in informal community control in all societies, neighbourhoods and organisations. But with the fall of the Iron Curtain in 1989, both parts of Germany received the 'salutary shock' of a sudden leap in crime in a single year. The policing problem was confronted, and crime rates rapidly stabilised at the new higher level. In Germany, public concern about crime, and public dissatisfaction with the performance of the police function, have direct consequences in the loss of votes cast for the ruling party or coalition, with the threat that poses for the leadership's retention of power over a federal state or a federal city-state—the threat of the loss of power as the government of, say, Bavaria or Bremen.

In France, there was a long tradition of tough centralised policing and a long tradition of extreme hostility to the police. The very seriousness of the clash between these two traditions led to crises in the late 1960s and 1970s that resulted in the French confronting early the criminogenic problems of a permissive society.

In the United States, the decline of public order was catastrophic from the 1960s to the early 1990s. From the early 1990s the Unites States confronted the fact that there was a crisis, and dealt with it.

In Britain, the freedom of the police from political control was for many decades of broadly consensual public satisfaction with the state of law and order an ornament to the British system. But mounting dissatisfaction was dismissed as 'populism', 'gutter-press hysteria', 'the exaggerated fear of crime', 'moral panic at a time of historically low crime rates' and so forth. Effective discontent was stifled with the introduction of 'democratic control' by 'police authorities' (weak, even compared with the old local watch committees of the boroughs and the patriarchal lay element in the counties) composed of minor local politicians, 'representatives' of one 'community' or another, and inconspicuous officials sent along from government bureaucracies and voluntary associations to fill the places allocated to them.

England, with its benign history of consensual policing and social order, now suffered through the complacency that it engendered. The rise in crime was steep. But there was no sudden leap that gave ordinary people the confidence to dismiss the prevailing academic and establishment doctrine that crime and disorder were not increasing. It was a welcome relief for the police, overwhelmed by the number of incidents of crime and disorder, to be diverted into the priorities set by groups who had the greatest capacity to damage them publicly, namely, the London pressure groups who protected the new cultural icons.

When and to the extent that all the elements of the New York model are adopted by the police forces of England and Wales, to that extent the problems of crime and disorder in England and Wales will move towards a solution.

As we said at the end of *The Failure of Britain's Police,* Kelling attributed the successes of the NYPD in cutting street crime so early and so dramatically to the NYPD's return to the principles of law enforcement enunciated by Sir Robert Peel as the basis of effective policing. Peel's principles all stemmed from his conviction that 'the basic mission for which the police exist is to prevent crime and disorder' by watch and ward, and that the proper test of police efficiency is 'the absence of crime and disorder, not the visible evidence of police dealing with them'. And the NYPD was able to return to those principles not only because it obtained the *number* of 'constables' that enabled it do so, but also because it changed its own *culture* and, sufficiently, society's culture—the view that the media and the general public took of what the problem was, and what *policing* could do to combat it.[2]

Perhaps it needed a perceptive American to point all this out to us; and for the England that has neglected them, perhaps it is time to relearn the lessons of low-level policing that she taught to world, from the America that is successfully applying them.

Where the laws of a state or rules of an organisation are the product of free discussion and representative government, freedom of choice to all others is afforded by 'the law-abiding citizen' and by the 'rule-respecting participant'. By contrast, within the framework of democratically arrived-at rules, other people's freedom is subjected to arbitrary restriction by those who ignore the rules. Generally, petty blue-collar criminals or other sub-criminal anti-social elements, as well as often major and ignored white-collar criminals, consider that breaking the rules is beneficial or at least satisfying to themselves. Political fanatics and religious fundamentalists break the rules in their self-righteous belief that this is required by their own conception of what is socially just or religiously virtuous.

The immediate effects of their individual petty crimes and major outrages are pernicious enough. But more pernicious still is the erosion of the freedom of the law-abiding citizen that their depredations bring in their train, through the pressure brought upon 'the law-abiding citizen' to give up some of the freedom he has enjoyed in a society of considerate and law-abiding citizens, in order to improve his security against petty criminals who disturb him, or against those whose ambition is his indiscriminate murder, all in their own good cause. Law breakers begin by robbing the law-abiding citizen of his tranquillity, property and bodily safety. They end by robbing him and his children of the benefits of a free society.[3]

Notes

Foreword

1   *Confident Communities in a Secure Britain: the Home Office strategic plan 2004-08*, Cm 6287, London: TSO, July 2004 and http://news.bbc.co.uk/1/hi/uk_politics/3907651.stm dated 19 July 2004.

2   *Confident Communities in a Secure Britain: the Home Office strategic plan 2004-08*, Cm 6287, 2004, p. 44.

3   *Confident Communities in a Secure Britain: the Home Office strategic plan 2004-08*, Cm 6287, 2004, p. 12.

4   *Confident Communities in a Secure Britain: the Home Office strategic plan 2004-08*, Cm 6287, 2004, p. 13.

5   *Confident Communities in a Secure Britain: the Home Office strategic plan 2004-08*, Cm 6287, 2004, p. 20.

6   *Confident Communities in a Secure Britain: the Home Office strategic plan 2004-08*, Cm 6287, 2004, passim.

7   *Confident Communities in a Secure Britain: the Home Office strategic plan 2004-08*, Cm 6287, 2004, p. 106.

8   *Confident Communities in a Secure Britain: the Home Office strategic plan 2004-08*, Cm 6287, 2004, p. 21.

9   *Confident Communities in a Secure Britain: the Home Office strategic plan 2004-08*, Cm 6287, 2004, p. 28.

10   *Confident Communities in a Secure Britain: the Home Office strategic plan 2004-08*, Cm 6287, 2004, p. 31.

11   When a campaign was launched by the Department of Constitutional Affairs to encourage cohabiting couples to make 'Living Together Agreements', the director of the campaign was careful with his disclaimer: 'we are not encouraging people to get married'. *Daily Telegraph*, 15 July 2004, p. 12.

12   Dennis, N., *Rising Crime and the Dismembered Family: how conformist intellectuals have campaigned against common sense*, London: IEA Health and Welfare Unit, 1993, p. xi and pp. xiii and xiv.

13   Dodd, T., Nicholas, S., N., Povey, D. and Walker, A.,*Crime in England and Wales 2003/04*, HOSB 10/04, London: Home Office, July 2004. Table 2.04.

14   *Criminal Statistics England and Wales*, London: HMSO, annually.

15   Dodd, Nicholas, Povey and Walker, *Crime in England and Wales 2003/04*, HOSB 10/04, 2004, p. 33.

16   Dodd, Nicholas, Povey and Walker, *Crime in England and Wales 2003/04*, HOSB 10/04, 2004, p. 33.

17   From 7.34 a.m. 22 July 2004.
http://www.bbc.co.uk/radio4/today/listenagain/thursday.shtml

Preface

1   Radzinowicz, L. and King, J., *The Growth of Crime: the international experience*, Harmondsworth: Penguin, 1979, p. 351.

2   Bell, D., *The End of Ideology*, Free Press: New York, 1962, p. 154.

3   Radzinowicz and King, *The Growth of Crime*, 1979, p. 17.

4   Radzinowicz and King, *The Growth of Crime*, 1979, pp. 16-17.

5   MacIver, R.M. and Page, C.H., *Society: an introductory analysis*, London: Macmillan, 1961, p. 456.

6   Weber, M., 'Politics as a vocation' (1921), in Gerth, H.H. and Mills, C.W. (eds), *From Max Weber: essays in sociology*, London: Routledge and Kegan Paul, 1948, pp. 77-78.

7   Benedict, R., *Patterns of Culture* (1934), New York: Mentor, 1960.

8   Mead, M., *Sex and Temperament in Three Primitive Societies*, London: Routledge, 1935. Mead, M., *Male and Female: a study of the sexes in a changing world* (1950), Harmondsworth: Penguin, 1962. Klein, V., *The Feminine Character: history of an ideology*, London: Routledge and Kegan Paul, 1946.

9   Mead, M., *Coming of Age in Samoa* (1928), Harmondsworth: Penguin, 1943. When critics say that the work Mead or some other anthropologist has been discredited—a convenient excuse for not reading what the author actually says—it is important to ask what aspect of her work has been discredited, and how it affects the evidence for the author's conclusions. Mead's work has not been discredited so far as the points made above are concerned.

10 Benedict, R., *The Chrysanthemum and the Sword: patterns of Japanese culture* (1946), London: Routledge and Kegan Paul, 1977.

11 Weber, M., *The Protestant Ethic and the Spirit of Capitalism*, (1904-05), New York: Charles Scribner, 1958.

12 Gibbon, E., *The Portable Gibbon: The Decline and Fall of the Roman Empire* (1776-1788), Harmondsworth: Penguin, 1977, p. 144.

13 Gibbon, *The Portable Gibbon*, 1977, p. 1.

14 Skinner, A., 'Introduction' to Smith, A., *The Wealth of Nations* (1776), Harmondsworth: Penguin, 1970, pp. 27-28.

15 Saint-Just, 'Institutions Républicaines' (1794), *Œuvres complètes*, Paris: Lebovici, 1984.

16 Skinner, A., 'Introduction' to Smith, *The Wealth of Nations*, 1970, pp. 22-23.

17 Since 1748, Marx and Engels write, modern capitalism—in effect, British capitalism—had 'accomplished wonders far surpassing Egyptian pyramids, Roman aqueducts, and Gothic cathedrals; it has conducted expeditions that put in the shade all former Exoduses of nations and crusades. … Subjection of Nature's forces to machinery, application of chemistry to industry and agriculture, stream-navigation, railways, electric telegraphs, clearing of whole continents for cultivation, canalisation of rivers, whole populations conjured out of the ground—what earlier century had even a presentiment that such productive forces slumbered in the lap of social labour?' Marx, K. and Engels, F., 'Manifesto of the Communist Party' (1848), in Marx, K. and Engels, F., *Selected Works*, Vol. I, Moscow: Foreign Languages Publishing House, 1958, p. 37 and pp. 38-39.

18 Easton, D., *A Systems Analysis of Political Life*, New York: Wiley, 1965.

19 Parsons, T., 'On the concept of influence', *Public Opinion Quarterly*, 27, 1963.

20 Fox, A., *Beyond Contract: work, power and trust relations*, London: Faber and Faber, 1974.

21 'After … labour has become not only the means of life but life's prime want; after the productive forces have also increased with the all-round development of the individual, and all the springs of co-operative development flow more abundantly … ' Marx, K., 'Critique of the Gotha Progamme' (1875), in Marx, K. and Engels, F.,*Selected Works*, vol. II, Moscow: Foreign Languages Publishing House, 1951, p. 23 and p. 31.

1: Political Disorder in England before the 1960s

1 Green, J.R., *A Short History of the English People*, London: Macmillan, 1878, pp. 53-54.

2 Lord Macaulay, 'The Armada'.

3 Wingfield-Stratford, E., *The History of British Civilization*, London: Routledge, 1930, p. 79.

4 Bracton, H. de, *De legibus et consuetudinibus Anglicæ*. Bracton, or Bratton, died in 1268. His work was very popular before the fifteenth century. It was used by Sir Edward Coke at the beginning of the seventeenth century in his constant collisions with the absolutist claims of James I and Charles I. Bracton and Coke were again much referred to with approval in the eighteenth century. Through Coke's *Institutes*, the 1628 Petition of Right that Coke helped to draft, and the writings of John Locke and his eighteenth century followers, the ideas of Bracton and the English defenders of the Common Law passed eventually into the legal and political culture of the United States.

5 Wingfield-Stratford, *The History of British Civilization*, 1930, p. 178.

6 Wingfield-Stratford, *The History of British Civilization*, 1930, pp. 326-27.

7 Burkhardt, J., *Reflections on History* (1905), London: Allen and Unwin, 1943, p. 144.

8 Weber, M., 'Parliament and Government in a reconstructed Germany' (1917), in Weber, M., *Economy and Society*, vol. II, Berkeley: University of California Press, 1978. The version in *Economy and Society* is a revision and enlargement of articles published in the summer of 1917 in the *Frankfurter Zeitung*.

9 Weber, M., 'Politics as a vocation' (1918), in Gerth, H.H. and Mills, C.W.,*From Max Weber: essays in sociology*, London: Routledge and Kegan Paul, 1948, p. 128. Weber used the terms *Gesinnungspolitiker* and *Verantwortungspolitiker*. He did not mean at all that the responsible politician, the *Verantwortungspolitiker*, was an unprincipled politician.

10 Tocqueville, A. de, *Democracy in America* (1835, 1840), New York: New American Library, 1956.

11 Weber, 'Parliament and government in a reconstructed Germany' (1917), in Weber, *Economy and Society*, 1978, p. 1451 and p. 1453.

12 Talmon, J.L., *The Origins of Totalitarian Democracy*, London: Mercury, 1961.

13 Arendt, H., *The Origins of Totalitarianism* (1951), New York: Meridian, 1958, pp. 156-57.

14 Arendt, *The Origins of Totalitarianism*, 1958, p. 155.

15 Thompson, E.P., *The Making of the English Working Class* (1963), London: Gollanz, 1980.

16 Cole, G.D.H. and Postgate, R., *The Common People 1746-1946* (1938), 4th edn, London: Methuen, 1949, p. 226.

17 Trevelyan, G.M., *English Social History: a survey of six centuries Chaucer to Queen Victoria*, London: Longmans, Green, 1944, p. 478.

18 Cole and Postgate, *The Common People 1746-1946* (1938), 1949, pp. 259-60.

19 Briggs, A., *Victorian Cities*, Harmondsworth: Penguin, 1968, p. 149.

20 Engels, F., *The Condition of the Working Class in England in 1844* (1845), London: Allen and Unwin, 1892 (with a Preface by Engels, 1892), pp. 130-32.

21 Marx's account appeared in the *Neue Oder-Zeitung*, 28 June 1855. He says the crowd, which he estimated at 200,000, moved off to Oxford Market, 'ironically crying "God Save the Queen"'.

22 *The History of the T.U.C. 1868-1968: a pictorial history.* London: TUC, 1968, pp. 14 and 19.

23 Dickens, C., *Hard Times* (1854), New York: Bantam, 1964, p. 155.

24 Sombart, W., *Socialism and the Socialist Movement* (1896), London: Dutton, 1909, p. 287.

25 Jones, G.S., *Outcast London*: Oxford: Clarendon Press, 1971, pp. 315-16.

26 Booth, C., *Life and Labour of the People in London: a study of the relationship between the classes in Victorian society*, vol. I, London: 1892, pp. 38-39 and p. 131. Marx had similarly thought 50 years before that this section of society was responsible for counter-productive disorder. 'The "dangerous class", the social scum, that passively rotting mass thrown off by the lowest layers of the old society may, here and there, be swept into the movement by a proletarian revolution. Its conditions of life, however, prepare it far more for the part of the bribed tool of reactionary intrigue.' Marx, K. and Engels, F., 'Manifesto of the Communist Party', in Marx, K. and Engels, F., *Selected Works*, vol. I, Moscow: Foreign Languages Publishing House, 1958, p. 44. Some middle-class Marxists have been distressed by this libel by the master on their beloved underclass see, e.g. Bovenkerk, F., 'The rehabilitation of the rabble: how and why Marx and Engels wrongly depicted the lumpenproletariat', *Netherlands Journal of Sociology*, 20, 1984.

27 Hardie, J.K., 'Measures to solve unemployment' (1904), in Bealey, F. (ed.), *The Social and Political Thought of the British Labour Party*, London: Weidenfeld and Nicolson, 1970, p. 62.

28 Briggs, A., *Victorian People*, Harmondsworth: Penguin, 1965.

29 Roberts, R., *The Classic Slum: Salford life in the first quarter of the century* (1971), Harmondsworth: Penguin, 1973, pp. 100-01.

30 Sorel, G., *Reflections on Violence* (1906), Cambridge: Cambridge University Press, 1999.

31 Arnot, R.P., *The Miners: years of struggle*, London: Allen and Unwin, 1953, pp. 114-16.

32 Roberts, *The Classic Slum: Salford life in the first quarter of the century* (1971), 1973, p. 99.

33 Arendt, H., 'Rosa Luxemburg', *Men in Dark Times*, Harmondsworth: Penguin, 1973, pp. 40-41.

34 *South Shields Volunteer Life Brigade Coast Rescue Unit*, South Shields: VLB, 2001.

35 *South Shields Volunteer Life Brigade Coast Rescue Unit*, South Shields: VLB, 2001.

36 Arnot, R.P., *The Miners: a history of the MFGB 1889-1910*, London: Allen and Unwin, 1949, p. 239.

37 Cole and Postgate, *The Common People 1746-1946* (1938), 1949, p. 422.

38 Cole and Postgate, *The Common People 1746-1946*, (1938), 1949, pp. 564-65.

39 Orwell, G., 'The English People' (1944), in Orwell, S. and Angus, I. (eds), *The Collected Essays, Journalism and Letters of George Orwell*, vol. III, London: Secker and Warburg, 1968, pp. 2-3 and p. 8.

40 Orwell said somewhere that he could never bring himself to dislike Hitler's face. He also said that some German Jewish refugees disliked the liberalism of interwar England, and would have preferred 1930s Germany if it had not been for the anti-

semitism of National Socialism. Either of these remarks is sufficient to make Orwell unquotable in support of any situation he has ever described or point of view he has ever expressed.

41 Smellie, K.B., *The British Way of Life*, London: Heinemann, 1955, pp. 24-25.

42 Cole and Postgate, *The Common People 1746-1946* (1938), 1949, p. 5.

43 Mr Justice McCardie's summing up is in *The Times*, 6 June 1924. The criticisms of him in Parliament are in *Hansard*, 9 June 1924. For an influential contemporaneous English 'left-wing' view of Amritsar see, Laski, H.J., *A Grammar of Politics* (1925), London: Allen and Unwin, 1938, p. 552.

44 Grant, A.J. and Temperley, H., *Europe in the Nineteenth and Twentieth Centuries (1789-1939)*, London: Longmans, Green, 1939, p. 568.

45 On the importance of distinguishing Islamism and Islamists from Islam and Muslims, see Cox, C. and Marks, J., *The 'West', Islam and Islamism: is ideological Islam compatible with liberal democracy?*, London: Civitas, 2002, pp. 5 and 6.

46 'En Algérie, les deux principaux dirigeants du FIS sont libérés après douze années de prison', *Le Monde*, 3 July 2003.

47 Gorer, G., *Exploring English Character*, London: Cresset, 1955, p. 16.

2: Crime in England before the Nineteen-Sixties

1   Engels, F., *The Condition of the Working Class in England in 1844* (1845), London: Allen and Unwin, 1892, pp. 130-32.

2   Mill, J.S., 'On the probable futurity of the labouring classes', *Principles of Political Economy* (1849), Oxford: Oxford University Press, 1994.

3   Mayhew, H., *London Labour and the London Poor; a cyclopædia of the condition and earnings of those that will work, those that cannot work, and those that will not work* (1861-62), London: Frank Cass, 1967.

4   Quennell, P. (ed.), *Mayhew's London: being selections from* London Labour and the London Poor *by Henry Mayhew*, London: Spring Books, no date (c. 1954), pp. 64-65.

5   *Judicial Statistics England and Wales: returns for 1860*, lx, London: HMSO, 1861, p. vii.

6   Quennell, (ed.), *Mayhew's London: being selections from* London Labour and the London Poor *by Henry Mayhew* (c. 1954), p. 38.

7   Quennell, (ed.), *Mayhew's London: being selections from* London Labour and the London Poor *by Henry Mayhew* (c. 1954), p. 36.

8   Quennell, (ed.), *Mayhew's London: being selections from* London Labour and the London Poor *by Henry Mayhew* (c. 1954), p. 45.

9   Quennell, (ed.), *Mayhew's London: being selections from* London Labour and the London Poor *by Henry Mayhew* (c. 1954), p. 43.

10 Quennell, (ed.), *Mayhew's London: being selections from* London Labour and the London Poor *by Henry Mayhew* (c. 1954), pp. 44-45.

11 Quennell, (ed.), *Mayhew's London: being selections from* London Labour and the London Poor *by Henry Mayhew* (c. 1954), p. 38.

12 Quennell, (ed.), *Mayhew's London: being selections from* London Labour and the London Poor *by Henry Mayhew* (c. 1954), pp. 53-54.

NOTES

NOTES 209

13 Quennell, (ed.), *Mayhew's London: being selections from* London Labour and the London Poor *by Henry Mayhew* (c. 1954), p. 52

14 Quennell, (ed.), *Mayhew's London: being selections from* London Labour and the London Poor *by Henry Mayhew* (c. 1954), p. 42.

15 Eliot, G., *Felix Holt the Radical* (1866), London: Panther, 1965, p. 21.

16 Kingsley, C., *Anton Locke: tailor and poet* (1850), London: no date (c. 1892), pp. 18-19.

17 Stevenson, R.L., *Treasure Island* (1883), New York: Bantam Classics, 1981, pp. 7-8.

18 Giffen, R., 'Presidential Address to the Statistical Society 1883', in Abrams, P., *The Origins of British Sociology 1834-1914*, Chicago: Macmillan, 1968.

19 Marshall, A., *Memorials of Alfred Marshall*, (ed. Pigou, A.C.) London: Macmillan, 1925, pp. 105 and 116.

20 Toynbee, A., *Lectures on the Industrial Revolution in England* (1884), Newton Abbot: David and Charles, 1969, p. 147.

21 Webb, B., *My Apprenticeship* (1926), Harmondsworth: Penguin, 1971, pp. 171 and 179.

22 Hobson, J.A., *Work and Wealth: a human valuation*, New York, 1916, pp. 155-56.

23 Engels, 'Preface', *The Condition of the Working Class in England in 1844*, 1892, pp. v-vi.

24 Engels, F., 'Introduction to *Socialism: utopian and scientific*', in Marx, K. and Engels, F., *On Religion*, Moscow: Foreign Languages Publishing House, 1957, p. 306.

25 Booth, C., *Life and Labour of the People in London*, vol. I, London: Williams and Norgate, 1892, p. 158.

26 Booth, *Life and Labour of the People in London*, vol. I, 1892, pp. 177-78.

27 Booth, *Life and Labour of the People in London*, vol. I, 1892, pp. 38-39 and p. 131.

28 *Judicial Statistics England and Wales, 1908, Part I, Criminal Statistics*, Cd. 5096, London: HMSO, 1910, pp. 9 and 11.

29 Home Office, *Criminal Statistics England and Wales 1998*, Cm 4649, London: The Stationery Office, March 2000.

30 McGregor, O.R., Blom-Cooper, L. and Gibson, C., *Separated Spouses*, London: Duckworth, 1970.

31 Marris, P., 'Review of *The Classic Slum*', *British Journal of Sociology*, 23, 1, March 1972.

32 Roberts, R., *The Classic Slum: Salford life in the first quarter of the century* (1971), Harmondsworth: Penguin, 1973, pp. 24-25.

33 Roberts, *The Classic Slum: Salford life in the first quarter of the century* (1971), 1973, p. 53.

34 http://www.met.police.uk/crimestatistic/index.htm

35 Engels, *The Condition of the Working Class in England in 1844* (1845), 1892, pp. 130-32.

36 Lenin, V.I., 'The State and Revolution: the Marxist doctrine of the state and the tasks of the proletariat in the revolution' (1917), in *Lenin: selected works*, vol. II, Moscow: Foreign Languages Publishing House, 1947, p. 203. Emphasis added.

37 'The indictment against Christianity' (1917), Inge, W.R., *Outspoken Essays*, London: Longman, Green, 1921, p. 245.

38 Childers, E., *The Riddle of the Sands* (1903), Ware, Herts: Wordsworth, 1993, p. 13.

39 Her Majesty's Chief Inspector of Constabulary, *Annual Report 2000/01*, HCP 230, London: SO, October 2001.

40 Daley, H., *This Small Cloud: a personal memoir*, London: Weidenfeld and Nicolson, 1986, p. xi.

41 Daley, *This Small Cloud: a personal memoir*, 1986, p. xi. Emphasis in original.

42 Daley, *This Small Cloud: a personal memoir*, 1986, p. 83.

43 Daley, *This Small Cloud: a personal memoir*, 1986, p. 81.

44 Daley, *This Small Cloud: a personal memoir*, 1986, pp. 81-82.

45 Daley, *This Small Cloud: a personal memoir*, 1986, p. 86.

46 Daley, *This Small Cloud: a personal memoir*, 1986, pp.101-02.

47 Daley, *This Small Cloud: a personal memoir*, 1986, p. 167.

48 Dennis, N., Erdos, G. and Robinson, D.,*The Failure of Britain's Police: London and New York compared*, London: Civitas, 2003, pp. 32-33.

49 Simmons, J. and Dodd, T.,*Crime in England and Wales 2002-2003*, HOSB 07/03, London: Home Office, July 2003, unnumbered preliminary page.

3: Conscience and Community Controls in England from the Nineteen-Sixties

1 Green, D.G., Grove, E.M. and Martin, N.A.,*Crime and Civil Society: can we become a more law-abiding people?*, London: Civitas, 2004.

2 The term was made current in sociology by Talcott Parsons. See, for example, Parsons, T., *The Social System*, New York: Free Press, 1951; various essays in Parsons, T.,*Essays in Sociological Theory* (1949), New York: Free Press, 1954; and Parsons, T. and Bales R.F., *Family, Socialisation, and Interaction Process*, London: Routledge and Kegan Paul, 1956. The replacement of Parsonian sociology by various species of Marxian sociology was an important aspect of the transformation of the social sciences in the 1960s.

3 *Orandum est ut sit mens sana in corpore sano.* You should pray for a sound mind in a healthy body. *Satires X.*

4 Dennis, N., *The Uncertain Trumpet: a history of Church of England education to* AD *2001*, London: Civitas, 2001, pp. 78-83.

5 Engels, F., 'Introduction to Socialism: Utopian and Scientific' (1892), in Marx, K. and Engels F., *On Religion*, Moscow: Foreign Languages Publishing House, 1957, p. 306. Emphasis added.

6 Trotsky, L., *Where is Britain Going?* (1925), London: New Park, 1978.

7 Evans, J.E., *Twelve Talks on Christian Citizenship for Leaders of Youth*, London: Christian Social Council, no date, p. 64.

8 Brontë, C.,*Jane Eyre: an autobiography* (1847), Ware: Wordsworth Classics, 1992, Chapter 5. The pupils, some of them 'full grown girls or rather young women', sleep two to a bed. Miss Miller sleeps in the dormitory with them. On the first night Jane, as a new pupil, is undressed by Miss Miller, and is her 'bedfellow'. There is no hint of the possibility of impropriety. In contrast to current inculcated perceptions and morals, inculcated perceptions and morals in Charlotte Brontë's time excluded salaciousness in this context from the mind of both the intention of what the author intended to convey and from the meaning the normal Victorian reader drew from the passage.

9 Adamson, J.W., *English Education 1789-1902*, Cambridge: CUP, 1902, p. 210.

10 National Education Union, *A Verbatim Report of the Debate in Parliament during the Progress of the Education Bill 1870*, Manchester: National Education Union, no date, pp. 5 and 18.

11 Lowndes, G.A.N., *The Silent Social Revolution: an account of the expansion of public education in England and Wales 1895/1935*, London: OUP, 1937, pp. 239-40.

12 Lowndes, *The Silent Social Revolution*, 1937, p. 239.

13 Lowndes, *The Silent Social Revolution*, 1937, p. 239.

14 Glass, D.V., 'Education and social change in modern England', in Halsey, A.H., Floud, J. and Anderson, C.A., *Education, Economy and Society: a reader in the sociology of education*, New York: Free Press, 1961, p. 395.

15 Johnson. P., 'A sense of outrage', in MacKenzie, N. (ed.), *Conviction*, MacGibbon and Kee, 1958.

16 *New Reasoner*, 1960. These were the goals set out in the first editorial.

17 'The trajectory of English social structure—*above all* the non-emergence of a powerful revolutionary movement of the working class—is *the* explanation of this arrested development.' Anderson, P., 'Components of the national culture', *New Left Review*, 1968. Emphasis added.

18 A Group Appointed by the Archbishop of Canterbury, *Putting Asunder: a divorce law for contemporary society*, London: SPCK, 1966.

19 Office for National Statistics, 28 August 2003.

20 Marshall, G. (ed.), *The Concise Oxford Dictionary of Sociology*, Oxford: OUP, 1994, p. 342.

21 Attlee, C.R., 'Socialism' (1908), *Attlee as I Knew Him*, London: London Borough of Tower Hamlets, 1983.

22 General Register Office, *Census 1951 England and Wales: housing report*, London: HMSO, 1956.

23 Office for National Statistics, *Census 2001: national report for England and Wales*, London: TSO, 2003.

24 General Household Survey, *Living in Britain: results from the 2001 GHS*, London: TSO, 2002.

25 Office for National Statistics, *Census 2001: national report for England and Wales*, London: TSO, 2003.

26 *Social Trends*, annually since 1971.

27 *Monthly Digest of Statistics No. 691*, July 2003.

28 *Annual Abstract of Statistics No. 90*, London: HMSO, 1953, Table 110, p. 91.

29 *Report of the Committee on Higher Education Appointed by the Prime Minister* [The Robbins Report], London: HMSO, 1961/63.

30 *Social Trends*, annually since 1971.

31 Department for Education and Skills, *Education and Training Statistics for the United Kingdom*, London: TSO annually from 1997; also available on: http://www.dfes.gov.uk/statistics. The small number of students in Northern Ireland have to be added to the 1951 figures to make the comparison exact.

32 Dennis, N., *The Invention of Permanent Poverty*, London: Civitas, 1997.

33 *British Social Attitudes 1984*. The results are based on 1,675 interviews in Great Britain.

34 City of Sunderland College, *On Course No. 4*, Autumn 2003.

35 City of Sunderland College, 'Policy for equal opportunities (students)', AJ/JW/Equal Op Stud 2. 'Student handbook, student diary and College Charter 2003/2004', September 2003.

36 Black, F., Letters to the Editor, *Sunday Times*, 17 August 2003.

37 *Social Trends*, annually since 1971.

38 Why start with 1951? In 1951 many people who are still alive were already adults then. They are therefore relatively immune to current misrepresentations about English life that, on the one hand, underplay the material hardship and squalor, and, on the other, exaggerate their social and moral failings of those years. It is only when all the pre-1960s generations have passed away that it will at last be possible to claim in full *Nineteen Eighty-Four* style, without being contradicted, that all those strange old tales of England 's low-crime neighbourhoods and safe town centres in the nineteenth and twentieth centuries were fantasies about 'a golden age that never existed'.

It can be made to appear to young people that the poor today are materially and educationally as badly off as their predecessors. There is low resistance to them accepting that view, for it is then 'reasonable' as a victim of injustice and unfairness 'to take action to harm society' (to use the words of the *Sunday Times* correspondent referred to in note 36).

It can be made to appear to them that there was as much or more anti-social behaviour in the residential areas and centres of England 's towns then as now—as much or more crime, as much child abuse, as much or more domestic violence, as much drunkenness. There is low resistance to accepting that view, for it means that the present generation has nothing correct in itself, and nothing to learn from the past.

39 The Archbishop of Canterbury's Commission on Urban Priority Areas, *Faith in the City: a call for action by Church and Nation*, London: Church House Publishing, 1985, p. 37. The least serious, both nationally and in urban priority areas, were problems of 'race and community relations'.

40 The Archbishop of Canterbury's Commission on Urban Priority Areas, *Faith in the City*, 1985, p. 10.

41 Coad, P., 'Crime will always pay under the present system', *Sunday Times*, 17 August 2003.

42 Home Office, *Criminal Statistics England and Wales 1948*, London: HMSO, 1949.

43 Plato, *Republic*, II, 359b-360b.

4: The Idea of Increasing Crime and Disorder Dismissed as Moral Panic and Exaggerated Fears

1 Pearson, G., *Hooligan: a history of respectable fears*, London: Macmillan, 1983, p. 208.

2 Pearson, *Hooligan: a history of respectable fears*, 1983, p. 231.

3 Burford, B., *Among the Thugs*, London: Secker and Warburg, 1991.

4 Pearson, *Hooligan: a history of respectable fears*, 1983. There are many references to disorder among spectators and lack of sportsmanship on the field of play throughout the book.

5 Pearson, *Hooligan: a history of respectable fears*, 1983, p. 131.

6   The Security from Violence Act 1863. Davis, J., 'The London garrotting panic of 1862', in Gatrell, V.A.C., Lenman, B. and Parker, G. (eds),*Crime and the Law*, London: Europa, 1980, p. 191. Cited in Pearson, *Hooligan: a history of respectable fears*, 1983, p. 144.

7   *The Times*, 10 June 1863.

8   *The Times*, 14 November 1856.

9   *Hansard*, 30 June 1933.

10   Pearson, *Hooligan: a history of respectable fears*, 1983, p. 35. Pearson takes his three 'brute facts' from *Reynold's News*, 1 November 1931, 17 November 1935 and 20 December 1936.

11   Pearson, *Hooligan: a history of respectable fears*, 1983, p. 35.

12   Home Office, *Criminal Statistics England and Wales 1928*, London: HMSO, 1930, p. xiv.

13   http://www.met.police.uk/crimestatistics/index.htm

14   Cohen, S., *Folk Devils and Moral Panics*, London: Macgibbon and Kee, 1972. Cohen, S. and Young, J., *The Manufacture of News: deviance, social problems and the mass media*, London: Constable, 1973. Cohen, S. (ed.),*Images of Deviance*, Harmondsworth: Penguin, 1976. Pearson, *Hooligan: a history of respectable fears*, 1983.

15   Kershaw, C., Budd, T., Kinshott, G., Mattinson, J., Mayhew, P. and Myhill, A.,*The 2000 British Crime Survey England and Wales*, London: Home Office, October 2000.

16   Simmons, J. and Dodd, T.,*Crime in England and Wales 2002/2003*, HOSB 07/03, London: Home Office, July 2003, p. 134.

17   http://www.met.police.uk/crimestatistics/index.htm

18   *Information on the Criminal Justice System*, Digest 4, London: Home Office, no date. http://www.homeoffice.gov.uk.rds.digest41.htm

19   Povey, D., Ellis, C. and Nicholas, S.,*Crime in England and Wales: quarterly update 12 months to September 2002*, HOSB, 02/03, London: Home Office, January 2003.

20   Povey, D., Nicholas, S. and Salisbury, H.,*Crime in England and Wales: quarterly update to December 2002*, HOSB 05/03, London: Home Office, April 2003, p. 1. (Emphasis added.)

21   Simmons and Dodd, *Crime in England and Wales 2002/2003*, HOSB 07/03, July 2003, summary page, p. 3 and p. 26.

22   http://www.crimereduction.gov.uk/statistics28.htm

23   Home Office, *Respect and Responsibility: taking a stand against anti-social behaviour*, Cm 5778, London: TSO, March 2003, p. 7. (Emphasis added.)

24   Simmons and Dodd, *Crime in England and Wales 2002/2003*, HOSB 07/03, July 2003, p. 82.

25   The robbery statistics were very little affected by the recording changes introduced in April 1998. Changes in recording rules introduced by all forces not later than April 2002 affected the police-recorded figures on robbery by raising the figure by three per cent (as contrasted with a 25 per cent effect on violence against the person, and 10 per cent overall). The 14 per cent fall in 2002/2003 is the figure that removes the 'artificial' three per cent rise attributable to the new counting rules of the National Crime Recording Standard. Simmons and Dodd,*Crime in England and Wales 2002/2003*, HOSB 07/03, July 2003, pp. 35 and 75.

26   Kershaw, C., Chivite-Matthews, N., Thomas, C. and Aust, R.,*The 2001 British Crime Survey: first results England and Wales*, London: Home Office, October 2001.

27 The raw figure for the year ending March 2003 was 5.9 million. From this must be subtracted 627,000 extra crimes added as a result of the rule changes introduced on 1 April 1998. (For a discussion of the way in which this change affected the series see Home Office Statistical Bulletin 18/99, London: Home Office, October 1999.) Also to be subtracted are 490,000 crimes attributable to the rule changes of the ACPO National Crime Recording Standard, that had to be adopted by all police forces from 1 April 2002. (The impact of introducing the National Crime Recording Standard was assessed in Povey, D. and Prime, J., *Recorded Crime Statistics: England and Wales April 1998 to March 2001*, HOSB 12/01, London: Home Office, 1999 and Simmons, J., *An Initial Analysis of Police Recorded Crime Data to End of March 2001 to Establish the Effects of the Introduction of the ACPO NCRS*, London: Home Office, 2001.) These two adjustments give a figure for the year ending March 2003 of 4.8 million.

28 Home Office, *Respect and Responsibility: taking a stand against anti-social behaviour*, Cm 5778, London: TSO, March 2003, p. 7.

29 Simmons and Dodd, *Crime in England and Wales 2002/2003*, HOSB 07/03, July 2003, p. 3.

30 Kershaw *et al.*, *The 2000 British Crime Survey*, HOSB 18/00, October 2000, p. 61, note 5.

31 Population aged 16 and older in private households in 1981: *Census 1981: national report for Great Britain*, London: HMSO, 1983. Population aged 16 and older in households in 2001: *Census 2001: national report for England and Wales*, London: TSO, 2002. Mid-year estimates of resident population aged 16 and older:
www.statistics.gov.uk/statbase/Expodata/spreadsheets/D6548.xls.
www.statistics.gov.uk/statbase/Expodata/spreadsheets/D7024.xls.
HOSB 18/00, Table A2.8, p. 67, gives the 1981 victimisation figure as 27.7 per cent. At least part of the difference between this victimisation rate of 27.7 per cent and our two possible victimisation rates for 2002/03, 29.3 per cent using the 2001 Census, and 30.3 per cent using the 2002 midyear estimates, is due to an adjustment of the raw figures by the Home Office. The raw figures of the household and personal crimes in 2002/03 had been subjected by the Home Office to 'calibration weighting' using an algorithm called CALMAR (and the raw figures back to 1996 but not the 1981 figures had been similarly recalibrated) to take into account the known differentials of response rates of different age and gender subgroups and of different household types. Simmons and Dodd, *Crime in England and Wales 2002-2003*, HOSB 07/03, Office, July 2003, p. 157.

32 Smith J., *The Nature of Personal Robbery*, HORS 254, London: Home Office, 2003.

33 Harrington, V. and Mayhew, P., *Mobile Phone Theft*, HORS 235, London: Home Office, January 2001.

34 Ainsworth, B., reported on Ananova, aol.com news pages, 6 April 2003.

35 Kershaw *et al.*, *The 2001 British Crime Survey*, HOSB 18/01, October 2001.

36 Mirlees-Black, C., Budd, T., Partridge, S. and Mayhew, P., *The 1998 British Crime Survey England and Wales*, 21/98, London: Government Statistical Service, 1998.

37 Simmons and Dodd, *Crime in England and Wales 2002/2003*, HOSB 07/03, July 2003, p. 18.

38 Simmons and Dodd, *Crime in England and Wales 2002/2003*, HOSB 07/03, July 2003, p. 23.

39 Simmons and Dodd, *Crime in England and Wales 2002/2003*, HOSB 07/03, July 2003, pp. 23 and 86.

40 Simmons, J. *et al.*, *Crime in England and Wales 2001/2002*, HOSB 07/02, London: Home Office, July 2002.

41 *Social Trends No. 32,* London, TSO, 2002, Table 9.10, p. 155.

42 Simmons *et al., Crime in England and Wales 2001/2002,* HOSB 07/02, July 2002.

43 Simmons *et al., Crime in England and Wales 2001/2002,* HOSB 07/02, July 2002.

44 Simmons *et al., Crime in England and Wales 2001/2002,* HOSB 07/02, July 2002,
    pp. 81 and 83. In 2001/2002, in addition to the 15 per cent who were 'very worried'
    about being mugged, another 26 per cent were 'fairly worried'. The proportion who
    were 'very worried about being mugged' was, of course, lower than the proportion
    who thought that it was 'very likely that they would be mugged in the following
    twelve months'. Two per cent thought it was 'very likely that they would be mugged
    in the following twelve months', and another 13 per cent thought it was 'fairly likely'.

45 Simmons *et al., Crime in England and Wales 2001/2002,* HOSB 07/02, July 2002.

46 Simmons *et al., Crime in England and Wales 2001/2002,* HOSB 07/02, July 2002. Povey,
    Nicholas and Salisbury, *Crime in England and Wales: quarterly update to December 2002,*
    HOSB 05/03, April 2003.

5: Police Powers and Numbers in Response to Rising Disorder and Crime

1   *Royal Commission on the Police 1960: interim report,* Cmnd. 1222, London: HMSO,
    November 1960, p. 17.

2   *Report of Her Majesty's Inspectors of Constabulary,* H.C. 1959-60 257, London: HMSO, July
    1960. *Royal Commission on the Police 1960: interim report,* Cmnd. 1222, 1960, p. 17.

3   *Royal Commission on the Police 1960: interim report,* Cmnd. 1222, 1960, p. 17.

4   *Royal Commission on the Police 1960: interim report,* Cmnd. 1222, 1960, p. 18.

5   *Royal Commission on the Police 1960: interim report,* Cmnd. 1222, 1960, p. 19.

6   *Royal Commission on the Police 1960: interim report,* Cmnd. 1222, 1960, p. 19.

7   *Royal Commission on the Police 1960: interim report,* Cmnd. 1222, 1960, p. 18.

8   *Annual Abstract of Statistics 100,* London: HMSO, 1963. *Annual Abstract of Statistics 120,*
    London: HMSO, 1984. The figures are for the police strength. The authorised establish-
    ment figures were 80,000 in 1960 and 117,000 in 1977. In 1884 there had been 35,000
    officers in total, and they had had to deal not with two million crimes, but with 92,000.

9   *The Red Lion Square Disorders of 15 June 1974* (Chief Justice Scarman), Cmnd. 5919,
    London: HMSO, February 1975.

10 Clutterbuck, R., *Britain in Agony: the growth of political violence,* Harmondsworth:
    Penguin, 1980.

11 *Report of the Royal Commission on Criminal Procedure,* Cmnd. 8092, London: HMSO, 1981,
    and *Report of the Royal Commission on Criminal Procedure: the investigation and prosecution
    of criminal offences in England and Wales,* Cmnd. 8092-1, London: HMSO, 1981.

12 *Report of an Inquiry into the Brixton Disorder 10-12 April 1981,* Cmnd 8427, London:
    HMSO, November 1981. Scarman said: 'The direction and policies of the Metropolitan
    police are not racist. I totally and unequivocally reject the attack made upon the
    integrity and impartiality of the senior direction of the force', para. 4.62. Scarman
    recognised that racial prejudice did manifest itself 'occasionally' in the behaviour of 'a
    few officers in the street', para. 4.63. By contrast, Macpherson reported that 'we have
    not heard evidence of overt racism or discrimination, unless it can be said that the use
    of inappropriate expressions such as "coloured" or "negro" fall into this category ... a
    number of officers used such terms, as some did not even during their evidence seem

CULTURES AND CRIMES

to understand that the terms were offensive and should not be used'. *The Stephen Lawrence Inquiry*, Cm 4262, London: TSO, February 1999. p. 20.

13 *Report of an Inquiry into the Brixton Disorder 10-12 April 1981*, Cmnd 8427, 1981, para. 4.76.

14 Carole Willis studied the stop-and-search records of four police stations. She found that the annual stop rates for blacks was 'markedly higher' than for that the general population. Willis, C., *The Use, Effectiveness and Impact of Police Stop and Search Powers*, Home Office Research and Planning Unit Paper No. 15, London: HMSO, 1983, p. 14.

15 Bourn, C., 'The police, the Acts and the public', in Benyon, J. and Bourn, C. (eds),*The Police: powers, procedures and proprieties*, Oxford: Pergamon, 1986, p. 281.

16 Bourn, 'The police, the Acts and the public', in Benyon and Bourn (eds),*The Police: powers, procedures and proprieties*, 1986, p. 283.

17 Buck, M., 'Questioning the suspect', in Benyon and Bourn (eds),*The Police: powers, procedures and proprieties*, 1986, p. 160. Maurice Buck represented the Association of Chief Police Officers in consultations with the government about the Police and Criminal Evidence Bill. He was Deputy Commandant of the Police Staff College at Bramshill before his appointment as Chief Constable of Northamptonshire.

18 Softley, P., *Police Interrogation: an observational study in four police stations*, Royal Commission on Criminal Procedure Research Study No. 4, London: HMSO, 1980. Barnes, J.A. and Webster, N., *Police Interrogation: tape recording*, Royal Commission on Criminal Procedure Research Study No. 8, London: HMSO, 1980.

19 *Report of the Royal Commission on Criminal Procedure*, Cmnd 8092, 1981, pp. 52-53.

20 An arrestable offence is one that could be the subject of a sentence of five years or longer. Under section 25 of PACE a constable could make an arrest for an otherwise non-arrestable offence if certain 'general arrest conditions' are satisfied. The general arrest conditions were satisfied if the name of the person was unknown, or could not be readily ascertained, or the constable had reasonable grounds for doubting that either the name or the address was correct; if the person was causing physical injury to himself or others; or damaging property; or committing an offence against public decency; or causing an unlawful obstruction of the highway; or if an arrest was necessary to protect a child or vulnerable person.

21 Buck, 'Questioning the suspect', in Benyon and Bourn (eds), *The Police: powers, procedures and proprieties*, p. 158.

22 *Report of the Royal Commission on Criminal Procedure*, Cmnd 8092, 1981, pp. 97-98.

23 Under the stringent conditions of section 58 of PACE, a superintendent or an officer of higher rank could delay access for up to 36 hours.

24 The Supreme Court judgement in the case of *Mapp v Ohio*. This extended the rule that already applied in Federal courts to state courts.

25 Monroe, D.G. and Garrett, E.W., *Police Conditions in the United States: report to the National Commission on Law Observance and Enforcement*, Washington, DC: GPO, 1931.

26 *Kuruma son of Kiniu* [1955] 1 All ER 236—Lord Chief Justice Goddard. *Callis v Gunn* [1963] 3 All ER 677—Lord Chief Justice Parker. *Jeffery v Black* [1978] 1 All ER 555—Lord Chief Justice Widgery.

27 A farmer named Tony Martin lived in a farmhouse near the village of Emneth Hungate in the Norfolk fens, far from police assistance. He was imprisoned for the murder in April 2000 (reduced to manslaughter on appeal in October 2001) for killing one burglar, Fred Barras, and wounding another, Brendan Fearon, in August 1999. The burglar he

wounded sued the farmer for damages from the cell where he was imprisoned on yet another occasion for yet other crimes in his criminal career. The burglar was entitled to legal aid to prosecute his claim; the farmer was not entitled to legal aid to defend himself. Amid reports that associates of the dead burglar had put a price of £60,000 on the farmer's head, the Norfolk police said that they would advise the farmer on burglar alarms and other security devices. His MP said that there would not be around the clock policing, but that there would be a 'fairly constant' police presence in the 'early weeks' after his release in July 2003. *Daily Express*, 8 July 2003.

28 JUSTICE was founded about 1956. It objective is 'the maintenance of the liberties of the subject and the highest standards of the administration of justice in those territories for which the Westminster Parliament is directly responsible'. 'The two most important liberties of the ordinary citizen, namely, to be free from people who want to hit him over the head or steal from him, and the *equally* important liberty not to be unnecessarily harassed by the police.' Siegart, P., 'Reliable evidence, fairly obtained', in Benyon and Bourn (eds), *The Police: powers, procedures and proprieties*, 1986. p. 277. Emphasis added. This formulation puts protection from the police officer and protection from criminal at exactly the same level of importance.

29 *The PACE Briefing Guide*, London: Home Office, 1983, para. 11.10.

30 Siegart, 'Reliable evidence, fairly obtained', in Benyon and Bourn (eds), *The Police: powers, procedures and proprieties*, 1986. pp. 274-75.

31 Police Numbers Task Force, *Report and Recommendations*, London: Home Office, December 2001. In addition to what people normally think of as 'the police'— the Home Office police, those covered by the 1996 Act—there are about 21 other 'bodies of people attested as constables'. Even the Home Office does not know exactly how many such police forces there are. The Police Numbers Task Force give the numbers of the largest non-Home Office forces as 3,800 for the Ministry of Defence police and 2,073 for the British Transport police. In addition they enumerated the UK Atomic Energy Authority Constabulary (500) and the Royal Parks police (155), Smaller police forces are responsible for various borough parks in the London area, various ports, tunnels and airports, and the universities of Oxford and Cambridge. (Annex F.) The armed forces have their own 'police' forces, but they are not 'constables'.

32 Her Majesty's Chief Inspector of Constabulary, *Annual Report 2001/02*, London: TSO, December 2002, p. 5.

6: Failure of Prevention is Followed by Failure of Detection—and Failure in Confidence in the Police and Criminal Justice System

1 *Report of the Royal Commission on Police Powers and Procedure*, Cmd 3297, London: HMSO, 1929.

2 Reith, C., *A New Study of Police History*, London: Oliver and Boyd, 1956, Appendix.

3 Simmons, J. and Dodd, T. (eds), *Crime in England and Wales 2002/2003*, HOSB 07/03, London: Home Office, July 2003, p. 110.

4 Simmons and Dodd (eds), *Crime in England and Wales 2002/2003*, HOSB 07/03, July 2003, p. 118.

5 Pike, M.S., *The Principles of Policing*, London: Macmillan, 1985, p. 185.

6 Simmons and Dodd, (eds.), *Crime in England and Wales 2002/2003*, HOSB 07/03, July 2003, p. 120.

7 Simmons and Dodd, (eds.), *Crime in England and Wales 2002/2003*, HOSB 07/03, July 2003, pp. 110-11.

8   Simmons and Dodd, (eds.), *Crime in England and Wales 2002/2003*, HOSB 07/03, July 2003, p. 109.

9   Jowell, R. and Airey, C. (eds), *British Social Attitudes: the 1984 report*, Aldershot: BSA, 1983.

10 Sims, L., 'Policing and the public', in Flood-Page, C. and Taylor, J. (eds),*Crime in England and Wales 2001/2002: supplementary volume*, HORB 01/03, London: Home Office, January 2003, p. 108.

11 Sims, 'Policing and the public', in Flood-Page and Taylor,*Crime in England and Wales 2001/2002: supplementary volume*, HORB 01/03, January 2003, p. 105.

12 Sims, 'Policing and the public', in Flood-Page and Taylor,*Crime in England and Wales 2001/2002: supplementary volume*, HORB 01/03, January 2003, p. 110 and p. 117.

13 Simmons and Dodd (eds), *Crime in England and Wales 2002/2003*, HOSB 07/03, July 2003, p. 130.

14 Sims, 'Policing and the public', in Flood-Page and Taylor,*Crime in England and Wales 2001/2002: supplementary volume*, HORB 01/03, January 2003, p. 110 and p. 117.

15 Sims, 'Policing and the public', in Flood-Page and Taylor,*Crime in England and Wales 2001/2002: supplementary volume*, HORB 01/03, January 2003, p. 118.

16 Whitehead E. and Taylor, J., 'Confidence in the criminal justice system', in Flood-Page and Taylor, *Crime in England and Wales 2001/2002: supplementary volume*, HOSB 01/03, 2003, p. 123. See also, Mirrlees-Black, C., *Confidence in the Criminal Justice System: findings from the 2000 British Crime Survey*, Research Findings 137, London: Home Office, 2001; Mattinson, J. and Mirrlees-Black, C.,*Attitudes to Crime and Justice: findings from the 1998 British Crime Survey*, HORS 200, London: Home Office, 2000.

17 Yougov poll, *Daily Telegraph*, 23 September 2003.

18 Simmons and Dodd, *Crime in England and Wales 2002/2003*, HOSB 07/03, July 2003, p. 130. The figures for the black and Asian respondents refer to the calendar year 2002—see Povey, D., Nicholas, S. and Salisbury, H., *Crime in England and Wales: quarterly update to December 2002*, HOSB 05/03, London: Home Office, April 2003.

19 Whitehead and Taylor, 'Confidence in the criminal justice system', in Flood-Page and Taylor, *Crime in England and Wales 2001/2002: supplementary volume*, HOSB 01/03, 2003, p. 122.

7: The Historical Roots of German Policing

1   Voltaire, *Lettres philosophiques*.

2   *Wenn alle untreu werden,*
    So bleiben wir doch treu,
    Daß Dankbarkeit auf Erden
    Nicht ausgestorben sei.
    Wir wollen stets uns halten
    Zu Thron und zu Altar,
    Woll'n treu sein wie die Alten
    In Sturm und in Gefahr.

3   Schmidt, P., *Die koenigliche Schutzmannschaft zu Berlin von 1898 bis 1908: als Nachtrag zur Geschichte des Korps aus Anlaß der 60jährigen Bestehens*, Berlin: Mittler, 1908, p. 7.

4   Schmidt, *Die koenigliche Schutzmannschaft zu Berlin von 1898 bis 1908: als Nachtrag zur Geschichte des Korps aus Anlaß der 60jährigen Bestehens*, 1908.

5   Röhl, J.C.G., '«Wehe, wenn ich zu befehlen haben werde!»—Kaiser Wilhelm II', in
    Studt, C. (ed.), *Die Deutschen im 20. Jahrhundert: ein historisches Lesebuch*, München:
    Beck, 1999, p. 19.

6   Röhl, '«Wehe, wenn ich zu befehlen haben werde!»—Kaiser Wilhelm II', in Studt,*Die
    Deutschen im 20. Jahrhundert: ein historisches Lesebuch*, 1999, p. 19.

7   Röhl, '«Wehe, wenn ich zu befehlen haben werde!»—Kaiser Wilhelm II', in Studt,*Die
    Deutschen im 20. Jahrhundert: ein historisches Lesebuch*, 1999, p. 20. William II had no
    direct experience of the 'year of revolutions', 1848. He was born on 27 January 1849.

8   Hundold, T., *Die Polizei in der Reform: was Staatsbürger und Polizei voneinander erwarten
    könnten*, Düsseldorf: Econ Verlag, 1968, p. 22.

9   Hundold, *Die Polizei in der Reform*, 1968, p. 19.

10 Hundold, *Die Polizei in der Reform*, 1968, p. 19.

11 *Gab dem obrigkeitlichen Denken noch sehr viel Spielraum, den Untertan bis hin zur Pflege, ans
    Gängelband zu nehmen.* Hundold, *Die Polizei in der Reform*, 1968, p. 21.

12 Hundold, *Die Polizei in der Reform*, 1968, pp. 21-22.

13 Hundold, *Die Polizei in der Reform*, 1968, p. 28. Emphasis added.

8: The Culture of Totalitarian Law and Order and Policing in East Berlin and East Germany

1   *Polizeiliche Kriminalstatistik Berlin 1990*, Berlin: Polizeipräsident in Berlin, no date, p. 2.

2   *Jahresbericht*, Berlin: Landeskriminalsamt Berlin, Landeskriminalamt, annually.
    Polizeiliche Kriminalstatistik, Berlin: Landeskriminalamt, annually. *Statistisches Jahrbuch
    der Deutschen Demokratischen Republik*, Berlin: VEB Deutscher Zentral Verlag, later
    Rudolf Haufe Verlag. Annually from 1955 to 1990.

3   *Statistisches Jahrbuch der Deutschen Demokratischen Republik*, Berlin: VEB Deutscher
    Zentral Verlag, later Rudolf Haufe Verlag. Annually from 1955 to 1990.

4   *Jahresbericht 1965*, Berlin: Landeskriminalsamt Berlin, no date. Annually until 1966.
    Kriminalität in Berlin, Berlin: Landeskriminalsamt Berlin, no date. Annually until 1985
    Polizeiliche Kriminalstatistik Berlin, Berlin: Landeskriminalsamt Berlin, no date. Annually
    from 1986.

5   *Kriminalität in Berlin*, Berlin: Landeskriminalsamt Berlin, no date. Annually until 1985
    Polizeiliche Kriminalstatistik Berlin, Berlin: Landeskriminalsamt Berlin, no date. Annually
    from 1986.

6   *Kriminalität in Berlin*, Berlin: Landeskriminalsamt Berlin, no date. Annually until 1985
    Polizeiliche Kriminalstatistik Berlin, Berlin: Landeskriminalsamt Berlin, no date. Annually
    from 1986.

7   *Kriminalität in Berlin*, Berlin: Landeskriminalsamt Berlin, no date. Annually until 1985
    Polizeiliche Kriminalstatistik Berlin, Berlin: Landeskriminalsamt Berlin, no date. Annually
    from 1986.

8   The Deutsche Volkspolizei were known as the DV, pronounced 'day-fow'.

9   Nawrocki, J. and Rexin, M., *Ostberlin: eine Politografie*, Berlin: Landeszentral für
    politische Bildungsarbeit and Presse- und Informationsamt des Landes Berlin, 1975,
    p. 13.

10 The main Police Act for the last 20 years of the East German régime was the 'VP Gesetz', the *Gesetz über die Aufgaben und Befugnisse der Deutschen Volkspolizei*, 11 June 1968.

11 Meiniger, H., Fechter, B. and Heyser, D., *Volkspolizei und freiwilliger Helfer*, Berlin: Staatsverlag der DDR, 1988.

12 Meiniger, Fechter and Heyser, *Volkspolizei und freiwilliger Helfer*, 1988, p. 9.

13 Meiniger, Fechter and Heyser, *Volkspolizei und freiwilliger Helfer*, 1988, pp. 10-11.

14 Meiniger, Fechter and Heyser, *Volkspolizei und freiwilliger Helfer*, 1988, p. 10.

15 Meiniger, Fechter and Heyser, *Volkspolizei und freiwilliger Helfer*, 1988, p. 9.

16 Saint-Just, 'Rapport sur la nécessité de declaré le gouvernement révolutionaire jusqu'á la paix', speech to the Convention, 10 October 1793.

17 Paczkowski, A., *Terror und Überwachung: die Function des Sicherheitsdienstes im kommunistisichen System in Polen von 1944 bis 1956*, Berlin: Unterlagen des Stasi der ehemaligen DDR, 1999, p. 3.

18 Meiniger, Fechter and Heyser, *Volkspolizei und freiwilliger Helfer*, 1988, p. 7.

19 *Verordnung über die freiwilligen Helfer der Deutschen Volkspolizei vom 1. April 1982.*

20 Surkau, W., *Die Aufgaben der Deutschen Volkspolizei bei der Gewährleistung von Ordnung, Sauberkeit und Hygiene in den Städten, Gemeinden und Erholungsgebieten*, Berlin: Ministerium der Innern, April 1979. The author, Prof dr sc Wolfgang Surkau, was a lieutenant in the Volkspolizei.

21 Surkau, *Die Aufgaben der Deutschen Volkspolizei*, 1979, pp. 8-9.

22 *Die weiteren Aufgaben der politischen Massenarbeit der Partei: Beschluß des Politbüros des Zentralkomitees der DDR*, Berlin: Dietz, 1977, p. 75.

23 «*In die Revieren sind mehrere Abschittsbevollmächtige in Offiziersrang tätig, die gemeinsam mit freiwilligem Helfern der VP nicht nur die Achtung der Gesetze, sondern auch die politische und moralische Entwicklung in den Wohngebieten überwachen.*» Nawrocki and Rexin, *Ostberlin: eine Politografie*, 1975, p. 12.

24 *Die Augaben der Deutschen Volkspolizei ... zur Festigung und weiter Entwicklung des Rechtsbewußtseins der Werktätigen*, Berlin: Ministerium der Innern, 1979. With a foreword by Professor Dr Habil Rödszus (a colonel in the People's Police).

25 *Die Augaben der Deutschen Volkspolizei ... zur Festigung und weiter Entwicklung des Rechtsbewußtseins der Werktätigen*, 1979, p. 11.

26 *Die Augaben der Deutschen Volkspolizei ... zur Festigung und weiter Entwicklung des Rechtsbewußtseins der Werktätigen*, 1979, p. 13.

27 *Die Augaben der Deutschen Volkspolizei ... zur Festigung und weiter Entwicklung des Rechtsbewußtseins der Werktätigen*, 1979, p. 12.

28 *Statistisches Jahrbuch der Stadt Berlin 34. Jahrgang*, Berlin: Stankiewicz, 1920.

29 Childers, E., *The Riddle of the Sands* (1903), Ware, Herts: Wordsworth, 1993, p. 123.

30 Schmidt, P., *Die königliche Schutzmannschaft zu Berlin von 1898 bis 1908*, Berlin: Mittler, 1908.

31 Meiniger, Fechter and Heyser, *Volkspolizei und freiwilliger Helfer*, 1988, pp. 7 and 9.

32 Diemer, G. and Kuhrt, E., *Kurze Chronik der Deutschen Frage*, München: Olzog, 1994, p. 238.

33 Glaeser, A., *Divided in Unity: identity, Germany and the Berlin police*, Chicago: University
    of Chicago Press, 2000.

9: The Culture of Policing by Consent in West Germany and West Berlin

1   Hundold, T., *Die Polizei in der Reform: was Staatsbürger und Polizei voneinander erwarten
    könnten*, Düsseldorf: Econ Verlag, 1968, pp. 43-44.

2   No particular terminology is used here when referring to East Germany and East Berlin
    and West Germany and West Berlin. In Germany itself their own terms were carefully
    used by East and West. The communist East used the acronyms DDR as its own desc-
    ription (*Deutsche Democratische Republik*) and BRD for West Germany (*Bundesrepublik
    Deutschlands*). In West Germany the acronym BRD was banned from official use. The
    name had either to be spelled out fully, or shortened to *Bundesrepublik*. East Germany
    was referred to as the DDR, often in quotation marks to disparage the claim that it was
    democratic. The East Germans first called Berlin 'Greater Berlin, democratic sector' and
    then 'Capital City Berlin'. They referred to West Berlin as 'Westberlin'. 'Westberlin'
    was considered an affront by West Germans, who referred to West Berlin as 'Berlin',
    or when clarity required it, 'West-Berlin' or 'Berlin (West)'. East Berlin was one of the
    15 'regions' (*Bezirke*) of East Germany, and was itself divided into regions. The other 14
    regions were divided into 'districts' (*Kreise*).

3   Hundold, *Die Polizei in der Reform*, 1968, p. 43. Emphasis in original.

4   Wolff, R.P., Moore, B. and Marcuse, H., *A Critique of Pure Tolerance*, Boston: Beacon
    Press, 1969.

5   Hundold, *Die Polizei in der Reform*, 1968, pp. 110-12.

10: Crime and Policing in a Reunited Berlin

1   Glaeser, A., *Divided in Unity: identity, Germany and the Berlin police*, Chicago: University
    of Chicago Press, 2000, p. 97.

2   Glaeser, *Divided in Unity*, 2000, p. 92.

3   The other two departments were Administration and Police Training. Until 2000, when
    it was wound up, there was also the federal-wide *Zentrale Polizeiliche Ermittlungstelle*
    (ZERV) that deal with criminal conduct of East Germans in connection with control of
    the Wall and the rest of the frontier.

4   Glaeser, *Divided in Unity*, 2000, p. 35.

5   *Organisationsstruktur der Berliner Polizei*, Berlin: Landespolizeiverwaltungsamt (LPVA),
    October 2001.

6   Glaeser, *Divided in Unity*, 2000, p. 182 note.

7   Glaeser, *Divided in Unity*, 2000, pp. xii-xiii.

8   Glaeser, *Divided in Unity*, 2000, p. 34.

9   Glaeser, *Divided in Unity*, 2000, p. 35.

10 BBC Radio Four's 'Today' programme, and its 8 a.m. news broadcast, 3 October 2003.
    The Home Secretary had announced at the Labour party conference the day before that
    136,000 police officers, a record number, were employed in England and Wales. There
    was no question, however, of a record number of police officers being 'on the streets' as
    either car or foot patrol officers, and certainly no question at all of there being a record
    number of 'beat' officers.

11 *Statistisches Jahrbuch Berlin*, Berlin; Statistisches Landesamt, annually.

12 *Statistisches Jahrbuch Berlin 2002*, Berlin; Statistisches Landesamt, 2002, pp. 31-32.

13 *Erfaßte Fälle und Häufigkeitszahlen auf Polizei-Abschnittsebene Berlin*, Berlin; Statistisches Landesamt, 2002.

14 «Kriminalitätsbelastungszahl (KBZ) nach Nationalitäten», *Kriminalität*, Berlin: die Polizeipräsident in Berlin, annually.

15 *Kriminalität 1979*, Berlin: die Polizeipräsident in Berlin, 1979. *Kriminalitätsentwicklung in Berlin 2002*, Berlin: Statistisches Landesamt Berln, 2003.

16 These are crimes recorded by the police. In the Berlin police definition these consist of, 'any criminal offence, including any punishable attempt, that appears in police records as a result of a police report' (*bekanntgewordene Fälle*). A detected case or a case cleared up (*aufgeklärte Fall*) is 'a criminal offence which after a police investigation has resulted in at least a suspect being known by name, or in someone being caught red handed'. A suspect (*Tatverdächtiger*) is someone who the police after an investigation have sufficient evidence (*zureichende tatsächliche Anhaltspunkte*) for them to believe that he or she has committed an offence. *Statistisches Jahrbuch Berlin 2002*, Berlin: Statistisches Landesamt, 2002, p. 176.

11: Policing a Politically Split Society

1 Ministère de l' Intérieur, Direction Générale de la Police Nationale, Direction Générale de la Police Judiciaire, *Aspects de la criminalité et de la délinquance constatée en France en 2000 par les services de police et les unités de gendarmerie*, Paris: La Documentation française, 2001.

2 Huntington, S.P., *The Clash of Civilisations and the Remaking of World Order*, New York: Simon and Schuster, 1996, pp. 137-54. Among counties without a cultural consensus, Huntington distinguishes between those that are 'cleft' and those that are 'torn' between mutually hostile groups. Switzerland, with its four distinct language areas is not 'cleft', because the difference in language spoken has not been the basis of hostility within a an otherwise strongly consensual culture—at any rate until the consensual culture began to be 'torn' by questions of Swiss participation in the European Union and NATO. The examples he gives of 'cleft' countries where there is a geographically distinct split include Nigeria, with its Muslim north and Christian south. On Huntington's definition, were North Ireland part of the Irish Republic, the strongest Unionist districts would remain for some indefinite time culturally 'cleft' from the rest of the country. In a 'torn' country there are, geographically mixed up, large and long-lasting competing cultures, one might or might not be dominant. The examples Huntington give of 'torn' cultures include Russia where, since the time of Peter the Great, important élites have tried to orient the country more to the West.

3 A prominent case was that of Winston Silcott. He was wrongly convicted for his part in the murder of a policeman who was hacked to death with machetes and knives by a mob of rioters at Broadwater Farm, Tottenham, in 1985. While serving a different sentence for murder (of which he continued to insist he was innocent, as he had killed in self-defence) his Broadwater Farm conviction was found unsafe, and he was paid £20,000 compensation in an out of court settlement by the Metropolitan Police. Among other honours paid to him by students, while in prison he was elected to office by the London School of Economic Students' Union.

4 Aron, R., *Democracy and Totalitarianism*, Lecture 11, London: Weidenfeld and Nicolson, 1968, p. 123. The 19 lectures that make the book were delivered at the Sorbonne during the academic year 1957-58. Aron can be criticised for being ignorant of the depth of alienation of African-Americans. But his lectures were delivered shortly after the United States Supreme Court judgement of 1954, that education that was separate could not be equal. This was regarded by the African-American civil rights

establishment at the time as the culmination of the work of the National Association for the Advancement of Colored People and its supporters, and as the portent of further peaceful gains. Until well into the 1960s, the civil rights movement asked for nothing but this: that what it promised to all Americans, American culture should deliver also to African-Americans. That is the whole point of Martin Luther King's 'I have a dream' speech.

5   Aron, *Democracy and Totalitarianism*, Lecture 12, 1968, p. 143.

6   Madelin, L., *Fouché 1759-1820* (1901), Paris: Nouveau Monde, 2002. Zweig, S., *Fouché: the portrait of a politician*, London: Cassell, 1930.

7   Quoted by Sir Frank Newsam in his history of the Home Office. Newsam, F., *The Home Office*, London: Allen and Unwin, 1954.

8   *Morning Chronicle*, 6 January 1812.

9   Halévy, E., *A History of the English People in 1815: political institutions* (1912), Harmondsworth: Penguin, 1937, p. 69.

10 *Report of the Select Committee on the Police of the Metropolis,* Parliamentary Papers, 440, IV, London, 17 June 1822.

11 Delacroix' 'Liberty guiding the People'.

12 Tocqueville deals with the enormous exceptions of the African-Americans and of the Amerindians of the United States. Even in the 1830s, in Tocqueville's account, the Amerindians were being dealt with by extermination.

13 Tocqueville, A. de, *Democracy in America* (1835-40), New York: New American Library, 1956, p. 40 and pp. 70 and 71.

14 Tocqueville, *Democracy in America* (1835-40), 1956, pp. 68-69.

15 Tocqueville, *Democracy in America* (1835-40), 1956, p. 86.

16 Marx, K., 'The eighteenth brumaire of Louis Bonaparte' (1850), in *Karl Marx and Frederick Engels Selected Works*, vol I, Moscow: Foreign Languages Publishing House, 1958.

17 Caussidière, M., *Secret History of the Revolutions of 1848: memoirs of Citizen Caussidière*, London: 1848.

18 Raisson, H.N., *Histoire de la Police de Paris, 1667-1844,* Paris: 1844.

19 Tocqueville, A. de, *Recollections* (1893), London: Macdonald, 1970, p. 118.

20 O'Brien, P., 'The revolutionary police in 1848', in Price, R. (ed.),*Revolution and Reaction: 1848 and the Second French Republic*, London: Croom Helm, 1975, p. 143.

21 Marx, K., 'Class struggles in France 1848-1850', in *Karl Marx and Frederick Engels Selected Works*, vol. I, 1958, pp. 161 and 162.

22 Tocqueville, *Recollections*, 1970, p. 136.

23 Bury, J.P.T., *France 1814-1940*, London: Methuen, 1949, p. 132.

24 Marx, K., 'The Civil War in France' (1871), in *Karl Marx and Frederick Engels Selected Works*, vol. I, 1958, pp. 516-17. Marx list also the standing army the clergy and the bureaucracy as part of the public force organised for social enslavement.

25 Bury, *France 1814-1940*, 1949, p. 132.

26 Marx, K., 'The Civil War in France' (1871), in *Karl Marx and Frederick Engels Selected Works*, vol. I, 1958, p. 519. Emphasis added.

27 Marx, 'The Civil War in France' (1871), in *Karl Marx and Frederick Engels Selected Works*, vol. I, 1958, pp. 529 and 534.

28 Engels, F., 'Introduction to *The Civil War in France* (1891), in *Karl Marx and Frederick Engels Selected Works*, vol. I, 1958, pp. 478-79.

29 Chapman, G.P., *The Third Republic: the first phase 1871-1894*, Macmillan, 1962, p. 13.

30 Hampden, J.H., *Clemenceau and the Third Republic*, London: Hodder and Stoughton, 1946, pp. 39-40.

31 Bury, *France 1814-1940*, 1949, p. 234.

32 *The Times*, 29 May 1871.

33 Engels, 'Introduction to *The Civil War in France* (1891)', in *Karl Marx and Frederick Engels Selected Works*, vol. I, 1958, p. 475.

34 Engels, 'Introduction to *The Civil War in France* (1891)', in *Karl Marx and Frederick Engels Selected Works*, vol. I, 1958, pp. 480-81.

35 Engels, 'Introduction to *The Civil War in France* (1891)', in *Karl Marx and Frederick Engels Selected Works*, vol. I, 1958, p. 481.

36 Chapman, *The Third Republic: the first phase 1871-1894*, 1962, p. 13.

37 Kleeblatt, N.L.(ed.) *The Dreyfus Affair: art, truth and justice*, Berkeley: UCP, 1987, p. xxvii. Emphasis added.

38 *The Times*, 7 February 1934. *Les Camelots du roi* were a militant royalist group in the 1930s. One of the causes of the Royalist riot was the sacking of the Paris police chief, Chiappe.

39 Aron, R., *Democracy and Totalitarianism*, London: Weidenfeld and Nicolson, 1968, p. 135.

40 Burke, E., *Reflections on the Revolution in France and Other Writings*, in *The Works of Edmund Burke*, vol. IV, London: OUP, p. 88.

41 Sartre, J.P., *Saint Genet: actor and martyr* (1952), London: W.H. Allen, 1964.

42 Direction générale de la police nationale et Direction générale de la police judiciaire, Service centrale d'étude de la délinquance, *La criminalité en France d'après les statistiques de la police judiciaire en1973*, La Documentation française, no date [c. 1974]. French 'recorded crime' figures include 'major crimes', 'moderate crimes' and 'delinquencies'. Robbery is classed as a major crime.

43 Ministre de l'Intérieur, *La criminalité en France d'après les statistiques de la police judiciaire en 1973*, no date [c. 1974], p. 89. In 1973 the four departments of the Paris region were the City of Paris, plus les Hautes-de-Seine, la Seine-Saint-Denis and le Val-de-Marne.

44 Merton, R.K., 'Social structure and anomie', in Merton, R.K., *Social Theory and Social Structure* (1947), Glencoe, Ill: Free Press, 1957.

45 Ministre de l'Intérieur, *La criminalité en France d'après les statistiques de la police judiciaire en 1973*, no date [c. 1974], p. 89.

46 Ardagh, J., *France in the 1980s: the definitive book*, Harmondsworth: Penguin, 1982, pp. 15-27.

47 Mairie de Paris, *Livre blanc du Conseil parisien de sécurité et de prévention de la délinquance*, Paris: Hôtel de Ville, no date [c. 1985], p. 59.

48 Mairie de Paris, *Livre blanc du Conseil parisien de sécurité et de prévention de la délinquance* [c. 1985], p. 60.

49 Mairie de Paris, *Livre blanc du Conseil parisien de sécurité et de prévention de la délinquance* [c. 1985], p. 38.

50 Mairie de Paris, *Livre blanc du Conseil parisien de sécurité et de prévention de la délinquance* [c. 1985], p. 39.

51 Mairie de Paris, *Livre blanc du Conseil parisien de sécurité et de prévention de la délinquance* [c. 1985], p. 44.

52 Mairie de Paris, *Livre blanc du Conseil parisien de sécurité et de prévention de la délinquance* [c. 1985], p. 84.

53 Elected members of the Council included Alain Juppé. Government representatives included the regional commissioner for the Ile-de-France (who was also the departmental commissioner for Paris), the prefect of police, with his directors the judicial, traffic and security police, and the president of the regional transport authority for Paris (*Régie autonome des transports parisiens*—the RATP). Non-voting representatives of various organisations, nominated by the mayor, included the Golden Age Clubs of France, the Departmental Union of Family Associations in Paris, the Olga Spitzer Association, the Jean Cotxet Association, the Pedestrians Association, the Drugs and Youth, and the National Federation of Chambers of Commerce of Watchmakers, Jewellery Retailers, Jewellers, Goldsmiths and Artisans. Non-voting individuals and representatives of various organisations were nominated by the government commissioner and the prefect of police. The associations included the Parisian Chamber of Commerce and Industry, the Association of Parisian Hoteliers and Restaurateurs, the French Association for Information and Research on Child Abuse, the Association for the Protection of Adolescents, the National Léo Lagrange Federation, and the Aid to Emigrants [*sic*] Service. The individuals included the president of the probation committee and the president of the Infants Tribunal in Paris.

54 Mairie de Paris, *Livre blanc du Conseil parisien de sécurité et de prévention de la délinquance* [c. 1985], p. 60. In the departments the police are the responsibility of the all-purpose departmental prefects. In Paris, the suburban communes, Lyon and Marseille they are the responsibility of the prefects of police. The municipal police forces are responsible to the mayor. The national gendarmerie is responsible to the minister of defence and is of particular importance in the rural areas.The police force is divided into public security forces and specialised police forces, such as the vice squad. The security police include the State Security Police (*Compagnies Républicaines de Sécurité*—the CRS), responsible for public order; the judicial police, who carry out criminal investigations and hunt down suspects; and the complex internal intelligence and anti-espionage units.

55 Mairie de Paris, *Livre blanc du Conseil parisien de sécurité et de prévention de la délinquance* [c. 1985], pp. 62-63.

56 Mairie de Paris, *Livre blanc du Conseil parisien de sécurité et de prévention de la délinquance* [c. 1985], pp. 63-64.

57 Direction de la Formation des Personnels de Police, *Cahiers de Formation*, Paris: January 1983.

58 Mairie de Paris, *Livre blanc du Conseil parisien de sécurité et de prévention de la délinquance* [c. 1985], p. 43.

59 Mairie de Paris, *Livre blanc du Conseil parisien de sécurité et de prévention de la délinquance* [c. 1985], pp. 71-72.

60 Mairie de Paris, *Livre blanc du Conseil parisien de sécurité et de prévention de la délinquance* [c. 1985], p. 76.

61 Mairie de Paris, *Livre blanc du Conseil parisien de sécurité et de prévention de la délinquance* [c. 1985], pp. 80-81.

62 Mairie de Paris, *Livre blanc du Conseil parisien de sécurité et de prévention de la délinquance* [c. 1985], p. 81.

63 Mairie de Paris, *Livre blanc du Conseil parisien de sécurité et de prévention de la délinquance* [c. 1985], p. 82.

64 Mairie de Paris, *Livre blanc du Conseil parisien de sécurité et de prévention de la délinquance* [c. 1985], p. 82-83.

65 Mairie de Paris, *Livre blanc du Conseil parisien de sécurité et de prévention de la délinquance* [c. 1985], pp. 4-5.

66 Mairie de Paris, *Livre blanc du Conseil parisien de sécurité et de prévention de la délinquance* [c. 1985], pp. 5-6.

67 Mairie de Paris, *Livre blanc du Conseil parisien de sécurité et de prévention de la délinquance* [c. 1985], p. 15.

68 Mairie de Paris, *Livre blanc du Conseil parisien de sécurité et de prévention de la délinquance* [c. 1985], p. 16.

69 Mairie de Paris, *Livre blanc du Conseil parisien de sécurité et de prévention de la délinquance* [c. 1985], p. 21.

70 Frydman, N. and Martineau, H., *La Drogue: où en sommes-nous? Bilan des connaissances en France en matière de drogues et de toxicomanies*, Paris: La documentation française, 1997, p. 105. Source: Statistical Service of the Ministry of Social Affairs (SESI).

71 Direction de la recherche des études de l'évaluation et des statistiques (DREES), Ministère de l'Émploi et de la solidarité, *Annuaire des statistiques sanitaires et sociales 2000*, Paris: La documentation française, [no date], p. 73.

72 Direction de la recherche des études de l'évaluation et des statistiques (DREES), Ministère de l'Émploi et de la solidarité, *Annuaire des statistiques sanitaires et sociales 2000*, [no date], p. 73, p. 83 and p. 149.

73 Thefts with violence (*vols avec violence*). The subcategories were thefts with violence where firearms were used (*á main armée (armes á feu)*) and thefts with violence where firearms were not used (*sans arme á feu*). A separate sub-category is thefts with violence against women on a street or in a public place with or without the use of firearms. Ministère de l' Intérieur, Direction Générale de la Police Nationale, Direction Générale de la Police Judiciaire, *Aspects de la criminalité et de la délinquance constatées en France en 2000 par les services de police et les unités de gendarmerie*, vol. I, Paris: La Documentation française, 2001, p. 15.

74 Ministère de l' Intérieur, Direction Générale de la Police Nationale, *Aspects de la criminalité et de la délinquance constatées en France en 2000 par les services de police et les unités de gendarmerie*, vol. I, 2001.

75 Calan, J. de, 'La prevention situationelle en Angleterre', *Les Cahiers de la sécurité intérieure*, 21, 1995.

76 Delhome, D. and Landauer, P., 'La sécurisation des grands ensembles', *Urbanisme et sécurité vers un projet urbain ?'*, Paris: Institut des Hautes Études de la Sécurité Intérieure (IHESI), 2001, p. 49.

77 Delhome and Landauer, 'La sécurisation des grands ensembles', *Urbanisme et sécurité vers un projet urbain ?'*, 2001, p. 53.

78 Calan, de, 'La prevention situationelle en Angleterre', *Les Cahiers de la sécurité intérieure*, 21, 1995.

79 Ocqueteau, F., 'Cinq ans après la loi "video-surveillance" en France, que dire de son application ?', *Urbanisme et sécurité vers un projet urbain ?*, Paris: Institut des Hautes Études de la Sécurité Intérieure (IHESI), 2001, p. 104.

80 Police strength (*effectives budgétaires*). Ministère de l'Intérieur, Direction Générale de la Police Nationale, *Aspects de la criminalité et de la délinquance constatées en France en 2000 par les services de police et les unités de gendarmerie*, vol. I, 2001, pp. 6-7.

81 Gaudin, *Présentation á la presse des aspects de la criminalité et de la délinquance constatées en 2002 par les services de police et de gendarmerie*, no publication details given, pp. 1-2. French 'street crime' includes theft of automobiles and freight vehicles, cycle theft, theft from vehicles, pick-pocketing, vandalism to private or public property (not arson), robbery and armed robbery.

82 Palle, C. and Godefroy, T., *Les dépenses de sécurité 1992-1996*, Études et données pénales, Guyancourt: CESDIP, Ministère de la Justice, 1998. Palle, C. and Godefroy, T.,*Coûts du crime: une estimation monétaire des délinquances 1992-1996*, Études et données pénales, Paris: Guyancourt: CESDIP, Ministère de la Justice, 1998. (http://www.msh-paris.fr/cesdip)

83 Palle and Godefroy, *Coûts du crime: une estimation monétaire des délinquances 1992-1996*, 1998, pp. 39 and 42. The armed robbery figure was that of the Central Office for the Control of Major Crime (*Office central pour la Répression de grand Banditisme*—the OCRB). No figures are given for robberies without the use of firearms.

84 Ministre de l'Intérieur, *La criminalité en France d'après les statistique de la police judiciaire en 1973*, no date [c. 1974]. Ministère de l' Intérieur, Direction Générale de la Police Nationale, *Aspects de la criminalité et de la délinquance constatées en France en 2000 par les services de police et les unités de gendarmerie*, 2001.

85 'Le Code pénal en avance sur Sarkozy', *Le Canard enchaîné*, 13 November 2002.

12: Dealing with Diversity: Extermination, Segregation, Assimilation

1 Rose, T. (ed.), *Violence in America: a historical and contemporary Reader*, New York: Vintage, 1970.

2 Debo, A., *A History of the Indians of the United States* (1970), London: Pimlico, 1995, p. 101, p. 106 and p. 234.

3 Collier, J., *Indians of the Americas: the long hope*, New York: Mentor, 1948, p. 143. Collier was a US Commissioner for Indian Affairs. It is not clear whether 'liquidate' is his word or the Assistant Commissioner's he quotes.

4 *The Stephen Lawrence Inquiry: report of an inquiry by Sir William Macpherson of Cluny*, Cm 4262-I, 1999. This was the only sense given the word until the Macpherson report succeeded in redefining 'institutional' as its opposite, that which is not enforced by the institutions —the rules—of an organisation. In Macpherson's definition, 'institutional' suddenly became what was individually 'unwitting', 'unconscious', 'thoughtless' or 'ignorant', leading to, from the point of view of the institution, *prohibited* individual conduct and even forbidden thoughts (p. 28). He says explicitly that he was persuaded to define institutional racism in this way because he had 'not heard evidence of overt racism or discrimination' in the course of his long and hostile inquiry, with the exception of the 'inappropriate use' of the words 'coloured' and 'negro' (p. 20).

5   Whitman, W., 'Democratic Vistas', in his *Collected Poetry and Collected Prose*, New York: Library of America, 1982.

6   McMaster, J.B., 'The rise of Nativism and anti-Catholic violence', in Rose, (ed.), *Violence in America: a historical and contemporary Reader*, 1970.

7   Morison, S.E. and Commager, H.S., *The Growth of the American Republic*, vol. II, New York: OUP, fourth edn 1950, p. 151 and p. 174.

8   McWilliams, C., 'The Los Angeles riots of 1943', in Rose, (ed.), *Violence in America: a historical and contemporary Reader*, 1970.

9   Benedict, L.A., *Chicago and the Metropolitan Area: population, decennial censuses 1840-1990*, Chicago: Chicago Municipal Reference Library, 1992, amended to include the census of the year 2000.

10 *Report of the General Superintendent of Police of the City of Chicago for the Year Ending 31 December 1885*, Chicago: Department of Police, 1886.

11 Wilson, S.P., *Chicago by Gaslight*, Chicago: Douglas Neighborhood Club, 1910. He was also author of *Chicago and its Cess-Pools of Infamy*, and *Wilson's Epitome of Historical and Chronological Facts*. (No publication details shown in either case.)

12 Wilson, *Chicago by Gaslight*, 1910, pp. 113-17.

13 Wilson, *Chicago by Gaslight*, 1910, pp. 14-15.

14 Peterson, V.W., *Barbarians in Our Midst: a history of Chicago crime and politics*, Boston: Little, Brown, 1952.

15 Citizens' Police Committee, *Chicago Police Problems*, Chicago: University of Chicago Press, 1931, p. vii.

16 Citizens' Police Committee, *Chicago Police Problems*, p. 193.

17 Citizens' Police Committee, *Chicago Police Problems*, Chicago: 1931, p. 194.

18 Citizens' Police Committee, *Chicago Police Problems*, 1931, p. 205.

13: Dealing with Diversity: Libertarianism and Multiculturalism

1   Kefauver, E., *Crime in America*, Garden City, NY: Doubleday, 1951.

2   Kerouac, J., *On the Road* (1957), Harmondsworth: Penguin, 1972. Mailer, N., 'The White Negro: superficial reflections on the Hipster' (1957) in *Advertisements for Myself* (1959), New York: New American Library, 1960.

3   Illinois Institute of Technology and the Chicago Crime Commission, *A Study of Organised Crime in Illinois*, Chicago: ITT and CCC, 1971, p. 169.

4   Illinois Institute of Technology and the Chicago Crime Commission, *A Study of Organised Crime in Illinois*, 1971, p. 281.

5   Illinois Institute of Technology and the Chicago Crime Commission, *A Study of Organised Crime in Illinois*, 1971, p. 283.

6   See, for example, Jacobs, P. and Landau, S., *The New Radicals: the student groups that are making a social revolution*, Harmondsworth: Penguin, 1967.

7   Rogers, C. R., *Freedom to Learn: a view of what education might become*, Columbus, Ohio: Merrill, 1969.

8   Editorial, 'A look into the house of torture', *Chicago Tribune*, 27 April 2002.

9   Euripides, *Medea*.

10 Biderman, A.D., Johnson, L.A., McInyre, J. and Weir, A.W., *Report on a Pilot Study in the District of Columbia on Victimisation and Attitudes Towards Law Enforcement,* Washington, DC: Government Printing Office, 1967. President's Commission on Law Enforcement and Administration of Justice, *The Police,* Washington, DC: Government Printing Office, 1967. President's Commission on Law Enforcement and the Administration of Justice, *The Challenge of Crime in a Free Society,* Washington DC: US Government Printing Office, 1967.

11 DiPasquale, D. and Glaeser E.L., *The Los Angeles Riot and the Economics of Urban Unrest,* NBER Working Papers 5456, Cambridge, Mass: National Bureau of Economic Research, January 1998.

12 Benedict, L.A., *Chicago and the Metropolitan Area: population, decennial censuses 1840-1990,* Chicago: Chicago Municipal Reference Library, 1992, amended to include the census of the year 2000.

13 *Chicago Police Statistical Report 1965,* Chicago: Director of Public Information, April 1966, p. 10. *Chicago Police Department Statistical Summary 1975,* Chicago: Chicago Police Department, July 1976.

14 *Chicago Police Department Statistical Summary 1975,* Chicago: Chicago Police Department, July 1976.

15 Jacobs, J.J., *The Death and Life of Great American Cities,* New York: Vintage Books, 1961, p. 72.

16 Jacobs, *The Death and Life of Great American Cities,* 1961, p. 72.

17 Wilson, J.Q. and Kelling, G.L., 'The police and neighborhood safety',*The Atlantic,* March 1982, p. 16.

18 Wilson, J.Q., *Varieties of Police Behavior,* Cambridge, Mass: Harvard University Press, 1968. Stead, P.J. (ed.), *Pioneers in Policing,* Montclair, NJ: Patterson Smith, 1977. Stinchcombe, A.L. *et al., Crime and Punishment in Public Opinion,* San Francisco: Jossey-Bass, 1980. Skogan, W.G. and Maxfield, M., *Coping with Crime: individual and neighborhood reactions,* Newbury Park, Calif: Sage, 1981. Fowler, F.J. Jnr and Mangione, T., *Neighborhood Crime, Fear and Social Control: a second look at the Hartford program,* Washington DC: National Institute of Justice, US Government Printing Department, 1982. Trojanowicz, R., *An Evaluation of the Neighborhood Foot Patrol in Flint, Michigan,* East Lansing: Michigan State University, 1982. Pate, T. *et al., Reducing Fear of Crime in Houston and Newark,* Washington DC: Police Foundation, 1986. Hope, T. and Hough, M., 'Area, crime and incivilities: a profile from the British Crime Survey', in Hope, T. and Shaw, M., (eds), *Communities and Crime Reduction,* London: HMSO, 1988. Skogan, W.G., *Disorder and Decline: crime and the spiral of urban decay in American neighborhoods,* New York: Free Press, 1990. *Criminal Victimisation in the United States 1993,* Washington DC: Department of Justice, US Government Printing Department, 1995. *Crime in the United States,* Washington DC: Federal Bureau of Investigation, Department of Justice, US Government Printing Department, annually.

19 Biderman *et al., Report on a Pilot Study in the District of Columbia on Victimisation and Attitudes Towards Law Enforcement,* 1967.

20 Hobbes, T., *Leviathan* (1651), London: Dent, 1914, p. 67.

21 Wilson and Kelling, 'The police and neighborhood safety',*The Atlantic,* March 1982, p. 34.

22 Wilson and Kelling, 'The police and neighborhood safety',*The Atlantic,* March 1982.

23 Kelling, G.L. and Coles, C.M., *Fixing Broken Windows: restoring order and reducing crime in our communities,* New York: Touchstone, p. 9.

24 Wilson and Kelling, 'The police and neighborhood safety', *The Atlantic*, March 1982.

25 Wilson and Kelling, 'The police and neighborhood safety', *The Atlantic*, March 1982.

26 Wilson and Kelling, 'The police and neighborhood safety', *The Atlantic*, March 1982.

27 Wilson and Kelling, 'The police and neighborhood safety', *The Atlantic*, March 1982, p. 12.

28 'The New York Newsday Interview with Jeremy Travis', *Newsday*, 11 August 1994, p. 13. Emphasis added.

29 Wilson and Kelling, 'The police and neighborhood safety', *The Atlantic*, March 1982, p. 13.

30 Bird, J., *Retreat from the Streets*, London: Politeia, December 2002.

14: Dealing with Diversity: Destroying Crime and Disorder

1   Fanon, F., *The Wretched of the Earth* (1961), Harmondsworth: Penguin, 1969. Foucault, M., *Madness and Civilization: a history of insanity in the Age of Reason* (1971), London: Routledge, 2001.

2   Wilson, J.Q. and Kelling, G.L., 'The police and neighborhood safety', *The Atlantic*, March 1982, p. 15.

3   Chicago Community Police Consortium, *Community Policing in Chicago, Years Five-Six: an interim report*, Chicago: Institute for Policy Research, Northwestern University, May 1999, p. 70. See www.nwu.edu/IPR/publications/policing.html.

4   Chicago Community Police Consortium, *Community Policing in Chicago, Years Five-Six: an interim report*, May 1999, pp. 1 and 33.
    See www.nwu.edu/IPR/publications/policing.html.

5   This account is an updated version of that published in our *The Failure of Britain's Police: London and New York compared*, London: Civitas, 2003,

6   Magnet, M., *The Dream and the Reality: the sixties' legacy to the underclass*, New York: Morrow, 1993.

7   New York's 'fiscal crisis' began in 1975 during the mayoralty of A.D. Beame, and continued during the first years of the mayoralty of Edward Koch. The city did not recover until 1983, when Koch's administration managed a successful issuance of new city notes.

8   New York City Police Department, *Annual Report 1968*, New York: City of New York, 1969.

9   New York City Police Department, *Annual Report 1974*, New York: City of New York, 1975.

10 New York City Police Department, *Annual Report 1982*, New York: City of New York, 1983.

11 Epstein, J., *The Great Conspiracy Trial: an essay on law, liberty and the constitution*, New York: Random House, 1970. The classic account of the 1968 riots is Norman Mailer's *Miami and the Siege of Chicago: an informal history of the American political conventions of 1968*, Harmondsworth: Penguin, 1969.

12 Dennis, N., Erdos, G. and Al-Shahi, A., *Racist Murder and Pressure Group Politics: the Macpherson report and the police*, London: Civitas, 2000.

13 *Report of Chief of Department to the Police Commissioner on the Tompkins Square Park Incident*, New York: NYPD, 23 August 1988.

14 Dennis, N., *Rising Crime and the Dismembered Family: how conformist intellectuals have campaigned against common sense*, London: Civitas, 1993.

15 Burns, R. and Saunders, J., *New York: an illustrated history*, New York: Knopf, 1999.

16 Management Analysis and Planning, Crime Analysis Unit, *Statistical Report: complaints and arrests*, New York: NYPD, different dates of issue.

17 See, for example, *Policing New York City in the 1990s: the strategy for community policing*, New York: NYPD, January 1991; *Problem Solving Annual for Community Police Officers: disorderly groups*, New York: NYPD, October 1993.

18 New York City Civilian Review Board, *Status Report 2000*, New York: CCRB, 2001, graph 2, entitled 'NYPD average uniformed headcount'. Our thanks are due to William H. Sousa, of the Police Institute, School of Criminal Justice, Rutgers University, for this information. The New York City Department of Personnel's *Annual Reports* (New York: City Hall) are intermittent, and give a somewhat different set of statistics. The numbers are complicated by the fact that formerly independent forces were amalgamated with the NYPD during the 1990s, notably the federal Housing Police, and the Transport Police. They were added to the numbers of NYPD as the Housing Bureau and the Transit Bureau, without adding to the numbers of 'police' in the city.

19 The 'public protection police' in Times Square and the surrounding area are the employees of the 'Times Square Business Improvement District (BID) Inc.'. This is a not-for-profit organisation set up in 1992 to combat the economically disastrous decline in the area owing to it having been invaded and occupied by the heterogeneous 'homeless'. In the early 2000s it had a $7 million annual budget, $6 million of which is raised by mandatory assessments on local property owners, and $1 million from grants and sponsorships. Besides its security patrols, it undertakes public improvements, for example, in lighting the area, and provides tourist and sanitation services. The power of the propaganda that claimed that all the areas problems were those of 'homelessness' is echoed in its programme of 'homeless outreach'.

20 Bratton, W.J., 'Crime is down in New York City: blame the police', in Dennis, N. (ed.), *Zero Tolerance: policing a free society*, London: Civitas, 1997.

21 Management Analysis and Planning, Crime Analysis Unit, *Statistical Report: complaints and arrests*, New York: NYPD, different dates of issue. The December statistics were those analysed. These give the figures for the calendar year 2000. For the precincts, the latest figures for December are those of December 2000.

22 Bureau of Justice Statistics, *Criminal Victimization in the United States, 1995: a National Crime Victimization Survey Report*, Washington DC: US Department of Justice, May 2000.

23 Jacobs, J.J., *The Death and Life of Great American Cities*, London: Jonathan Cape, 1962.

24 See, for example, *Breaking the Cycle of Domestic Violence*, Police Strategy No. 4, New York: NYPD, April 1994; *Reducing Auto-Related Crime in New York*, Police Strategy No. 6, New York: NYPD, February 1995; *Reclaiming the Roads of New York*, Police Strategy No. 8, New York: NYPD, November 1995. One of the earliest successes of the Giuliani/Bratton régime was due to the implementation of the recommendations contained in Kelling, G.L., Julian, M. and Miller, S., *Managing 'Squeegeeing': a problem-solving exercise*, New York: NYPD, 1994. Possibly this report was the first to use the term 'no tolerance'—soon to become 'zero tolerance'. The report said that the problem of 'squeegeeing' could be managed and largely stopped *by patrol officers* if a no tolerance approach was adopted—and it was.

25 Kelling, G.L. and Sousa, W.H. Jr, *Do Police Matter?: an analysis of the impact of New York City's police reforms*, Civic Report No. 22, New York: Center for Civic Innovation, Manhattan Institute, December 2001.

26 The BID public safety officers are uniformed, but have no more powers than any other citizen. Most of their time is spent in being helpful to visitors. In case of trouble, their job is to call the police. But because they are on the spot, and *will* call the police, crime and disorder have been reduced to a low level, to the benefit of the vast majority of businesses and people working in and visiting the area.

27 *Uniform Crime Report*, Washington, DC: FBI, 2003.

28 McArdle, A. and Erzen, T. (eds), *Zero Tolerance: quality of life and the new police brutality in New York City*, New York: NYU Press, 2001.

29 NYPD Compstat, vol. 10, no. 42.

30 Phillips, M., *America's Social Revolution*, London: Civitas and the *Sunday Times*, 2001, p. 37.

15: Making Up Lost Ground

1 In October 2004 the High Court in London considered a case brought against Brent borough Council and the Metropolitan Police on behalf of three youths who had been made the subjects of Anti-Social Behaviour Orders (ASBOs). The ASBOs had been obtained from a district judge after a 15-day hearing and upheld on appeal. The ASBOs were imposed on the grounds that the youths were part of a gang that for two years on their Neasden estate had committed theft and criminal damage, used foul and abusive language, regularly possessed drugs and knives, thrown bricks through windows, urinated outside residents' doors, plunged the homes of elderly residents into darkness, and surrounded and pelted police cars with stones and mud. No residents dare give their name in commenting to the press on the case. A disabled resident said that she was afraid to leave the house, or even sit in her own garden. A man said, 'They are wannabe gangsters, who go around instilling fear into others'. Maps had been distributed as leaflets and shown on a website showing the exclusion areas covered by the ASBOs, with photographs of the youths to whom the ASBOs applied, and with a description the youths' offences. Lawyers backed by the human rights group Liberty claimed that the youths' human right to privacy and family life, guaranteed under Article 8 of the Human Rights Convention, had been violated. The case was dismissed, but in an obiter dictum Lord Justice Kennedy emphasised the need for those considering publicity to have in mind the rights of those against whom ASBOs are made. 'Teenage gang members lose plea for privacy', *Daily Telegraph*, 8 October 2004.

2 Kelling, G.L. and Sousa, W.H. Jr, *Do Police Matter?: an analysis of the impact of New York City's police reforms*, Civic Report No. 22, New York: Center for Civic Innovation, Manhattan Institute, December 2001.

3 Dennis, N., Erdos, G. and Robinson, D., *The Failure of Britain's Police: London and New York compared*, London: Civitas, 2003, pp. 46-47.

Index